This is an exceptional and exhaustive work regarding victim participation and the crucial value of victim impact statements in the context of the sentencing of sexual assault victims. Davies and Bartels have produced a remarkable analysis of this area in the Australian legal context. Through powerful case examples, the authors give context to the therapeutic value of such statements. Beyond its obvious relevance and importance to an Australian readership, the book makes a major contribution to the area of therapeutic jurisprudence and assures its relevance to audiences internationally.

David B Wexler, Honorary President, International Society for Therapeutic Jurisprudence, Distinguished Research Professor of Law Emeritus, University of Arizona, Professor of Law, University of Puerto Rico

This volume greatly enhances our understanding of victims' perspectives of the use of victim impact statements in sexual offence cases. Based upon original research, the authors make a number of key recommendations to improve sentencing policy and/or legislative reform from a victim-focused perspective. The primary focus is upon Australia but this important book contains lessons for all common law jurisdictions.

Julian Roberts, Professor of Criminology, University of Oxford and Executive Director, Sentencing Academy of England and Wales

Ever since the criminal courts began to give recognition to the important roles that victims can and should play in criminal justice processes, policymakers have been keen to see how victims' experiences may have changed and whether the reforms that were put in place met expectations. Combining qualitative interviews with victims and justice professionals with an analysis of sentencing remarks, Dr Davies and Professor Bartels present a timely and unique victim-focused perspective that now provides those involved in judicial processes with guidance for effective acknowledgment of victims at sentencing. The evidence presented is convincing. The recommendations for future policy development are persuasive.

Rick Sarre, Emeritus Professor, University of South Australia and Past President, Australian and New Zealand Society of Criminology

By combining interviews with victims and justice professionals with the analysis of sentencing transcripts, Davies and Bartels provide unique insights into the complexity of ensuring that victim impact statements achieve their potential to give victims voice, validation, and vindication. Their findings and recommendations are relevant to all jurisdictions that make use of victim impact statements in the sentencing process. This book is essential reading for judicial officers, justice professionals, and policymakers interested in supporting victims of sexual assault through the criminal process, as well as providing compelling new material for lecturers and students.

Kate Warner AC, Governor of Tasmania and Professor Emerita, University of Tasmania

The Use of Victim Impact Statements in Sentencing for Sexual Offences

Drawing on extensive research from Australia, this book examines the experiences of sexual offence victims who submit a victim impact statement. Victim impact statements are used in sentencing to outline the harm caused to victims. There has been little research on the impact statement experiences of sexual offence victims. This book fills this gap, examining the perspectives of six adult female victims and 15 justice professionals in Australia. This is supplemented by analysis of 100 sentencing remarks, revealing how courts use such statements in practice.

This book examines victims' experiences of preparing and submitting statements, justice professionals' experiences of working with victims to submit statements, and the judicial use of impact statements in sentencing. It identifies an overarching lack of clarity around the purpose of impact statements, which affects the information that can be included and the way they can be used by the court. It consequently explores the issues associated with balancing the expressive and instrumental purposes of such statements, and the challenges in communication between professionals and victims of crime. The findings highlight several issues with the operation of impact statement regimes. Based on these findings, the book makes recommendations to clarify such regimes, to improve communication between justice professionals and victims of crime, and to enhance the therapeutic goals of such statements.

An accessible and compelling read, this book is essential reading for all those engaged with victimology, sentencing, and sexual violence.

Rhiannon Davies is a public servant in Australian government. She has previously worked in legal practice and in the law faculties at Flinders University in South Australia and the University of Tasmania.

Lorana Bartels is the Criminology Program Leader in the Centre for Social Research and Methods at the Australian National University. She is an Adjunct Professor of Law at the University of Canberra and University of Tasmania and a Fellow of the Australian Academy of Law.

Routledge Frontiers of Criminal Justice

Policing and Mental Health
Theory, Policy and Practice
Edited by John L.M. McDaniel, Kate Moss and Ken G. Pease

The Making of a Police Officer
Comparative Perspectives on Police Education and Recruitment
Edited by Tore Bjørgo and Marie-Louise Damen

Police Integrity in South Africa
Sanja Kutnjak Ivkovich, Adri Sauerman, Andrew Faull, Michael E. Meyer and Gareth Newham

Emotional Labour in Criminal Justice and Criminology
Edited by Jake Phillips, Chalen Westaby, Andrew Fowler and Jaime Waters

Predictive Policing and Artificial Intelligence
Edited by John L.M. McDaniel and Ken G. Pease

The Use of Victim Impact Statements in Sentencing for Sexual Offences
Stories of Strength
Rhiannon Davies and Lorana Bartels

Understanding the Educational Experiences of Imprisoned Men
(Re)education
Helen Nichols

For more information about this series, please visit: https://www.routledge.com/Routledge-Frontiers-of-Criminal-Justice/book-series/RFCJ

The Use of Victim Impact Statements in Sentencing for Sexual Offences

Stories of Strength

Rhiannon Davies and Lorana Bartels

Routledge
Taylor & Francis Group
LONDON AND NEW YORK

First published 2021
by Routledge
2 Park Square, Milton Park, Abingdon, Oxon OX14 4RN

and by Routledge
52 Vanderbilt Avenue, New York, NY 10017

Routledge is an imprint of the Taylor & Francis Group, an informa business

British Library Cataloguing-in-Publication Data
A catalogue record for this book is available from the British Library

Library of Congress Cataloging-in-Publication Data
A catalog record has been requested for this book

ISBN: 978-0-367-52419-7 (hbk)
ISBN: 978-0-367-52422-7 (pbk)
ISBN: 978-1-003-05785-7 (ebk)

Typeset in Bembo
by Deanta Global Publishing Services, Chennai, India

Contents

Figures

Tables

Acknowledgements

Rhiannon would like to acknowledge Julia Davis, without whom her PhD research would never have commenced. She thanks her University of Tasmania colleagues and friends, Charlotte Hunn, Helen Cockburn, Caroline Spiranovic, and Rosalie and Rich Martin. She thanks Cat Hoffman for her friendship and editorial support, and Jordan Tutton for his encouragement. She thanks her family – Bernie, Malcolm, Brendan, Lauren, Joshua, Georgie, Artie, Emmy, Liam, Alice, Sian, and most of all, Mike – for their love and emotional support.

Lorana would like to acknowledge her current and former colleagues at the Australian National University, University of Canberra and University of Tasmania. She would also like to thank her family – Tim, Maxie, and Jimmy – for once again putting up with the distraction that comes with completing a book.

Rhiannon and Lorana would especially like to thank Terese Henning for co-supervising the PhD research on which this book is based, and Professor Julian Roberts, Professor David Wexler and Professor Rick Sarre for their gracious endorsements. Most of all, we would like to thank Her Excellency Professor the Honourable Kate Warner AC, who co-supervised Rhiannon's PhD (and Lorana's before that), wrote an endorsement, and is a wise and generous friend and mentor.

Abbreviations

ACT	Australian Capital Territory
Cth	Commonwealth (of Australia)
DPP	Director of Public Prosecutions
NSW	New South Wales
NT	Northern Territory
ODPP	Office of the Director of Public Prosecutions
OPP	Office of Public Prosecutions
Qld	Queensland
SA	South Australia
Tas	Tasmania
UK	United Kingdom
US	United States of America
Vic	Victoria
VIS	Victim impact statement
VSO	Victim support officer
WA	Western Australia
WAO	Witness assistance officer
WAS	Witness assistance service

Chapter 1

Introduction

Introduction

One night in 2015, Brock Turner, a promising athlete who was a student at Stanford University, was found in the act of raping an unconscious young woman behind a dumpster (for discussion, see Sheley 2017). In 2016, Turner was convicted at trial of three charges of felony sexual assault and was sentenced to six months' imprisonment and three years of probation. He was ultimately released after serving three months in jail. The so-called 'Stanford rape' case became a *cause célèbre*; as a result of the leniency of the sentence imposed, the sentencing judge became the first judge in California to be removed from office in over 80 years (Astor 2018). However, the case assumed even greater prominence because of the actions and courage of the victim, referred to in court documents as 'Emily Doe'. Before Brock was sentenced, 'Emily' stood up in court and delivered her powerful 7,200-word impact statement. It commenced as follows:

> Your Honor, if it is all right, for the majority of this statement I would like to address the defendant directly.
>
> You don't know me, but you've been inside me, and that's why we are here today.
>
> (cited in Baker 2016: np; Miller 2019: 333)

After chronicling the circumstances and aftermath of the assault in searing detail, including the trial process, her responses to claims made by the defence, and her reaction to the pre-sentence report, 'Emily' concluded her statement:

> And finally, to girls everywhere, I am with you. On nights when you feel alone, I am with you. When people doubt you or dismiss you, I am with you. I fought everyday for you. So never stop fighting, I

> believe you. *Lighthouses don't go running all over an island looking for boats to save; they just stand there shining.* Although I can't save every boat, I hope that by speaking today, you absorbed a small amount of light, a small knowing that you can't be silenced, a small satisfaction that justice was served, a small assurance that we are getting somewhere, and a big, big knowing that you are important, unquestionably, you are untouchable, you are beautiful, you are to be valued, respected, undeniably, every minute of every day, you are powerful and nobody can take that away from you. To girls everywhere, I am with you. Thank you.
>
> (cited in Baker 2016: np; Miller 2019: 357, emphasis added)

The statement 'went viral, becoming a kind of manifesto for assault survivors all over the world' (Whittaker 2020: np). It reportedly inspired Hillary Clinton's 2016 Presidential candidacy concession speech. She also quoted the final paragraph of Miller's statement in her autobiography, adding: 'I hope Emily Doe knows how much her words and her strength meant to so many' (Clinton 2017, cited in Miller 2019: 291). But there was more to come. In September 2019, Chanel Miller participated in a *60 Minutes* interview, in which she 'reclaimed her identity as the author of that statement' (Whittaker 2020: np) and discussed her forthcoming memoir, *Know My Name* (Miller 2019). In the book, which includes Miller's statement in full, she stated: 'I had written the statement to say stop. Stop treading on me, denying my truths, stop pushing back' (2019: 287). She went on to note: 'I had a voice, he stripped it, left me groping around blind for a bit, but I always had it. I just used it like I had never had to use it before' (2019: 288). She found that, when she 'wrote the ugly and painful parts into a statement, … [t]he world did not plug up its ears, it opened itself to me' (2019: 311). She observed that

> Victims are often accused of seeking revenge, but revenge is a tiny engine. I know better than to think my peace arrives when the gavel hits, when the handcuffs click shut … We don't fight for our own happy endings. We fight to say *you can't.* We fight for accountability. We fight to establish precedent. We fight because we pray we'll be the last ones to feel this kind of pain.
>
> (2019: 291, emphasis in original)

The implications of Miller's impact statement and memoir have already been the subject of extensive academic commentary (see e.g. Sheley 2017; Giles 2018; Kemph 2018; Serisier 2018; Roy 2019). We do not propose to add to that commentary, but Miller's statement and the ensuing discourse highlight the importance and salience of our empirical research on sexual offence victims' impact statements conducted in Australia between 2014 and 2016.

Background to our research

The physical and psychological effects of sexual offence victimisation can be traumatic, complex, and prolonged (see e.g. Morrison, Quadara, & Boyd 2007; Wall & Quadara 2014). Sexual offending is 'often under-reported and may be unrecorded' (Australian Bureau of Statistics 2013: 7; see also Hoyle & Zedner 2007). The Australian Bureau of Statistics has explained that, while this makes it difficult to measure the prevalence of sexual offending in the Australian community, 'the available evidence suggests that most victims of sexual violence do not report the crime to police' (2013: 7). There are a number of reasons for this, including the 'significant emotional stress' that 'even the most robust citizen' may experience as a consequence of involvement in legal proceedings (Herman 2003: 159). For victims of sexual offending, who are likely to have experienced psychological trauma as a result of the offending (Herman 2003; Hoyle & Zedner 2007; Konradi 2007), 'involvement in the justice system may compound the original injury' (Herman 2003: 159; Warner 2005).

While there are no simple solutions to improve the criminal justice experience of sexual offence victims, legal and policy reforms over the past 30 years have been intended, at least in part, 'to address factors and barriers' (Australian Law Reform Commission 2010: 1187) that contribute to high attrition rates in the prosecution of sexual offences (Naylor 2010) and address the identified justice needs of many victims (O'Connell 2015). Daly, who has indicated a preference for the term 'victims' justice interests' (2014: 388), has explained that these interests include the need:

- to participate in the justice process, which includes being provided with information about developments of the case as it progresses (see also Shapland, Willmore, & Duff 1985);
- for voice, including the ability to share the story of what has happened in a public setting, where the victim can receive public recognition and acknowledgement (see also Lievore 2005);
- for validation, involving affirmation that the victim is believed (see also Bluett-Boyd & Fileborn 2014); and
- for vindication, involving the recognition that what happened to the victim was wrong (see also Herman 2005).

Others have echoed Daly's list, but highlighted the particular trauma that may be experienced by victims of sexual offending as a consequence of the criminal justice process (see e.g. Clark 2010; Keenan 2017). The need to be treated with respect (Payne 2009; McGlynn 2011) and feel a sense of control over their experience of the justice process (Clark 2010; Bluett-Boyd & Fileborn 2014) have therefore also been emphasised in the context of victims of sexual offending.

As part of legal and policy reforms intended to meet victims' justice needs, including participation and voice, and to improve victims' experiences of the justice process, victim impact statements[1] were introduced as 'one of the earliest and most significant legislative responses that encourage victim participation during the sentencing stage of the criminal justice process' (Iliadis 2020: 48).

These statements are prepared by the victim prior to sentencing and outline the harms caused to them as a consequence of the offending and are read by the judicial officer prior to sentencing. They were introduced in Australia from the 1980s, among other reforms intended to address the re-traumatisation of sexual offence victims (Australian Law Reform Commission 2010) and reduce 'many of the anti-therapeutic tendencies entailed by [victim] involvement in [criminal justice] proceedings' (Erez, Ibarra, & Downs 2011: 37).

When first introduced in several jurisdictions around the world during the 1980s (for a timeline, see De Mesmaecker 2012), research into impact statement schemes was prolific and a number of researchers undertook empirical research to investigate the consequences of their implementation. These studies aimed to identify issues such as the financial and time implications of the schemes (see e.g. Erez, Roeger, & Morgan 1994), the effect that the submission of impact statements had on sentence length and type (Erez & Tontodonato 1990; Davis & Smith 1994), the reasons why victims chose to participate in impact statement schemes (e.g. Hoyle et al 1998), and victim satisfaction levels following the submission of their statements (e.g. Leverick, Chalmers, & Duff 2007). Since then, research on victim participation in the sentencing process has continued sporadically and has become a renewed priority for Australian governments in recent years (see e.g. Victorian Law Reform Commission 2016; New South Wales (NSW) Sentencing Council 2018).

A key finding from the research is that victims' satisfaction with their justice system experience tends to increase significantly when judicial officers acknowledge the harm they have suffered, by making reference to the victim and the content of their impact statement during the sentencing process (Meredith & Paquette 2001; Erez 2004; Regehr & Alaggia

2006). Other research suggests that many judicial officers are aware of this beneficial effect and self-report their endeavours to make reference to, and consequently validate, victims' experiences when preparing their sentencing remarks (O'Connell 2006; 2009; Victorian Victim Support Agency 2009). However, at the time we undertook our research, only one study had presented empirical research exploring actual judicial practice in acknowledging victims at sentencing (Booth 2014) and this examined the victim impact statement experiences of family members of homicide victims, not the primary victims themselves (see also Booth 2011; 2012; 2013; 2015).

There has also been little empirical research into victim participation in sentencing in the context of sexual offences (Du Mont, Miller, & White 2008). We were able to find only two previous research projects that explored the views of victims of sexual offending on victim impact statements (Walberg-Hegan 1997; Konradi & Burger 2000). Although such statements were introduced, in part, to address problems arising from the justice system experience of victims of sexual offending, research on such statements has generally excluded victims of sexual offending, not distinguished their experiences from those of other crime victims, and not involved interviews with victims themselves (for discussion, see Miller 2013). Du Mont, Miller, and White (2008) recommended that further research be undertaken by way of in-depth interviews with victims of sexual offending, to explore their experiences of victim impact statements and of the sentencing process. In this book, we begin to address this research gap by presenting the findings of our interviews with victims of sexual offences in two Australian jurisdictions.

Our research

As set out above, victim impact statements are used in the sentencing process to outline the harm caused to victims by the offending committed against them. Legislative frameworks for courts to accept these statements were introduced across Australia from the 1980s. They were also introduced across a range of other countries, including the United States (US), United Kingdom (UK), Canada, and New Zealand, as part of reforms designed to address barriers to successful sexual offence prosecutions and to reduce harmful aspects of victims' involvement in the criminal justice process. To date, however, little research has been undertaken to explore victim impact statements in the context of sexual offending. Previous research has generally excluded victims of sexual assault, not distinguished their experiences from those of other victims, or not involved interviews with victims themselves. As Tait has noted, '[f]ew VIS studies have asked [victims of crime] directly about their experiences of the VIS, using individual in-depth interviews' (2015: 36).

In this book, we address this gap, by providing the perspectives of six victims of sexual offences in Australia on the use of the impact statements in their case. We supplement this with the findings from interviews with 15 justice professionals who work with such victims and analysis of sentencing remarks in 100 sexual offence cases involving a victim impact statement, to determine the extent to which the harm experienced by the victims is acknowledged by judicial officers.

Structure of the text

The remainder of this chapter provides an overview of our research methodology, including the aims, scope, approach, and theoretical lens, as well as the limitations of our approach (for a more detailed overview, see Davies 2017).

Chapter 2 presents our literature review on victim participation in sentencing. It first outlines the development of victims' rights, including the right to present a victim impact statement. It then examines the prior research conducted to evaluate impact statement regimes and identifies the gaps in the literature that this book begins to fill.

Chapter 3 reviews impact statement legislation, case law, policies, and guidelines in Australia. It identifies, compares, and contrasts laws and policies relating to the preparation of victim impact statements and their presentation at sentencing. It focuses on the jurisdictions in which the research was conducted, especially the legislation, case law, policies, and guidelines that were identified as problematic in the interviews and the analysis of sentencing remarks.

Chapter 4 presents the first research findings. It analyses the sentencing remarks in 100 sexual offence cases from four Australian jurisdictions, supplemented by key findings from interviews with victims and professionals who work with victims. This chapter critically evaluates judicial practice in relation to the use of, and reference to, victims and their impact statements at sentencing. It identifies a range of approaches that judges take to acknowledge victims in their remarks and uses a series of examples to explore judicial practice from a victim-focused perspective. It makes two recommendations for educative processes that will assist judges to develop an understanding of how best to acknowledge victims, while still balancing the other requirements of sentencing.

Chapter 5 extends our findings, drawing on our interviews with both victims and justice professionals in relation to impact statements and sentencing processes across the research jurisdictions. The chapter focuses on a significant problem identified from the interviews and literature review, namely a pervasive lack of understanding of the purpose and use of victim impact statements in sentencing. In order to resolve this uncertainty, the chapter recommends a model that will, if adopted, achieve consistency and clarity in victim impact statement regimes.

Chapter 6 is the final findings chapter. It examines common problems raised by victims around the lack of information they received throughout their justice process experience, including a lack of information about sentencing. The chapter identifies a number of issues within current victims' rights regimes that may prevent justice professionals sharing information effectively with victims. It then explores the evidence-based literature on effective communication skills to propose strategies for improving communication between justice professionals and victims of crime.

Chapter 7 summarises our findings and consolidates our recommendations. It also highlights the importance of these recommendations and reaffirms their implications for improved policy and practice for judicial officers, justice professionals who work with victims throughout the sentencing process, and policymakers. These recommendations are of significance not only to the research jurisdictions examined within the book, but also to other jurisdictions with impact statement regimes, both in Australia and internationally. If adopted, they have the potential to improve the administration of justice in relation to victims of sexual violence.

Each of the foregoing substantive chapters is interspersed with vignettes, documenting the experiences of the six victims interviewed for this project. In her ground-breaking doctoral research with four victims of sexual abuse aged between 13 and 16, Walberg-Hegan (1997) included key aspects of her participants' stories, including their perspectives on the impact statements they prepared and suggestions for other victims. More recently, Elva and Stranger (2017) and Lee (2018) have prepared memoirs documenting their experiences as victims of sexual offending, although they did not examine sentencing issues. In her memoir, Miller (2019) made the following plea:

> When you hear a story about rape, all the graphic and unsettling details, resist the instinct to turn away; instead, look closer, because beneath the gore and police reports is a whole, beautiful person, looking for ways to be in the world again.
>
> (2019: 312)

Our research provides a rare opportunity to hear and learn from the experiences of adult victims of sexual offending who have participated in empirical research, especially in relation to the specific topic under examination, impact statements.

Our research method

This section provides a brief overview of our research aims, scope, approach, and theoretical lens (for further detail, see Davies 2017). Before providing this information, however, it is important to note that there are nine criminal justice jurisdictions in Australia: six states and two territories, as well as the Commonwealth (Cth) or federal government. Each of these has their own criminal law and sentencing frameworks. All substantive criminal laws in relation to sexual offending (e.g. rape) are dealt with at the state/territory level; federal offences only account for 2% of all crime in Australia and, in the context of sexual offending, relate to issues such as sexual offending committed outside of Australia and online. Most federal criminal matters are dealt with in the state/territory courts; there are also federal courts, but they mostly deal with civil matters. There are no federal prisons in Australia, so federal prisoners are housed in state/territory prisons. In descending order of population, the states and territories are NSW, Victoria (Vic), Queensland (Qld), Western Australia (WA), South Australia (SA), Tasmania (Tas), the Australian Capital Territory (ACT) and the Northern Territory (NT).

The literature shows that 'the study of VIS and their ability to meaningfully satisfy victims by giving them input into the sentencing phase remains a work in progress' (Sankoff & Wansborough 2006: 29). This is particularly true of victims in sexual offence matters. Our research had three major aims:

1. to gain a better understanding of victim perspectives of victim impact statement and sentencing processes and procedures in sexual offence cases;
2. to explore judicial practice in relation to the use of and reference to victim impact statements at sentencing in sexual offence cases; and
3. to determine whether any recommendations can be made for policy or legislative reform, to achieve best practice for impact statement processes and procedures from a victim-focused perspective.

We adopted a mixed-methods design, involving content analysis of 100 sentencing remarks and qualitative interviews with victims of sexual offending (n = 6) and justice professionals (n = 15). Our research was conducted in four jurisdictions: Victoria, South Australia, Tasmania, and the

ACT; this allowed for both the comparison of different approaches and identification of best practice across these jurisdictions.

The victim impact statement experiences of victims of sexual offending have never been explored in this way, in Australia or elsewhere. Accordingly, this combination of research approaches produces original insights into sexual offence victims' experiences of the impact statement process before, during, and after sentencing. Our findings and recommendations have significant implications for victims' experiences of impact statement and sentencing processes, judicial practice, and the practice of justice professionals who regularly work with victims, including prosecutors and witness assistance and victim support officers.

Sentencing remarks

Our content analysis of judges' sentencing remarks sought to determine the extent to which and how judicial officers acknowledge victim harm and the information in victim impact statements when sentencing. We also sought to assess the extent to which current judicial practice in that regard meets victims' expectations and needs.

We selected our study jurisdictions on the basis of those that make their sentencing remarks readily available. At the time of our research, sentencing remarks for the ACT and Tasmania were published permanently on the ACT and Tasmanian Supreme Court websites, respectively. South Australian sentencing remarks were published on the Courts Administration Authority website for a period of time after the sentence, while some, though not all, remarks from Victoria are published on the Australasian Legal Information Institute website.

We examined the sentencing remarks for every sexual offence conviction between 2014 and 2016 involving both an adult victim and adult offender in the ACT (n = 22), South Australia (n = 22), and Tasmania (n = 16) (for a full list, see Davies 2017: Appendix 2). Victoria had a far greater number of published remarks, reflecting its significantly larger population. Consequently, a random selection of Victorian remarks from the same period was collected (n = 40). The sentencing remarks were determined by five judges in Tasmania, eight in the ACT, 14 in South Australia, and 21 in Victoria. In 66 cases, the sentences were imposed following pleas of guilty, while sentencing occurred after a guilty verdict in 33 cases. In one case, there was a combination of guilty plea and verdict.

Table 1.1 displays the type of offending dealt with in each set of remarks. Only the most serious offence for which the offender was convicted is listed. For example, if the offender was convicted of both rape

Table 1.1 Offence type, by jurisdiction

Most serious offence	*ACT*	*SA*	*Tas*	*Vic*	*Total*
Rape[2]	15	15	10	26	66
Attempted rape	0	1	0	1	2
Aggravated sexual assault	0	0	4	0	4
Sexual penetration by fraud	0	0	0	2	2
Indecent assault	7	5	2	11	25
Indecent filming	0	1	0	0	1
Total	22	22	16	40	100

and indecent assault, this was listed as ‘rape’, which accounted for nearly two-thirds of all sentences.

The remarks from each jurisdiction tended to follow the same general format, starting with a description of the course of the offending. This was often, though not always, followed by a description of the effect of the crime on the victim and/or their family or community. Then the offender’s personal circumstances were described, including their previous criminal history, before setting out the sentence imposed.

The remarks were systematically coded, with a focus on determining frequency (how many cases involved judicial reference to victim harm) and substance (extent of discussion of victim harm). The remarks were coded for manifest, rather than latent, content, as we sought to determine the effect that judicial comments at sentencing have on victims, who are likely to take the remarks at face value. Coding for manifest content also involves a lower degree of interpretation (Maxfield & Babbie 2015) and reduces the subjectivity of any results.

Interviews

This project had ethics approval from the University of Tasmania. We conducted 21 interviews between September 2015 and June 2016. The interviews sought to ascertain and explore victims’ expectations and experiences of impact statement and sentencing processes and identify the judicial approaches they found beneficial or detrimental. We completed interviews with six victims of sexual offending and 15 justice professionals in a variety of roles:

- prosecutors who work with victims in the conduct of the prosecution of defendants (n = 3);

- witness assistance officers (WAOs), who work to support victims from within a prosecuting agency (n = 5); and
- victim support officers (VSOs), who work to support victims, but who do not work for a prosecuting agency (n = 7).

Table 1.2 sets out the jurisdiction and role of each interviewee. Justice profession participants were recruited through the agencies for which they worked. Victim participants were recruited with the assistance of victim support and witness assistance agencies in all four study jurisdictions, but ultimately only participated in South Australia and Tasmania (for discussion, see Davies 2017).

To be included in the study, participants were required to be adult female victims of sexual offending that had resulted in a conviction. Female victims were chosen because they are approximately five times

Table 1.2 Interview participants

ACT (n = 2)	
Jacqui	Prosecutor
Suzanna	VSO
SA (n = 6)	
Samuel	WAO
Cathy	VSO
August	Victim
Laura	Victim
Philippa	Victim
Jessica	Victim
Tas (n = 6)	
Michael	Prosecutor
Robert	VSO
Harriet	WAO
Clare	VSO
Rachel	Victim
Eve	Victim
Vic (n = 7)	
Rose	Prosecutor
Hannah	WAO
Andie	WAO
Colette	VSO
Jane	VSO
Trish	VSO
Alisa	VSO

Each interviewee was allocated a pseudonym to preserve their anonymity.

more likely than males to be a victim of sexual assault (Australian Bureau of Statistics 2016). They needed to be receiving or have received support from a victim support or witness assistance agency and have submitted an impact statement during the sentencing process. They were also required to have had access to their statement and the sentencing remarks from their case, to minimise the risk of re-traumatisation. If the victim no longer had these documents, their support workers were asked to provide copies. It was considered important that they had already read, processed, and understood the sentencing remarks in their case, as it would not have been appropriate to ask them to read the remarks for the first time in the lead-up to the interview. As researchers, having access to the impact statement and sentencing remarks was important to enable triangulation of the data. These documents provided background information on both the offending and its effect on the victim, allowing the interview to complete an otherwise 'incomplete picture' (Webley 2010: 940). This approach also ensured the interviewer knew the circumstances of the offending prior to the interview, which obviated the need to ask for this information from the victim participants and allowed the interviews to focus only on the victim impact statement and sentencing processes, unless the participant chose to share information about the offending of their own volition.

The semi-structured interview questions were modelled on Booth's (2013; 2015) research on the victim impact statement experiences of 14 family victims of homicide. Justice professionals were asked about the type of support they provide to victims prior to and during the court process, as well as their opinions on the effectiveness of the impact statement processes and how victims tend to be acknowledged by judicial officers in the courtroom. Victim participants were asked about their experience of completing and presenting an impact statement and the process of viewing or participating in a sentencing hearing. They were also asked about the support they received from various agencies prior to and during the court hearing and their feelings about the way they were acknowledged by the judge in court.

The interviews took place between September 2015 and June 2016. As they progressed, it became increasingly evident from the victim interviews that there were pervasive problems around the receipt of information arising in each victim's case. Because of these problems, which are explored in Chapter 6, the questions were refined to add discussion about how justice professionals provide information during the justice process and victims' receipt of such information.

Undertaking interviews with both victims and justice professionals allowed for a rich analysis of victim experiences from multiple and sometimes contradictory perspectives. The importance of exploring a diversity of views is clearly demonstrated by our findings, especially in Chapter 6, which identify systemic problems affecting victims' right to information about court and sentencing processes. The victim interviews demonstrate that some issues may be misunderstood or overlooked even by experienced justice professionals.

Our research lens

The lens of victim-focused therapeutic jurisprudence is brought to bear in analysing and discussing the research data in this book. A victim-focused approach was chosen for two reasons. First, because this research specifically concerns victims of sexual offending, only a victim focus would have allowed us to develop a comprehensive understanding of the nature and consequences of sexual victimisation. Second, this approach was required because of the nature and function of victim impact statements, as they are inherently victim-focused instruments introduced to alleviate the re-traumatisation of victims that may be caused by the criminal justice process. Consequently, it is arguable that any research seeking to explore whether and how victim impact statement processes and procedures are working must be approached from a victim-focused perspective.

We chose therapeutic jurisprudence as our research lens because of its law reform agenda (Winick 2011). Therapeutic jurisprudence is not strictly a theory, but rather a way of looking at the law (Wemmers 2008). It recognises that '[l]egal rules, legal procedures, and the roles of legal actors (such as lawyers and judges) constitute social forces that, whether inten[tionally] or not, often produce therapeutic or anti-therapeutic consequences' (Winick 1997: 185). In acknowledging that the justice system can have a 'far-reaching impact on those that become involved with it' (Cattaneo & Goodman 2010: 482), including victims, therapeutic jurisprudence uses the 'tools of the social sciences to … ascertain whether the law's anti-therapeutic effects can be reduced, and its therapeutic effects enhanced' (Winick 1997: 185). This may involve examining legal rules and 'legal practices and the way various legal actors – judges, lawyers, police officers, etc. – play their roles' (Winick 2009: 536), with the goal of 'restructur[ing] legal arrangements to … maximize their potential for healing and rehabilitation' (Winick 2009: 536).

It is important to emphasise that therapeutic jurisprudence does not 'suggest that therapeutic goals should trump other ones' (Wexler 2000: 125), nor does it attempt to 'subordinate … due process and other justice values' (Winick 1997: 185) or interfere with any established rights of others within the justice system, including the principle of fairness to the accused. Rather, it is 'a way of looking at the law in a richer way, and then bringing to the table some of these areas and issues that previously have gone unnoticed' (Wexler 2000: 125).

Victim-focused reform research has often utilised a feminist legal perspective and/or restorative justice approach (see e.g. Konradi & Burger 2000; McPhail 2016; Rossner 2017; Erez, Jiang, & Laster 2020), rather than a therapeutic jurisprudence lens. These three theoretical approaches share many common features and this book explores many themes that are relevant to both feminist and restorative justice analyses. However, we chose the therapeutic jurisprudence lens because, in using the tools of the social sciences to focus attention on the harms and benefits that may be caused by the law or legal processes, as distinct from harms caused by the offending, it aligns most closely with our research aims. In essence, our research seeks to identify legal processes that work, and those that do not, from a therapeutic, victim-focused perspective and make recommendations for change on this basis. Therapeutic jurisprudence has previously been criticised for being too focused on defendants (see e.g. Cannon 2007; Lopez & Koss 2017), rather than victims (Holder 2006). However, it has more recently begun to focus on victims' experiences of the law (Wemmers 2008; 2011; Tait 2015; Freckelton 2018). Erez, Jiang, and Laster recently observed that, '[f]or victims, [therapeutic jurisprudence] holds the promise of ameliorating secondary victimization at all levels and stages of the criminal justice process' (2020: 13), while Iliadis suggested, in the context of a discussion on victim impact statements, that '[i]ncreasing victim participation rights in the criminal justice system is therefore often advocated on the basis of improved therapeutic outcomes' (2020: 48). Although 'it is one thing to provide a therapeutic opportunity, another to ensure its therapeutic consequences' (Tait 2015: 8), our approach contributes to the growing application of therapeutic jurisprudence to issues relating to victims of crime (King 2008), by thinking creatively about how 'legal processes can be reshaped to … maximize the potential for the healing of the victim' (Winick 2009: 540). Our recommendations, which have implications for judicial practice, as well as for the practice of other justice professionals, such as prosecutors, witness assistance officers, and victim support agencies, attempt to reduce the legal system's anti-therapeutic effects, and enhance outcomes for victims when preparing and submitting a victim impact statement.

A note on terminology

It is important to acknowledge that the term 'victim' can be problematic and 'survivor' is often preferred when discussing sexual violence (see e.g.

Brooks & Burman 2017). However, consistent with many law reform and legal policy documents, we use 'victim', because 'it is the term that the majority of agencies use and understand when referring to someone who has experienced victimisation, and is the term officially used in policies and legislation' (Wedlock & Tapley 2016: 7).

In victim-focused research, concepts such as 'healing', 'closure', and 'therapeutic benefits' have also been subject to criticism on a number of bases. The vagueness of their meaning has been noted as a point of concern (see e.g. Bandes 2009; Pemberton & Raynears 2011; Doak & Taylor 2013) and issues with the generalisability of potential therapeutic outcomes have also been raised. As Pemberton and Reynaers (2011) argued, general statements that concern the possible effects of particular criminal justice initiatives on victims tend to disregard variations in victims' backgrounds, experiences, and psychological characteristics, all of which have the potential to affect their experience of victimisation, as well as their experience of the criminal justice process. Accordingly, we conceptualise the terms 'healing', 'closure', and 'therapeutic benefits' consistently with the approach of narrative psychology (e.g. White & Epston 1990; Vassilieva 2016), which

> is founded on the premise that externalising traumatic experiences … constitutes an effective coping mechanism for many people facing upheavals from major life-changing events, including violent crime. It follows that, if victims are given an outlet through which they can channel their emotions, they may be able to recover from the effects of victimisation more readily.
>
> (Doak, Henham, & Mitchell 2009: 667)

Consequently, where we argue that therapeutic benefits may arise from victims' use of impact statements, this should be understood to mean that impact statements provide victims with an outlet through which they can share – with the court, the offender, and the public – the harm caused to them by the offending. Consistent with the practice of narrative psychology, this outlet is expected to provide victims with the benefit of the potential for swifter recovery from the effects of victimisation. According to McGovern,

> [m]aking a victim impact statement has the potential to assist sexual violence survivors with their recovery. It can provide an occasion for formal recognition of the wrongfulness of the offending and acknowledgement of the harm suffered. It may help survivors

> develop insight into the effects of the offending and the resources available to the survivor for addressing these effects. Writing a victim impact statement may facilitate the process of grief and growth for some survivors. The process of discussing the content of a victim impact statement with an empathetic listener might help to reduce any shame the survivor is experiencing.
>
> (2013: 29)

The extent to which such claims are supported empirically is explored further in Chapter 2. In subsequent chapters, we examine ways to enhance the therapeutic benefits of impact statements for victims of sexual offences, drawing on our analysis of case law, as well as interviews with victims and justice professionals.

Limitations of the research

There are a number of limitations to the research, largely due to the small and exploratory nature of the study. We found that we reached saturation with the 15 justice professionals, but the fact that the justice professional interviewees were self-selected limits the representativeness and generalisability of the interview findings arising from this cohort of participants. Furthermore, as mentioned above, it became apparent during the victim interviews that there were pervasive problems around the lack of information received by each victim. However, by the time this problem had emerged, several justice professional interviews had already been completed. Consequently, there were a number of interviewees who were not asked about this subject. Accordingly, we are unable to represent the views of all of the interviewed justice professionals in the discussion of victims' right to information in Chapter 6.

In addition, we were unfortunately able to access fewer victim interviewees than were originally planned and this small number cannot be seen as representative of all victims of sexual offending who complete impact statements. Furthermore, our study was focused on sexual offences and two-thirds of the sentencing remarks we examined were for rape. Accordingly, we are not able to make claims about the applicability of our findings to other offences more generally.

While we examined judicial use of impact statements at sentencing by analysing remarks from a sample of cases, we did not obtain copies of the impact statements in those cases. Each court has full discretion in choosing whether or not to release such documents to the public (see e.g. *District Court Act 1991* (SA) s54(2)); potential difficulties could have arisen in accessing the statements, due to concerns about victims' privacy, especially given the sensitive nature of the offending. Accordingly, it is impossible to estimate the content or length of any statement submitted at a hearing, except where the judge has quoted directly from it. This does not prevent critique of the way that judges used and referred to the impact statements at sentencing, but we do so without knowing the exact contents of each statement. This means that certain aspects of our critique are speculative in nature.

Financial and time constraints prevented our content analysis from being supplemented by the context that could have been provided by interviewing at least some of the judicial officers whose remarks were analysed. Also, due to resource constraints, we only conducted research in four of the eight Australian states and territories. While we attempted to identify best practice across the ACT, South Australia, Tasmania, and Victoria, it is quite possible that beneficial practices go unacknowledged in NSW, the Northern Territory, Queensland, and/or Western Australia.

Finally, we acknowledge that some of the recommendations we make would be inconsistent with the law and/or practice in some jurisdictions. As our original research draws on an Australian case study, our findings, recommendations, and conclusions may not be directly applicable in other countries. There is no suggestion that our proposals entail solutions that apply universally. However, we suggest that they provide a solid foundation for other jurisdictions that wish to adopt a more victim-focused approach to victim impact statements, especially in respect of the victims of sexual offences.

Conclusion

This chapter has laid the foundation for the remainder of the text. Subject to the limitations noted above, we found that our chosen research approaches were well suited to obtain valuable insights and to achieve our primary research aims. The content analysis of sentencing remarks allowed for an in-depth critique of current judicial practice in acknowledging victims at sentencing. Undertaking interviews with victims and with justice professionals has allowed for a rich analysis of victim experiences from multiple perspectives and the benefits of directly interviewing victim participants greatly outweighed the difficulties encountered in planning and conducting this component of the research.

Notes

1 These statements are referred to by different names in different jurisdictions. They are called victim impact statements in Australia and victim personal statements in England and Wales. While the acronyms 'VIS', VISs', 'VPS', and 'VPSs' are often used in other published research, the terms 'victim impact statement/s', 'impact statement/s', and 'statement/s' will be used in this book to refer to such schemes in all jurisdictions.

2 The offence of sexual intercourse with a person who does not consent is called 'sexual intercourse without consent' in the ACT under the *Crimes Act 1900* (ACT) s54, 'rape' in South Australia under *Criminal Law Consolidation Act 1935* (SA) s48, 'rape' under *Criminal Code Act 1924* (Tas) s185, and 'rape' under *Crimes Act 1958* (Vic) s38. To achieve consistency, the term 'rape' is used to describe this category of offending across all of the jurisdictions.

References

Astor, M (2018). 'California Voters Remove Judge Aaron Persky, Who Gave a 6-Month Sentence for Sexual Assault', *New York Times*, 6 June. https://www.nytimes.com/2018/06/06/us/politics/judge-persky-brock-turner-recall.html.

Australian Bureau of Statistics (2013). *Defining the Data Challenge for Family, Domestic and Sexual Violence*, Cat 4529.0. Canberra.

Australian Bureau of Statistics (2016). *Gender Indicators Australia*, Cat 4125.0. Canberra.

Australian Law Reform Commission (2010). *Family Violence—A National Legal Response*, Report 114. Sydney.

Baker, K (2016). 'Here's The Powerful Letter The Stanford Victim Read To Her Attacker', *BuzzFeed*, 3 June. https://www.buzzfeednews.com/article/katiejmbaker/heres-the-powerful-letter-the-stanford-victim-read-to-her-ra.

Bandes, S (2009). 'Victims, "Closure" and the Sociology of Emotion', *Law and Contemporary Problems*, 72, Spring, 1–26.

Bluett-Boyd, N & Fileborn, B (2014). *Victim/Survivor-Focused Justice Responses and Reforms to Criminal Court Practice*, Australian Institute of Family Studies. Melbourne.

Booth, T (2011). 'Crime Victims and Sentencing: Reflections on *Borthwick*', *Alternative Law Journal*, 36, 236–239.

Booth, T (2012). '"Cooling Out" Victims of Crime: Managing Victim Participation in the Sentencing Process in a Superior Sentencing Court', *Australian and New Zealand Journal of Criminology*, 45, 214–230.

Booth, T (2013). *Accommodating Justice: An Exploratory Study of Structures and Processes that Shape Victim Participation and the Presentation of Victim Impact Statements in the Sentencing of Homicide Offenders in the NSW Supreme Court*, Unpublished PhD Thesis, University of NSW. Sydney.

Booth, T (2014). 'The Restorative Capacities of Victim Impact Statements: Analysis of the Victim-Judge Communication Dyad in the Sentencing of Homicide Offenders', *Restorative Justice*, 2, 302–326.

Booth, T (2015). *Accommodating Justice: Victim Impact Statements in the Sentencing Process*, Federation Press. Sydney.

Brooks, O & Burman, M (2017). 'Reporting Rape: Victim Perspectives on Advocacy Support in the Criminal Justice Process', *Criminology and Criminal Justice*, 17, 209–225.

Cannon, A (2007). 'Therapeutic Jurisprudence in the Magistrates Court: Some Issues of Practice and Principle', in G Reinhardt & A Cannon (eds), *Transforming Legal Processes in Court and Beyond*, Australasian Institute of Judicial Administration. Melbourne.

Cattaneo, L & Goodman, L (2010). 'Through the Lens of Therapeutic Jurisprudence: The Relationship Between Empowerment in the Court System and Well-being for Intimate Partner Violence Victims', *Journal of Interpersonal Violence*, 25, 481–502.

Clark, H (2010). *'What Is the Justice System Willing to Offer?' Understanding Sexual Assault Victim/Survivors' Criminal Justice Needs*, Australian Institute of Family Studies. Melbourne.

Clinton, H (2017). *What Happened*, Simon & Schuster. New York.

Daly, K (2014). 'Reconceptualizing Sexual Victimization and Justice', in I Vanfraechem, A Pemberton & F Ndahinda (eds), *Justice for Victims: Perspectives on Rights, Transition and Reconciliation*, Routledge. Abingdon.

Davies, R (2017). *Stories of Pervasive Uncertainty: A Victim-Focused Analysis of Victim Impact Statements and Sentencing in Sexual Offence Cases*, Unpublished PhD Thesis, University of Tasmania. Hobart.

Davis, R & Smith, B (1994). 'The Effects of Victim Impact Statements on Sentencing Decisions: A Test in an Urban Setting', *Justice Quarterly*, 11, 453–469.

De Mesmaecker, V (2012). 'Antidotes to Injustice? Victim Statements' Impact on Victims' Sense of Security', *International Review of Victimology*, 18, 133–153.

Doak, J, Henham R & Mitchell B (2009). 'Victims and the Sentencing Process: Developing Participatory Rights?', *Legal Studies*, 29, 651–677.

Doak, J & Taylor, L (2013). 'Hearing the Voices of Victims and Offenders: The Role of Emotions in Criminal Sentencing', *Northern Ireland Legal Quarterly*, 64, 25–46.

Du Mont, J, Miller, K-L & and White, D (2008). 'Social Workers' Perspectives on the Victim Impact Statements in Cases of Sexual Assault in Canada', *Women and Criminal Justice*, 18(3), 1–23.

Elva, T & Stranger, T (2017). *South of Forgiveness*, Scribe. Melbourne.

Erez, E & Tontodonato, P (1990). 'The Effect of Victim Participation in Sentencing on Sentence Outcome', *Criminology*, 28, 451–474.

Erez, E, Roeger, L & Morgan, F (1994). *Victim Impact Statements in South Australia: An Evaluation*, South Australian Attorney-General's Department. Adelaide.

Erez, E (2004). 'Victim Voice, Impact Statements and Sentencing: Integrating Restorative Justice and Therapeutic Jurisprudence Principles in Adversarial Proceedings', *Criminal Law Bulletin*, 40, 483–500.

Erez, E, Ibarra, P & Downs, D (2011). 'Victim Welfare and Participation Reforms in the United States: A Therapeutic Jurisprudence Perspective', in E Erez, M Kilchling & J-A Wemmers (eds), *Therapeutic Jurisprudence and Victim Participation in Justice: International Perspectives*, Carolina Academic Press. Durham.

Erez, E, Jiang, J & Laster, K (2020). 'From Cinderella to Consumer: How Crime Victims Can Go to the Ball', in J Tapley & P Davies (eds), *Victimology*, Palgrave Macmillan. Cham.

Freckelton, I (2018). 'Foreword', in S Bronitt & P Easteal (eds), *Rape Law in Context: Contesting the Scales of Injustice*, Federation Press. Sydney.

Giles, F (2018). 'The Other-Directed Memoir: Victim Impact Statements and the Aesthethics of Change', in B Avieson, F Giles & S Joseph (eds), *Mediating Memory: Tracing the Limits of Memoir*, Routledge. Abingdon.

Herman, J (2003). 'The Mental Health of Crime Victims: Impact of Legal Intervention', *Journal of Traumatic Stress*, 16, 159–166.

Herman, J (2005). 'Justice from the Victim's Perspective', *Violence Against Women*, 11, 571–602.

Holder, R (2006). 'The Emperor's New Clothes: Court and Justice Initiatives to Address Family Violence', *Journal of Judicial Administration*, 16, 30–47.

Hoyle, C, Cape, E, Morgan, R & Sanders, A (1998). *Evaluation of the 'One Stop Shop' and Victim Statement Pilot Projects*, Home Office. London.

Hoyle, C & Zedner, L (2007). 'Victims, Victimization and Criminal Justice', in M Maguire, R Morgan & R Reiner (eds), *The Oxford Handbook of Criminology*, Oxford University Press, 4th ed. Oxford.

Iliadis, M (2020). *Adversarial Justice and Victims' Rights: Reconceptualising the Role of Sexual Assault Victims*, Routledge. Abingdon.

Keenan, M (2017). 'Criminal Justice, Restorative Justice, Sexual Violence and the Rule of Law', in E Zinsstag & M Keenan (eds), *Restorative Responses to Sexual Violence: Legal, Social and Therapeutic Dimensions*, Routledge. Abingdon.

Kemph, M (2018). 'Reconsidering the Use of Victim Impact Evidence', *Georgetown Journal of Legal Ethics*, 31, 673–688.

King, M (2008). 'Restorative Justice, Therapeutic Jurisprudence and the Rise of Emotionally Intelligent Justice', *Melbourne University Law Review*, 30, 1096–1126.

Konradi, A & Burger, T (2000). 'Having the Last Word: An Examination of Rape Survivors' Participation in Sentencing', *Violence Against Women*, 6, 351–395.

Konradi, A (2007). *Taking the Stand: Rape Survivors and the Prosecution of Rapists*, Praeger. Westport.

Lee, B (2018). *Eggshell Skull: A Memoir About Standing Up, Speaking Out and Fighting Back*, Allen & Unwin. Sydney.

Leverick, F, Chalmers, J & Duff, P (2007). *An Evaluation of the Pilot Victim Statement Schemes in Scotland*, Scottish Executive Social Research. Edinburgh.

Lievore, D (2005). *No Longer Silent: A Study of Women's Help-Seeking Decisions and Service Responses to Sexual Assault*, Australian Institute of Criminology. Canberra.

Lopez, E & Koss, M (2017). 'The RESTORE Program for Sex Crimes: Differentiating Therapeutic Jurisprudence from Restorative Justice with Therapeutic Components', in E Zinsstag & M Keenan (eds), *Restorative Responses to Sexual Violence: Legal, Social and Therapeutic Dimensions*, Routledge. Abingdon.

Maxfield, M & Babbie, E (2015). *Research Methods for Criminal Justice and Criminology*, Cengage Learning, 7th ed. Boston.

McGlynn, C (2011). 'Feminism, Rape and the Search for Justice', *Oxford Journal of Legal Studies*, 31, 825–842.

McGovern, D (2013). 'The Therapeutic Potential of Victim Impact Statements for Sexual Violence', *Sexual Abuse in Australia and New Zealand*, 5(2), 21–30.

McPhail, B (2016). 'Feminist Framework Plus: Knitting Feminist Theories of Rape Etiology into a Comprehensive Model', *Trauma, Violence, & Abuse*, 17, 314–329.

Meredith, C & Paquette, C (2001). *Summary Report on Victim Impact Statement Focus Groups*, Department of Justice Canada. Ottawa.

Miller, C. (2019). *Know My Name: A Memoir*, Viking. New York.

Miller, K-L (2013). 'Purposing and Repurposing Harms: The Victim Impact Statement and Sexual Assault', *Qualitative Health Research*, 23, 1445–1458.

Morrison, Z, Quadara, A & Boyd, C (2007). *'Ripple Effects' of Sexual Assault*, Australian Institute of Family Studies. Melbourne.

Naylor, B (2010). 'Effective Justice for Victims of Sexual Assault: Taking up the Debate on Alternative Pathways', *University of NSW Law Journal*, 33, 662–684.

NSW Sentencing Council (2018). *Victims' Involvement in Sentencing – Report*. Sydney.

O'Connell, M (2006). 'Evolving Mechanisms for Engaging Victims in the Sentencing Process: Should Victims Have a Stronger Voice in Court?', Paper presented at the Sentencing Principles Perspectives and Possibilities Conference, Canberra.

O'Connell, M (2009). 'Victims in the Sentencing Process: South Australia's Judges and Magistrates Give Their Verdict', *International Perspectives in Victimology*, 4, 50–57.

O'Connell, M (2015). 'The Evolution of Victims' Rights and Services in Australia', in D Wilson & S Ross (eds), *Crime, Victims and Policy: International Contexts, Local Experiences*, Palgrave Macmillan. Cham.

Payne, S (2009). *Rape: The Victim Experience Review*, UK Home Office. London.

Pemberton, A & Reynaers, S (2011). 'The Controversial Nature of Victim Participation: Therapeutic Benefits in Victim Impact Statements', in E Erez, M Kilchling & J-A Wemmers (eds), *Therapeutic Jurisprudence and Victim Participation in Justice: International Perspectives*, Carolina Academic Press. Durham.

Regehr, C & Alaggia, R (2006). 'Perspectives of Justice for Victims of Sexual Violence', *Victims and Offenders*, 1, 33–46.

Rossner, M (2017). 'Restorative Justice and Victims of Crime: Directions and Developments', in S Walklate (ed), *Handbook of Victims and Victimology*, Routledge. Abingdon.

Roy, A. (2019). 'Impact Statements: Giving Voice to Sexual Assault Survivors', *University of Maryland Law Journal of Race, Religion, Gender and Class*, 19, 370–394.

Sankoff, P & Wansborough, L (2006). 'Is Three Really a Crowd? Thoughts about Victim Impact Statements and New Zealand's Revamped Sentencing Regime', Paper presented at the International Conference of the International Society for the Reform of Criminal Law, Brisbane.

Serisier, S (2018). *Speaking Out: Feminism, Rape and Narrative Politics*, Palgrave Macmillan. Cham.

Shapland, J, Willmore, J & Duff, P (1985). *Victims in the Criminal Justice System*, Gower. Aldershot.

Sheley, E (2017). 'Victim Impact Statements and Expressive Punishment in the Age of Social Media', *Wake Forest Law Review*, 52, 157–192.

Tait, F (2015). *Testaments of Transformation: The Victim Impact Statement Process in NSW as Experienced by Victims of Crime and Victim Service Professionals*, Unpublished Master's Thesis, University of Sydney. Sydney.

Vassilieva, J (2016). *Narrative Psychology: Identity, Transformation and Ethics*, Palgrave Macmillan. Cham.

Victorian Law Reform Commission (2016). *The Role of Victims of Crime in the Criminal Trial Process: Report*. Melbourne.

Victorian Victim Support Agency (2009). *A Victim's Voice: Victim Impact Statements in Victoria*. Melbourne.

Walberg-Hegan, L (1997). *Voices of Victims: The Experience of Preparing a Victim Impact Statement for Use in Court, As Described by Adolescent Sexual Abuse Survivors*, Unpublished EdD Thesis, University of Toronto. Toronto.

Wall, L & Quadara, A (2014). *Acknowledging Complexity in the Impacts of Sexual Victimisation Trauma*, Australian Institute of Family Studies. Melbourne.

Warner, K (2005). 'Sexual Offending: Victim, Gender and Sentencing Dilemmas', in D Chappell & P Wilson (eds), *Issues in Australian Crime and Criminal Justice*, LexisNexis Butterworths. Sydney.

Webley, L (2010). 'Qualitative Approaches to Empirical Legal Research', in P Cane & H Kritzer (eds), *Oxford Handbook of Empirical Legal Research*, Oxford University Press. Oxford.

Wedlock, E & Tapley, J (2016). *What Works in Supporting Victims of Crime: A Rapid Evidence Assessment*, Report for the Victims Commissioner for England and Wales, University of Portsmouth. Portsmouth.

Wemmers, J-A (2008). 'Victim Participation and Therapeutic Jurisprudence', *Victims and Offenders*, 3, 165–191.

Wemmers, J-A (2011). 'Victims in the Criminal Justice System and Therapeutic Jurisprudence: A Canadian Perspective', in E Erez, M Kilchling & J-A Wemmers (eds), *Therapeutic Jurisprudence and Victim Participation in Justice: International Perspectives*, Carolina Academic Press. Durham.

Wexler, D (2000). 'Therapeutic Jurisprudence: An Overview', *Thomas M Cooley Law Review*, 17, 125–134.

White, M & Epston, D (1990). *Narrative Means to Therapeutic Ends*, WW Norton & Co. New York.

Whittaker, B (2020). '"Know My Name": Author and Sexual Assault Survivor Chanel Miller's Full "60 Minutes" Interview', *60 Minutes*, 9 August. https://www.cbsnews.com/news/chanel-miller-full-60-minutes-interview-know-my-name-author-brock-turner-sexual-assault-survivor-2020-08-09/.

Winick, B (1997). 'The Jurisprudence of Therapeutic Jurisprudence', *Psychology, Public Policy, and Law*, 3, 184–206.

Winick, B (2009). 'Therapeutic Jurisprudence Perspectives on Dealing with Victims of Crime', *Nova Law Review*, 33, 535–543.

Winick, B (2011). 'Therapeutic Jurisprudence and Victims of Crime', in E Erez, M Kilchling & J-A Wemmers (eds), *Therapeutic Jurisprudence and Victim Participation in Justice: International Perspectives*, Carolina Academic Press. Durham.

EVE

Eve met the offender through a dating website and arranged to meet for a drink at a pub near Eve's daughter's school, with Eve's child present too. After some drinks and conversation, they decided to go back to Eve's house with her child to talk more. When they got there, Eve made it clear that the offender was not welcome to stay and he said he had organised for a friend to pick him up after a few hours. They kissed consensually, but Eve repeatedly told him that she was not interested in having sex. The offender held Eve down on the couch and raped her. Afterwards, Eve said 'you raped me' and the offender agreed that he had done this. Eve reported the rape to the police while the offender was still in her house. The police arrived and questioned the offender.

The Director of Public Prosecutions (DPP) didn't contact Eve for 15 months after the rape. She called every so often for an update, but each time she rang, she spoke to a different person who was not familiar with her case, so she was forced to retell her story each time. About three weeks before the trial, the DPP's office called Eve and told her the trial was coming up. She had not heard anything else from the DPP, but then spent up to three days a week with the prosecutor, discussing her evidence. She said:

> If I have learned anything from this process, it's that nobody actually cares about the victim. I got a phone call out of the blue, 15 months after he raped me, saying 'can you come to the DPP's office?' No one got in contact with me after it happened. I went to the hospital, got the rape kit done and that's it.

Eve was familiar with victim impact statements before the trial, because she had completed one previously for a minor matter. She was encouraged to complete an impact statement by the witness assistance officer who supported her, but said that it was something that she wanted to do anyway, because she felt that she didn't have a voice through the process:

> the purpose of it is that I get a voice and I get to tell him how I am feeling, rather than just the facts of what happened that night. I don't necessarily think that anybody cares. That the judge or anybody takes it on board with sentencing. He might have. He got above minimum, which I was surprised about. And the judge was lovely. But I guess that they have probably heard them all before. … I wanted to do it because I wanted to get my power back, that he

had taken from me, but for the courts, I think it's probably more of a formality and a process, [rather] than them actually caring.

After the offender was convicted by the jury of one count of rape, Eve read out her impact statement to the court. She was happy that she was able to read the statement aloud to the offender. She said:

> I liked doing it to his face. And having his mum and dad there as well, because they were present during the whole trial, and were staring at me throughout the whole trial. So, I wanted them to know the impact that their son had on me.

However, Eve was very unhappy about the fact that the court was not closed for the reading and she wasn't given the option of this. As a result, the content of her impact statement was widely published in the media. Eve found this greatly traumatising:

> I wouldn't have even gone through the whole process if I had known how horrific it would be. If I was ever raped again, I would never report it. That's how horrendous the whole process was. I would never do it again. If it happened to a girlfriend, I wouldn't want them to go through it either. Which is awful because then all the rapists get to walk around thinking that's what they can do. So, something needs to be put in place to help people. The process is just crap.

Eve recognised that this would allow sexual offenders to escape the justice system, but felt this would be less traumatic than what she experienced. The judge made the following reference to Eve in the sentencing remarks:

> [Eve's] victim impact statement shows that the crimes had a significant impact on her. The crime made her feel humiliated and powerless. She had great difficulty reliving the event through the police investigation. The stress was exacerbated when told that the defendant had herpes. She had an immediate panic attack and vomited. She has suffered from nightmares and lack of sleep. All of this is on top of the emotional and psychological difficulties she suffered because of the earlier family tragedies. Because of those things she used alcohol as a method of trying to cope and had difficulties with self-harm. After this incident she had a number of admissions to a psychiatric unit in relation to self-harm and suicidal thoughts. She had finished

> her job a few weeks beforehand and was unable to work again for a period of about seven months before finding employment.

In her impact statement, she also explained that she trusted people less than she used to and felt worried about her daughter's wellbeing. She also did not feel comfortable in her home, which

> used to feel like a safe place before this happened. I … have to make sure that things are all locked and secure. I felt that the offender had a complete disregard for both me and for my daughter … I was also shocked at the offender's disregard for my welfare and disregard for the possibility of pregnancy. He showed further disregard by trying to add me as a Facebook friend some months after the crime occurred.

Eve's statement was edited slightly by the prosecutor before submission, including reference to the type of medication Eve was taking. Eve felt that victims should be allowed to write whatever they want in their impact statements:

> it's your statement. It's the only time you get a voice. You shouldn't be restricted. I wasn't allowed to say things. It happened to me. It didn't happen to him, or the judge or the jury or the lawyers. So I shouldn't be restricted, and I should be able to say what I want to say, without being stupid or anything.

Chapter 2

Victim participation in sentencing

Introduction

The study of victims' needs and the establishment of victims' rights are fairly recent developments in the adversarial criminal justice system. This chapter briefly summarises the evolution of these rights (for a general overview, see e.g. Erez, Jiang, & Laster 2020), before exploring victims' right to participate in sentencing by submitting a victim impact statement. Despite this process now being an accepted part of the modern criminal justice system (see O'Connell 2006; 2009), research is lacking on the use of impact statements by victims of sexual offending and the practical use of those statements by judicial officers in court. This chapter establishes the current state of the literature on these issues, framed by a focus on the two principal – and largely conflicting – approaches to the purpose of such statements. The chapter then identifies the knowledge gaps that this book begins to fill.

The historic role of the victim

The role of victims in the adversarial criminal justice system has changed dramatically over time. At least until the end of the 11th century, victims were active participants in the criminal process, because crimes were considered to be private in nature (see e.g. Kearon & Godfrey 2007; von Hirsch, Ashworth, & Roberts 2009). This meant that the victim and their family or community undertook action to rectify any injury suffered. According to Sankoff and Wansborough (2006: 6), this model had significant drawbacks for the community as a whole, because it allowed victims or their families to 'take laws into their own hands … [which] was liable to result in larger vendettas or blood feuds between clans or families'. It was also seen by the monarchy as obstructive to its ability to rule effectively and a breach of the King's peace (Young 2001).

Consequently, the King chose to take a more active role in the prosecution of defendants, by converting criminal injury into a public wrong. Thus began the decline of the victim's role in the criminal justice system and, by the 14th century, prosecution had become entirely the domain of the Crown (Young 2001; Kearon & Godfrey 2007).

This progression from a system of 'private vengeance to state administered justice' (Erez, Roeger, & Morgan 1994: 1) resulted in a criminal justice system where, for hundreds of years, the victim's role was limited to that of witness. This meant that victims had no power to compel prosecution or influence the sentence imposed, nor any standing to contest decisions. Christie described this as the theft of the conflict from the victim, arguing that the victim was a 'heavy loser in this situation. Not only has he suffered, lost materially or become hurt, physically or otherwise … above all he has lost participation in his own case' (1977: 7).

In more modern times, beginning in the 20th century, the victim's lack of formal role in the criminal justice process led to a larger societal perception of injustice (Erez, Roeger, & Morgan 1994). As Duff pointed out, 'it is hard to explain the sense in which [crimes] are "public" wrongs without denigrating the victim's standing by implying that they are wrongs against "the public" rather than the victim' (2009: 180). It became generally understood that, at best, the criminal justice system left victims feeling aggrieved; at worst, it caused them to feel disempowered, disenchanted, and alienated (Katz 2010), which could result in their re-victimisation (Ashworth 1993; Mossman 2012).

Victims' needs and the development of victims' rights

Beginning in the 1970s, the victims' rights movement emerged, drawing particular attention to the 'unenviable and essentially powerless position of victims of sexual crimes' (O'Connell 2015: 243). The movement advocated for the needs of victims that were largely ignored by the justice system, including the need for emotional support and information and to be heard, compensated, and acknowledged (see e.g. Hoyle & Zedner 2007). The movement successfully exerted pressure on governments across Australia and other jurisdictions to develop support services to address these needs.

In the 1980s, the goals of the movement shifted towards establishing formal rights for victims in the criminal justice system. Legislatures in some Australian jurisdictions responded quickly. For example, in 1981, South Australia established a Committee of Inquiry into Victims of Crime (O'Connell 2015). This trend was mirrored overseas, with the US President's Task Force on Victims of Crime proclaiming that:

> Victims, no less than defendants, are entitled to their day in court. Victims, no less than defendants, are entitled to have their views considered. A judge cannot evaluate the seriousness of a defendant's conduct without knowing how the crime has burdened the victim. A judge cannot reach an informed determination of the danger posed by the defendant without hearing from the person he has victimized.
>
> (1982: 76–77)

By 1985, the United Nations General Assembly had resolved to 'adopt and implement the Declaration of Basic Principles of Justice for Victims of Crime and Abuse of Power' (the Declaration) (Mossman 2012: 3). The Declaration recognised victims' need to be:

- treated with compassion and respect;
- informed of their role within the justice system, the progress of the proceedings, and of the disposition of their cases; and
- have their views presented and considered at appropriate stages of the proceedings.

(United Nations 1985)

It also urged the implementation of victims' rights legislation, proposing 'minimum standards for the treatment of victims, including to be treated fairly, to obtain compensation, and [to] be provided with assistance in healing and recovery' (Mossman 2012: 3).

Since that time, victims' rights instruments have been introduced in Australia and other jurisdictions worldwide (for a comparison between the UK and US, see Manikis 2019b). In Australia, these instruments are the *Victims of Crime Act 1994* (ACT); *Victims of Crime Act 1994* (WA); *Victims of Crime Act 2001* (SA); *Victims' Charter Act 2006* (Vic); *Victims of Crime Assistance Act 2009* (Qld); *Victims' Rights and Support Act 2013* (NSW); Northern Territory *Charter of Victims' Rights* and *Charter of Rights of Victims of Crime* (Tas). These instruments reflect many of the United Nations Basic Principles of Justice for Victims of Crime, such as victims' right to receive information about their case. Some provide guidance to assist state institutions to treat victims in a sympathetic and dignified way and protect victims' privacy. NSW, Queensland, South Australia, and Victoria also provide the right for information about the harm caused to the victim to be presented to the sentencing court through a victim impact statement. This is also covered by the relevant sentencing legislation (see *Criminal Law (Sentencing) Act 1988* (SA) s7A, which was in place at the time we conducted our research; see now *Sentencing Act 2017* (SA) s14; see also *Sentencing Act 1991* (Vic) ss8K–8S; *Sentencing Act 1995* (NT) ss106A–106B; *Sentencing Act 1995* (WA) s25; *Sentencing Act 1997* (Tas) s81A; *Crimes (Sentencing Procedure) Act 1999* (NSW) ss26–30; *Crimes (Sentencing) Act 2005* (ACT) ss47–53).

Victim impact statements and the modern role of the victim

Victim impact statements are reports provided to the court before the offender is sentenced. They outline the effect of the offending on the victim, including details such as the physical, psychological, and financial suffering the victim has experienced as a consequence of the offending. They are currently used in Australia, Canada, Ireland, the Netherlands, New Zealand, South Africa, the UK, and the US (see e.g. Garkawe 2006; De Mesmaecker 2012; McGovern 2013; Lens et al. 2015; Manikis 2015; Miller 2015; Erez, Jiang, & Laster 2020; van de Merwe & Mitchell 2020; Windsor & Roberts 2020). Accordingly, our findings have broad implications for all countries that use – or are considering using – victim impact statements as part of their criminal justice system.

While impact statements were introduced as early as the 1980s in some US (Erez 1990), Australian (see e.g. Erez, Roeger, & Morgan 1994), and Canadian (Walberg-Hegan 1997; Young, 2001) jurisdictions, they were not legislated for in England and Wales until 2001 and in Scotland until 2003 (Chalmers, Duff, & Leverick 2007; Garkawe 2007). The introduction of impact statements at sentencing reflects the modern conception of the victim within the criminal justice system, wherein their role is no longer limited to that of simply witness for the prosecution (Victorian Law Reform Commission 2016). This shift arose from a 'genuine and deeply rooted realisation that victims have a legitimate interest in the way that criminal justice is administered, in terms of substance, processes and outcomes' (Doak 2008: 243).

The recognition of the interests of the victim cannot, however, override the defendant's right to a fair trial, which Mason CJ and McHugh J of the High Court of Australia recognised in *Dietrich v The Queen* as 'a central pillar' of the criminal justice system ((1992) 177 CLR 292: 298). In *X7 v Australian Crime Commission* (2013) 248 CLR 92, French CJ and Crennan J held that this 'extends to the whole course of the criminal process' (2013: 116), including sentencing. As a result of the requirement to both adhere to fundamental criminal justice principles for the offender and promote the interests of the victim, impact statement schemes were described by Sully J in *R v FD; R v FD; R v* JD [2006] NSWCCA 31 as an 'attempt to balance interests that are not easily balanced' (2006: [97]). Arguably, the introduction of such statements has steered the criminal justice system into 'unfamiliar territory where the ideological lines are far from clear' (Garland 2001: 4), although Manikis has recently argued that 'the rhetoric of "balancing rights" or "balancing interests" of the accused with those of victims reinforces a zero-sum game perception of criminal processes' (2019b: 208; see also Kennedy, Easteal, & Bartels 2012).

As a result of this perceived tension, the introduction of victim impact statements at sentencing has not been without detractors, who are concerned that they may conflict with the 'central pillar' of the defendant's right to a fair trial (see e.g. Erez 1999; Sanders et al. 2001; Roberts & Manikis 2011; Booth 2015). However, the issue of fairness to the defendant arises only if judicial officers rely on the information in the statement when determining sentence. It is therefore critical to determine the purpose for which victim impact statements are intended to be used.

What are the possible purposes of victim impact statements?

Roberts (2003) has explained that the goals of victim impact statements are primarily to:

- increase victims' and society's satisfaction with the criminal justice system;
- increase offenders' awareness of the harms they have caused;
- promote healing and closure for victims; and
- apprise sentencing judges of the harms suffered by victims, which could be taken into account in determining sentences.

These goals reveal the two potential underlying purposes of impact statements, namely, as:

- *instrumental* tools, used by judicial officers in determining the sentence, where the impact statement can influence the sentence imposed; or
- communicative or *expressive* tools, which allow victims to achieve healing and catharsis by sharing with the court, offender, and public the harm caused to them by the offending (Roberts & Erez 2010; see also Erez 2000; Iliadis 2020).

Manikis (2015: 56) has described the fundamental divergence between these two approaches as a 'conflict', while Tait suggested that the 'potential probative value of the VIS to inform sentencing decisions is perhaps its poisoned chalice' (2015: 7).

The instrumental approach views impact statements as a tool for the judicial officer to assess the actual harm caused by the offending and, by taking that harm into account, determine the sentence to be imposed. This information about harm could enhance the retributive aims of sentencing (Booth 2005) and assist the judicial officer in determining relevant aggravating factors. If victim impact statements are used instrumentally, the fundamental principle of the offender's right to a fair trial requires that impact statements be treated as evidence and comply with the rules relating to evidence and proof. This is because, as noted by the majority of the High Court in *R v Olbrich*, 'the process by which a court arrives at the sentence to be imposed on an offender has just as much significance for the offender as the process by which guilt or innocence is determined' ((1999) 199 CLR 270: 270). Consequently, if used instrumentally, the content of impact statements must be limited to information that meets the standard of proof in the event of a challenge from the defence, and offenders must have the opportunity to challenge that information, for example through objection and submissions from the bar table (Booth 2011) or cross-examination of the victim (Edwards 2009).

In contrast, under an expressive approach to impact statements, Manikis has explained that the statement:

> understood solely as having an expressive function is not intended to affect the nature or quantum of the sentence … since its role is not to adduce evidence but rather to express emotion, there is no real need to ensure the factual reliability or the relevance of the information … Typically, this will allow more flexibility in terms of the content of the statement as well as in what methods of delivering the statement are permissible.
>
> (2015: 92)

When viewed expressively, an impact statement has no effect on the sentence imposed on the offender. Instead, it is seen only as a therapeutic tool, which should ideally assist the victim by providing a cathartic experience. As Sully J noted in *R v FD; R v FD; R v JD*, impact statements provide victims with

> a forum in which they can make a public statement in words of their own choosing in order to have the emotional catharsis of ensuring

> that their grief and loss has not been ignored altogether or expressed in what they see as an inadequate way.
>
> ([2006] NSWCCA 31: [100])

Accordingly, an expressive impact statement framework enables victims to share whatever information they choose, without being constrained by the rules of evidence and proof or fear of being questioned via cross-examination.

The expressive purpose may appear at first glance to be the more therapeutic approach, from a victim-focused perspective, since it seems to align more closely with the originating aims of impact statement schemes, namely to increase victims' involvement in, and improve their experience of, the justice process. However, if impact statements are used expressively, and victims are permitted the freedom to include any information they choose within their statement, without that information being verified via cross-examination, then it follows that judicial officers must ignore impact statements in determining sentence and must make it clear that they have done so. If this is not done, there is a danger that sentences may appear to be tainted by possibly irrelevant material. Yet, as will be discussed below, recent research reveals that victims derive great therapeutic benefit from judicial acknowledgement of their impact statements at sentencing. Consequently, if judicial officers cannot acknowledge impact statements when sentencing, then an expressive approach may also be anti-therapeutic from a victim-focused perspective.

The divergence between these two approaches, and the consequential outcomes for victims and offenders, raises questions of whether one purpose should be preferred or whether elements of both can be implemented in impact statement regimes. This is an important question, because the rules and requirements of any impact statement regime must be informed by the purpose of such statements (Markin 2017). One would therefore expect that victim impact statement legislation would contain clear direction in this regard. Yet, as will be discussed in Chapter 3, there is no explicit indication as to which purposes actually underlie impact statement regimes in Australia and the implied indicators are confusing and sometimes contradictory (see Booth 2015). This lack of clarity frames much of the analysis and discussion throughout the remainder of the book. Ultimately, Chapter 5 will argue that it is possible for a properly constructed and principled victim impact statement regime to balance instrumental and expressive approaches, in order to prioritise a victim focus, without jeopardising fairness to the offender.

Empirical research on impact statements

Objections to impact statements

In addition to the unresolved question of the purpose of victim impact statements, there have also been a number of practical objections arising from the implementation of such schemes. These objections are based on fears that:

- the use of impact statements may unfairly increase sentences for offenders;
- impact statement may:
    - cause court delays;
    - be superfluous;
    - contain information that is inflammatory or contradictory to what is already before the court;
- victims may:
    - be re-traumatised by the process of submitting an impact statement; and
    - expect their impact statement to influence the sentence imposed on the offender, which may lead to disappointment.

Many of these objections can be and have been subject to empirical research. In this chapter, we focus predominantly on the research from Commonwealth countries (i.e. Australia, UK, Scotland, and Canada), due to the ease of comparison across their adversarial justice systems (for discussion of the implications of the adversarial system for victims and impact statements, see e.g. Erez 2004; Garkawe 2006; Booth 2012; Walklate 2012; Tait 2015; Erez, Jiang, & Laster 2020; for discussion of the use of such statements in the inquisitorial context, see e.g. Booth, Bosma & Lens 2018; Braun 2013; Lens, Pemberton, & Bogaerts 2013; Lens et al. 2015). We found the literature from the US of lesser relevance, due to its focus on the use of impact statements in the context of capital offences (for an overview, see e.g. Englebrecht 2011), which is not relevant to the Australian context.

Objections on procedural grounds

Do impact statements unfairly increase sentences?

As noted above, Edwards (2009: 299) has argued that the 'central theoretical constraint' on the use of victim impact statements at sentencing is the risk of interfering with procedural fairness for the offender. In particular, a common argument is that this may result in victim-driven sentencing (see e.g. Ashworth 1993) and lead to 'a subjective approach [that] lets emotions shape legal decisions' (Hörnle 1999: 176). On this issue, a question often asked in the literature is whether an offender who kills a victim without a family should be punished less severely than one who kills a well-loved victim (Roberts & Manikis 2010). In cases where the primary victim is still alive, critics have expressed concern that similar cases might be treated differently, depending on factors such as the resilience and vindictiveness or forgiveness of the victim (see e.g. Ashworth 1993; 2015). It has also been suggested that impact statements could increase the unpredictability of sentencing, which should ideally demonstrate consistency in the punishment of offenders (Garkawe 2007).

However, extensive research (e.g. Erez & Tontodonato 1990; Erez, Roeger, & Morgan 1994; Manikis & Roberts 2011) indicates that impact statements have not led to victim-driven sentencing. Erez and Tontodonato (1990) found that specific requests for incarceration by the victim did not influence courts' choice of sentence. Other studies (see Davis & Smith 1994a; 1994b) found that impact statements affect neither the type of sanction imposed on the offender, nor the length of punishment. In Tait's (2015) research with justice professionals in NSW, 7% of respondents said impact statements affected the sentence, 40% said it did not, 30% said it did so sometimes, and 23% indicated they did not know. The direction and magnitude of any such impact was not discussed. O'Connell's research with judicial officers led him to conclude that 'victims have in general exercised restraint and not used impact statements as a means to appeal for harsher sentences' (2009: 56). It is accordingly commonly accepted that victim impact statements generally have no effect on sentencing severity (Erez & Rogers 1999; Manikis 2019b). Consequently, although impact statements could lead to more severe sentences, the literature suggests that critics' fears that they would lead to this have not been realised.

Do impact statements cause court delays?

Another early fear about the use of impact statements was that victims' participation in sentencing could lead to court delays and longer trials (O'Connell 2006). However, this fear was allayed by Erez, Roeger, and Morgan's (1994) research in South Australia with lawyers, judicial officers, and victims, which found that the use of impact statements did not lead to court delays or increased expense. O'Connell's (2006) surveys of judicial officers in South Australia found that no one believed that the statements significantly delayed the sentencing process, only that there could be a slight increase in the time spent on sentencing, since victims have the right to read or have their statements read out. However, it should be noted that, in a later publication based on this survey data (O'Connell 2009), seven out of 17 respondents did report an increase in the time required to conduct a hearing, although it did not appear that these delays were significant.

Objections based on concerns about the content of victim impact statements

Are victim impact statements superfluous?

According to Garkawe, some opponents of victim impact statements have argued that they are 'superfluous ... because the very nature and circumstances of the crime [are] enough to assess the relevant seriousness of the crime and its likely effect on the victims' (2006: 2). Similarly, Sanders et al. asserted that the reason impact statements do not affect sentence length is because, in most cases, the effect of a crime upon a victim is the effect one would expect, given the nature and seriousness of the crime committed. They argued, therefore, that if an impact statement 'says nothing unexpected, it inevitably makes no difference' (2001: 454).

However, there is a connection between the information about harm detailed by impact statements and the purposes of punishment in Australia, such as protection of the community, denunciation, rehabilitation, 'just' or 'adequate' punishment, and recognition of the victim (see *Sentencing Act 1991* (Vic) s5(1); *Penalties and Sentences Act 1992* (Qld) s9(1); *Sentencing Act 1995* (NT) s5(1); *Sentencing Act 1995* (WA) s 6(4); *Sentencing Act 1997* (Tas) s3; *Crimes (Sentencing Procedure) Act 1999* (NSW) s3A; *Crimes (Sentencing) Act 2005* (ACT) s7(1); *Sentencing Act 2017* (SA) s4(2); see also *Criminal Law (Sentencing) Act 1988* (SA) s10(2), which applied at the time of our research). Under current sentencing regimes, this information may be used to assist judicial officers in a number of ways. For example, information regarding victim harm can promote protection of the community by establishing whether the offender poses such a risk to the community that a term, or longer term, of imprisonment is warranted (see von Hirsch & Kazemian 2009; Victorian Sentencing Advisory Council 2012). The information may assist the judicial officer to denounce the offender's conduct, by publicly identifying the harmful effects that the offending has caused. The information contained in impact statements may also provide an opportunity for the offender to comprehend the harm they have caused to the victim.

This may promote rehabilitation, by changing their views about crime or future choices in relation to offending behaviour (see e.g. Shapland & Hall 2010; White, Perrone, & Howes 2019). Judicial determination of 'just' or 'adequate' punishment, as measured by the offender's culpability and the seriousness of the harm caused, may also be assisted by the description of harm contained in an impact statement (see Erez 2000; Booth 2015). Finally, recognition of the victim may be achieved through judicial acknowledgement of the victim and their impact statement when sentencing. Therefore, the information contained in an impact statement is relevant to a number of purposes of punishment and cannot be seen as superfluous when understood in this context.

In her research with judicial officers, Erez found that, while some were of the view that impact statements are sometimes redundant, or the harm caused to the victim could be inferred from the evidence on file, there were cases in which the statement contained new information. This was seen as helpful, as it prompted judicial officers to reconsider the penalty they had intended to impose and instead impose 'a more commensurate sentence' (1999: 548). Interestingly, in this 'minority of cases in which VIS made a difference', it was just as likely to lead to a more lenient sentence as to a harsher sentence than the judicial officer had planned. O'Connell likewise found that most South Australian judicial officers felt that impact statements contained useful information that would otherwise be unavailable to them. In fact, one stated: 'I can't conceive being able to sentence properly and take proper account of the effect of the crime without [an impact statement]' (2009: 51). O'Connell (2009) also noted that none of the 21 respondents said that an impact statement was 'never useful' and only one found it 'almost never' useful.

This research indicates that impact statements are not considered superfluous by the judicial officers who receive them. Moreover, any suggestion of superfluity disregards the utility that statements may have when not being used for instrumental purposes. As explored elsewhere in this chapter, the utility of impact statements extends beyond their assistance to sentencers, as they may provide significant benefits to victims when used expressively.

What if impact statements contain contradictory or inflammatory material?

Tait (2015: 200) observed that '[t]he VIS is a subjective document. It is truthfully made, but … is a constructed personal evaluation of facts, truly believed by the VIS author'. In her analysis of 38 impact statements in homicide cases in NSW, Booth (2012: 220) found it 'striking' that much of the approved content of the statements referred to inadmissible material. Chalmers, Duff, and Leverick (2007) considered the issue of how the court should respond when an impact statement contains information that contradicts other evidence before the court. This may arise particularly where an offender is convicted of only one or some of the offences for which they were charged. Chalmers, Duff, and Leverick argued, however, that this is not a matter for concern, because it is the judicial officer's role to disregard prejudicial material in any hearing. For example, in *Welch v R* ([2011] ACTCA 19: [70]), Justice Refshauge explained that 'judges are expected to be able to set aside material they have viewed which must be ignored because irrelevant or inadmissible'. As contradictory information will be disregarded, it will cause no unfairness to the offender.

This argument applies equally to fears that impact statements might contain inflammatory or prejudicial material; again, it is a judicial officer's role to disregard unfairly prejudicial material. Notably, Erez, Roeger, and Morgan found in their qualitative research with judicial officers that impact statements 'rarely include inflammatory, prejudicial or other objectionable statements. Similarly, exaggerations are not common place' (1994: 40). Our research on and recommendations for dealing with potentially problematic material in impact statements are discussed further in Chapters 3 and 5.

Objections based on concerns for victims

Can impact statements re-traumatise victims?

It was previously feared that victims may be re-traumatised by the process of submitting an impact statement. This is supported by Tait's (2015) quantitative findings, set out below. Tait also observed that:

> It could be argued that for each VIS to reach its full therapeutic potential it should be orally acknowledged and validated by the court in judicial summation. However, VOC also need to be made aware and reminded of the subjective nature of the truth of the impacts they present, which by the adversarial rules of justice must be viewed in conjunction with other truths to be considered …
>
> (2015: 200)

The principal fear is generally related to the risk of cross-examination on its content (O'Connell 2006). Being subject to cross-examination could arguably interfere with the therapeutic benefits that may otherwise be obtained from the impact statement process. However, Australian research indicates that this concern is overstated. In South Australia, 19 of the 21 judicial officers surveyed by O'Connell (2009) indicated that victims were never cross-examined on their impact statements, while the remaining two (both magistrates) said this almost never happened. The Victorian Victim Support Agency's (2009) research found that 98% of the 41 surveyed judicial officers (including 100% of judges) said that cross-examination of victims on their impact statements almost never or never happened. In NSW, Tait found that only one of the 29 victim service professionals in her study was aware of a victim being cross-examined on their statement. Therefore, although the potential for victims to be re-traumatised by cross-examination on their impact statement remains in theory, it does not appear to be a significant risk in practice, at least in Australia (in the international context, see also De Mesmaecker 2012). Furthermore, as set out below, few of the respondents in Tait's (2015) research indicated that they would be concerned if this were to occur.

Are victims disappointed if their impact statement fails to influence the sentence?

As noted above, confusion persists about the exact purpose for which impact statements are intended. According to Roberts (2009), some victims are under the impression that completing an impact statement will lead to the offender receiving a harsher sentence. This idea is supported by Hoyle et al. (1998), who found that, while 60% of the 298 victims they interviewed in England and Wales submitted their impact statements for expressive purposes, half also did so for instrumental reasons (i.e. to influence the sentence imposed).

Due to this confusion, some have argued that impact statement schemes should not exist at all (see e.g. Edwards 2009; Ashworth 2015). Research has shown that a lack of understanding or incorrect beliefs about impact statement schemes can have negative effects on victims. For example, the South Australian Parliament Legislative Review Committee's (2010) *Report on Victim Impact Statements* found that victims could become angry and confused when not made fully aware of how their statements might be used. Roberts (2003: 386) went so far as to say that there was a 'near-universal issue' in the gap between victim expectation and the actual use of impact statements in sentencing. This is unsurprising, given the noted lack of legislative clarity surrounding the purpose of impact statements.

However, other research suggests that confusion about the purpose of submitting an impact statement can be overcome by sufficient victim education. This was shown by Leverick, Chalmers, and Duff (2007), who evaluated the pilot project which introduced the use of impact statements in Scotland. As part of this scheme, victims were provided with a letter and leaflet explaining the scheme, with 90% of the 202 participants reporting that they read all or most of the letter and leaflet. In contrast to the results of earlier research, Leverick, Chalmers, and Duff found that only 5% of victims in their study submitted impact statements with the intention of influencing the sentence. This indicates that victims' understanding of the nature of impact statements is greatly improved by education about their role in sentencing. Erez argued that the problem of victims' confusion or unmet expectations 'can be resolved by explaining to victims that the VIS is only one of the factors judges use to determine the type and severity of penalties' (1999: 553). McGovern (2013: 28) likewise suggested that clinicians and specialist victims' advisors

> could provide survivors with basic information about how victim impact statements are taken into account in sentencing ... to avoid raising expectations about the effect of a victim impact statement that cannot then be met.

This view is also shared by the South Australian Legislative Review Committee (2010), which recommended that victims' confusion about court processes could be addressed by improving communication between victims and the courts.

Booth (2012: 225) noted that it would be 'unsurprising' if family victims of homicide in NSW 'harbour misguided hopes or expectations that their VISs could influence the penalty imposed', as the information provided to victims in NSW is 'misleading'. We are not aware of any empirical research that has specifically examined the effect improved education may have on victims' expectations about their impact statement. It is possible that providing educative materials may be insufficient in dispelling all victims' misconceptions about the role of impact statements. For example, Leverick, Chalmers, and Duff found that, even when victims were provided with extensive written materials explaining the purpose and function of their statements, some still misunderstood aspects of the scheme. As they noted,

> it may be that some of these misunderstandings were the result of victims simply not reading the statement scheme literature (where all of these issues are addressed) or it may be that a further educational effort is necessary.
>
> (2007: 91)

Nonetheless, this research clearly indicates that better-informed victims submit their impact statements for reasons other than to influence the sentence imposed on the offender. Accordingly, it appears that information and education are an effective means of reducing the potential of victim disappointment around the use of impact statements at sentencing.

Why do victims submit impact statements?

Research by the Victorian Support Agency (2009) estimated that 80–95% of victims who were eligible to make an impact statement in the County or Supreme Court did so, although this fell to 7% in the Magistrates' Court. To similar effect, O'Connell's (2009) research with judicial officers in South Australia suggested that statements were presented in 80% of Supreme Court matters and 60–90% of District Court matters, although uptake in the Magistrates' Court was only 3%. Accordingly, it appears that, in Australia at least, most victims of serious offences do choose to make a statement. A key question is why they choose to do so.

Communicative or expressive purposes are widely acknowledged by victims to be a significant reason for submitting impact statements. Research by the Commissioner for Victims and Witnesses in England and Wales (2011) with 30 victims found that many valued the opportunity to submit their statement, because it allowed them to share with the court the way that the crime had affected them. Similarly, 60% of the victims interviewed by Hoyle et al. (1998) and just over a third of the victims in the Scottish study conducted by Leverick, Chalmers and Duff (2007) submitted impact statements for expressive purposes.

Mastrocinque (2014) analysed data from the British Crime Survey to determine the influence of victim, offence, and offender variables on victims' decisions whether to submit a statement. She found that the odds of a female victim providing a statement were 80% higher than for male victims. Asian victims were also more likely to provide a statement. Crime seriousness and the presence of injury also made victims more likely to provide a statement, while offender characteristics, including whether the victim knew the offender, were not relevant. Lens, Pemberton, and Bogaerts (2013) conducted research with 170 victims who were eligible to submit a statement in the Netherlands. They found that three variables were positively associated with the likelihood of delivering a statement: post-traumatic stress symptoms, the type of crime, and the length of time since victimisation. More specifically, victims displaying signs of poorer psychological functioning as a consequence of their victimisation were more likely to provide a statement. Perhaps surprisingly, they found that victims' perceptions about the purpose and function of impact statements did not determine whether they chose to provide a statement.

Drawing on interviews with 24 relevant professionals in Northern Ireland, Moffatt (2017) concluded that victims make statements not purely out of retribution, but also to seek judicial acknowledgement of their harm. Relevantly for our research, Moffatt also found that hearing victims is 'muffled by the opaqueness of sentencing practices, whereby redactions limit the magnitude of victims' voices and the lack of sentencing remarks by judges on the role of the [impact statement] in determining the sentence' (2017: 575). Accordingly, he suggested that 'judges have an obligation to communicate to victims through their remarks that their voices are heard in order to engender a better sense of procedural justice' (2017: 576).

Tait's (2015) research in NSW is discussed further below in relation to sexual assault victims. Quantitative data from interviews with 29–33 victim service professionals (depending on the question) indicated that the main purposes of impact statements were to have a voice in the proceedings (100%) and inform the court of the impact of the crime (94%). Accordingly, statements were perceived to fulfil both expressive and instrumental purposes. In response to a separate question, 89% of respondents (n = 29) indicated that their clients made an impact statement in part to affect the sentence. Some of the key factors identified as influencing whether a victim makes a statement were not wanting the offender to know the full impact of the crime (91%), not wanting to present as a victim (90%), and 'VIS has no impact on sentence, so there is no point making one' (85%). In addition, 97% of respondents said that the main reason some victims do not make a statement is that they do not wish to engage further in the criminal justice process.

Tait's qualitative data from both victims and professionals indicated that the reasons victims make statements include: informing the court and offender of the impact of the offence; redressing the balance in sentencing proceedings; promoting community awareness; affecting the sentence; and achieving catharsis. The barriers to making a statement include a lack of desire to continue with the criminal justice process; lack of awareness of statements in the Local Court; the reaction of family members, victim support agencies, and prosecutors; not wanting the offender to know the effects of the crime; fear of retribution; ambivalence; trauma; shame, literacy, language, and perceived intellectual inadequacy; and fear of cross-examination.

We consider the limited empirical research on sexual offence victims and their impact statements further below, but the research on victims generally indicates that they submit impact statements for a variety of reasons, many of which are expressive and communicative. Some do submit a statement for the purpose of influencing the sentence imposed on the offender, but as noted above, this issue can be addressed by providing relevant victim support and education. This could also be improved by enhanced clarity around impact schemes generally, as will be explored throughout this book. There are also a number of reasons why victims may choose not to submit a statement.

How do victims feel after submitting their impact statement?

Because victim dissatisfaction was a key rationale for the introduction of victims' rights, including victim impact statements, numerous researchers have sought to determine whether victim satisfaction levels have actually increased as a result of the right to submit a statement. Most of this research has found that victims generally feel satisfied with their choice to submit an impact statement. For example, Tait's quantitative and qualitative research led her to conclude that 'the VIS is a useful therapeutic mechanism' (2015: 192) and that this derives 'not only from the participatory but also the self-reflective, validatory and empowering opportunities the VIS provides' (2015: 193). Many of Tait's participants even described their statement 'as a document that gave comfort, they were proud of and treasured and at times re-read' (2015: 195). Conversely, Iliadis (2020) reported on a Victorian case where

> the magistrate *refused* to hear the VIS of a sexual assault victim due to his view that the plea hearing was running overtime. The victim in this case described this experience as feeling like she "*didn't get justice at all*. I feel let down. It's just shattered me"
>
> (2020: 48, citing Houlihan & Johnston 2010; emphasis added)

In comparison to much of the other research discussed below, Davis and Smith (1994b) found that participating in the sentencing process did *not* increase victim satisfaction. However, it should be noted that their study involved victims who engaged in recorded interviews about their experience of victimisation. The interview transcripts were used by caseworkers employed by the researchers to draft each victim's impact statement. This research approach was similar to the then-current practice in England and Wales, where victims did not write or present their statement, which was instead taken in writing by a police officer and submitted to the court in that format (see Roberts & Manikis 2012). It is arguable that the cathartic and therapeutic effects experienced by many victims, through the process of putting their own thoughts on paper or verbally sharing their experiences with the court, cannot be compared to a situation where the impact statement is prepared and submitted by a person other than the victim (see Roberts & Erez 2010). Furthermore, it should be noted that since Davis and Smith's (1994a; 1994b) study was undertaken, impact statement procedures in England and Wales have been amended and victims are now entitled to present their statements personally to the court (see UK Ministry of Justice 2013), as is the case in all Australian jurisdictions.

In another less positive study, Sanders et al. (2001) found that, while 77% of victims in their UK study initially felt that submitting an impact statement was the right decision, only 57% continued to believe this by the time their case ended. They also found that one third of victims felt better after submitting their statement, but 18% felt worse. As a result, Sanders et al. argued that impact statement schemes are not particularly successful in terms of therapeutic benefits. However, Chalmers, Duff, and Leverick (2007) dismissed this criticism, on the basis that a satisfaction level of 57% is still a majority and not an indication of general dissatisfaction. In their research, Leverick, Chalmers, and Duff (2007) found that 86% of the victims in their study thought that submitting an impact statement was the right thing to do and nearly two-thirds found that submitting their statements made them feel better.

Erez found that victims reported feeling relieved and satisfied after completing their statement and that, 'for the majority of victims, filing the statement was a worthwhile therapeutic experience, and the cathartic effect of recording the impact of the offence had been an end in itself' (1999: 552). In addition, the Commissioner for Victims and Witnesses in England and Wales found that victims perceived impact statements to be useful for helping the court to understand what had happened to them, so that the victim was not just 'another number' (2011: 25) to the judicial officer.

In research with 41 victims in Canada, Meredith and Paquette (2001) found that completing an impact statement enabled victims to:

- vent their anger;
- confront their offender in a safe environment;
- include information they had been prevented from providing when giving evidence; and
- bring to the court's attention the total impact of the offence.

These victims also felt that impact statements gave offenders the opportunity to think more seriously about the harm they had caused. In addition, some victims found it cathartic to prepare their statements and that reviewing and listing the effects of the crime made them 'better able to put some issues behind them and move on with their lives' (2001: 6).

The Victorian Victim Support Agency (2009) found that victims generally had positive views about their impact statements, although sexual offence victims were excluded from this research. They found that several determinants affected satisfaction levels, including whether:

- victims understood, and had accurate expectations of, the impact statement process (in particular, an understanding of how their statement would be used);
- victims received adequate information and support in preparing their statement; and
- the experience of presenting the statement in court went well.

According to the Victorian Department of Justice (2014), for some victims, the process of reading their victim impact statement out loud, as opposed to having it handed up to the judge or having another person read it in court, provided a sense of power or strength. One victim reported that 'when I [read my statement aloud in court] he had to listen … I was in control … It was like a reverse role … he had to listen … It's something I'll never regret. It gave me strength' (2014: 30).

Finally, Lens et al. (2015) conducted surveys and interviews with 143 Dutch victims who were eligible to complete impact statements. They found that the act of delivering an impact statement did not directly give rise to therapeutic benefits for the participants. Nevertheless, they suggested that 'the effectiveness of delivering a VIS should not be viewed as a "black or white" issue' (2015: 31) because the victims' feelings of anxiety decreased when they felt a sense of procedural justice through the process of submitting their impact statement.

Sexual offence victims and their impact statements

As discussed in Chapter 1, this book focuses on sentencing in sexual offence cases, as there has been very little research on the impact statement experiences of such offences (see Du Mont, Miller, & White 2008). Likely out of concern about the prospect of re-traumatising victims, the research has commonly excluded victims of sexual offences or has failed to distinguish their experiences from those of other victims. Miller has explained that:

> The few studies that were designed to specifically examine VIS used by sexually assaulted women are now outdated, did not originally include empirical data from victims, or combined victims' use of the

> VIS with other forms of criminal justice participation, which made meaningful interpretation difficult.
>
> (2013: 1445)

The limited research highlights the range of purposes for which victims of sexual offending submit a statement. In the first identified research on this issue, Walberg-Hegan (1997) interviewed four Canadian adolescent female victims of sexual abuse about their experiences of preparing a victim impact statement for inclusion in court at sentencing. That this research involved child victims makes it particularly noteworthy, although of lesser relevance to our project, which focused on adult victims. Walberg-Hegan's participants sought to obtain recognition and acknowledgement of the harm they experienced (for discussion, see McGovern 2013). As one put it, '[w]hen I did mine I thought they can't just look at me like someone who doesn't exist. I'm here and I have feelings and I want to tell the court about them' (Walberg-Hegan 1997: 83). The participants also wanted to communicate their anger, demonstrate they were not afraid of the offender, express the hope that he would change, and ensure that similar abuse would not happen to others. They documented more positives than negatives about the experience, with comments such as 'I feel so much better about myself now … It's a great feeling knowing I got up and was strong enough to do that' (1997: 80) and 'I felt proud and strong' (1997: 103).

In their US research with 37 sexual assault victims, Konradi and Burger found that 52% of the 25 respondents who provided their motives for participating in sentencing wanted to influence the sentence, with 40% wanting to 'maximize punishment', while 32% 'wanted to ensure that the defendant did not have the capacity to strike again' (2000: 366) and 8% wanted to promote rehabilitation. However, these instrumental objectives were less common than the desire, by 68% of the participants, to promote procedural justice and engage with the justice process, with 44% wanting to put 'their story "on record"' (2000: 367). The same proportion (44%) wanted 'to reduce their fear of the defendant, to force him to acknowledge that he had injured them and to resolve nagging pain and feelings of guilt' (2000: 369). The other explanations were a desire to alter the power imbalance with the defendant (28%) and resolve other emotional aspects of the rape (24%). Most respondents nominated multiple objectives, and the findings 'suggest[ed] that the emotional aspects of the trial process for crime victims must be taken seriously' (2000: 382).

Du Mont, Miller, and White (2008) examined the perspectives of 15 Canadian social workers who had supported or counselled sexual offence victims in relation to those victims' impact statements. Their results were consistent with earlier research on impact statement schemes generally. The social worker respondents believed that their clients could find the completion of their statement therapeutic: 'words such as "closure," "healing," and "empowerment" were used to describe the writing process in and of itself' (2008: 17). It was also suggested that, by submitting their impact statements, victims felt listened to by judicial officers. However, it should be noted that Du Mont, Miller, and White did not conduct research directly with victims and recommended that such research be undertaken by way of in-depth interviews to continue the exploration of the benefits of, and issues with, impact statement schemes in sexual offence cases.

Miller (2013) found that the 11 sexual offence victims she interviewed in Canada had completed impact statements primarily to share with the offender the way the offence made them feel. Her research revealed that many victims also tended to 'repurpose' their statements outside of instrumental or expressive approaches and used them for a purpose other than sharing the harm they had suffered with the court. Specifically, Miller found that victims commonly used their statements to explain their suffering to other parties, such as families and loved ones, who may not otherwise have understood their experience. In related research drawing on the same interview data with 11 victims, 20 victim services workers, and four feminist advocates, Miller (2014) also found that the women were motivated to complete an impact statement out of a desire to prevent other women from being sexually assaulted. Many of the victims found it important to read their statement aloud in court, in order to communicate their experience to the public and thereby potentially protect the community. In line with our research, Miller noted that 'a VIS author is most often female, vulnerable, a victim of violent crime or personal injury, victimised at home, harmed by a known or male offender' (2014: 798). In the doctoral research on which these articles were based, Miller suggested that the 'protean, unpredictable, and persisting positive and negative effects of the VIS hold promise – and danger – for sexual assault victims' (2015: iii).

Research into the sentencing experiences of sexual offence victims, particularly empirical research with victims from Australia, is lacking. Even the ACT Government's (2009) research into sexual assault victims' experiences of the criminal justice system only mentions victim impact statements in passing, while Iliadis' (2020) research on the rights of sexual assault victims involved interviews with 26 professionals in Australia (as well as Ireland, England, and Wales), but not the perspectives of victims themselves.

Tait's research with 66 victims in NSW included 53 people who were eligible to make an impact statement. There were seven sexual assault victims, five of whom made a statement. The study also included family victims of homicide (n = 26), as well as victims of domestic violence (n = 7); historical child sexual abuse (n = 7); and physical assault (n = 6). Tait's approach included both qualitative and quantitative data. The quantitative data are summarised in Table 2.1 (see Tait 2015: 50–76; 230; 234–238) and provide extensive insights into the experiences of the sexual assault victims who provided responses. They also highlight the clear ways in which these victims' experiences differed from the response cohort as a whole.

In addition, Tait's research included quantitative and qualitative data from interviews with 35 prosecutors, witness assistance service (WAS) officers, and providers who offer victims legal, court, and personal support. Some of the general findings of relevance to the present research are presented above. However, it is also noteworthy that the respondents felt their clients were more likely to make a statement in cases involving sexual assault.

Tait's qualitative research also examined the experience of making a statement, although there were few comments specific to sexual offences. This material considered the process of writing the statement, including perceptions of the content's appropriateness and the role of the media; the support available to victims when preparing their statement; editing the statement and charge negotiations; presenting the statement, including the timing in the sentencing process and the position from which the statement is read; and offenders' and judicial reaction to the statement. The experience of writing the statement was often considered cathartic, 'liberating', and 'empowering' (Tait 2015: 159; 178), especially for victims of both sexual assault and historical child sexual abuse. One sexual assault victim engaged with a journalist, who 'helped in terms of looking at the expressionism. How it would come across' (2015: 164). Two male victims of historical child sexual abuse also wanted their experience to reach a wider audience through the media. A sexual assault victim who did not submit a statement indicated that this was because she did not feel she had enough time to do so, while another victim was 'angry that [the offender] was able to make me change my [statement]' (2015: 175) as a result of charge negotiations.

Tait's research is the most detailed Australian examination of sexual assault victims' impact statement experiences, although this cohort was not the particular focus of her research. We recognise the need for extreme caution when engaging with cohorts of victims who are particularly vulnerable. However, the exclusion of victims' perspectives, especially in the context of victim impact statements, is particularly striking, given

Table 2.1 Summary of Tait's quantitative data on sexual assault and total victims

Proportion of respondents	*Sexual assault*	*Total*
No factors affected the ability to understand information about VIS	71% (n = 7)	54% (n = 50)
Purpose/expectation of VIS is to:	(all n = 7)	(all n = 49)
a) inform the offender of the impact	71%	66%
b) inform the court of the impact	67%	88%
c) have a voice in proceedings	50%	86%
The purpose of VIS is to affect sentence	(n = 6)	(n = 49)
Expected VIS might affect sentence	17%	39%
Hoped VIS might affect sentence	17%	41%
	0%	65%
Was told by police/prosecution that VIS can affect sentence	17% (n = 5)	10% (n = 50)
Decided immediately to make a statement	67% (n = 6)	80% (n = 49)
Wrote the statement themself	60% (n = 5)	64% (n = 44)
WAS provided assistance with the statement	60% (n = 5)	23% (n = 44)
Support was useful when writing the statement	100% (n = 5)	64% (n = 47)
Required assistance with the statement's content	40% (n = 5)	27% (n = 44)
Writing the VIS was upsetting	100% (n = 5)	82% (n = 44)
Upsetting features of writing the VIS:	(n = 5)	(n = 44)
a) evaluating impact on personal life	100%	66%
b) emotional distress	80%	75%
c) having to acknowledge impact	80%	61%
d) reliving the trauma	80%	55%
e) not being able to describe the impact	80%	36%
f) not knowing where to start	60%	29%
Was given enough time to prepare statement	67% (n = 6)	78% (n = 45)
Writing the VIS was a positive experience	80% (n = 5)	74% (n = 46)
Knew how the VIS would be used in court	33% (n = 6)	51% (n = 49)
Wanted the offender to see VIS	83% (n = 6)	74% (n = 46)
Was aware offender would see VIS	67% (n = 4)	87% (n = 46)
Matter finalised at trial	57% (n = 7)	47% (n = 55)
Charges negotiated	33% (n = 6)	58% (n = 48)
Thought statement should be edited	0% (n = 4)	5% (n = 43)
Statement was edited	20% (n = 5)	48% (n = 44)
Prosecution edited statement	0% (n = 5)	32% (n = 44)
Would make the same statement again	50% (n = 2)	49% (n = 41)
Aware that could be cross-examined on VIS	33% (n = 6)	63% (n = 48)
Would be concerned if cross-examined on VIS	25% (n = 4)	29% (n = 42)
Read VIS in court	60% (n = 5)	59% (n = 44)
Judge positively acknowledged or commented on VIS	25% (n = 4)	46% (n = 39)
Judge did not supportively acknowledge or behaved dismissively to VIS	0% (n = 4)	36% (n = 39)
Offender responded to or acknowledged VIS	0% (n = 4)	8% (n = 39)

(Continued)

Table 2.1 (Continued)

Proportion of respondents	*Sexual assault*	*Total*
Supported by victim support services during VIS/sentencing process	71% (n = 7)	50% (n = 52)
Had no support during the VIS/sentencing process	0% (n = 7)	15% (n = 52)
Would make a statement again	100% (n = 5)	98% (n = 45)
Happy with the presentation of VIS to the court	80% (n = 5)	70% (n = 44)
Happy with the sentencing process	60% (n = 5)	40% (n = 47)
Happy with the sentence	25% (n = 4)	39% (n = 46)

Source: Tait 2015

that the act of submitting an impact statement meets two of the long-established justice needs of victims of sexual offending, namely, the need to participate in the justice process (Shapland, Wilmore, & Duff 1985; Daly 2014) and the need for voice (Lievore 2005; Daly 2014). Although it has been argued that 'completing a VIS or having the opportunity to do so … [is] essential to a sexually assaulted woman's therapeutic well-being' (Miller 2013: 1447), there is a clear gap in our understanding of the views of sexual offence victims on their experiences of impact statements. Accordingly, our interviews with six Australian victims of sexual offending, including the vignettes in this book detailing their experiences before, during, and after the criminal justice process, shed light on an under-examined issue.

Judicial acknowledgement of victim impact statements

One theme that has emerged in the literature is the value of judicial acknowledgment of the victim and their impact statement at sentencing (see e.g. Walberg-Hegan 1997; Roberts & Erez 2010; Schuster & Propen 2010). For example, 76% of the victim service respondents in Tait's (2015) NSW study felt that the judge's reaction was 'very important' to their clients, compared with 45% for the offender's reaction. The qualitative comments from both victims and professionals indicated that judicial acknowledgement occurred most frequently in cases involving death and, of greater relevance to this research, in sexual offence cases where an oral statement was made.

Erez (1999) revealed, through research with victim advocates, that victims' satisfaction with the criminal justice system increased when the judicial officer acknowledged or validated the harm suffered by the victim (see also Schuster & Propen 2006). This is particularly so when the judicial officer quotes the victim's own words in their sentencing remarks (Katz 2010). Erez has explained that:

> Victims feel gratified when their sense of harm is validated in judges' remarks. Victim advocates in Australia as well as in the United States indicate that victims who have heard or read sentencing comments in which judges quote their impact statements in sentencing remarks often say, 'I could not believe the judge has actually listened to what I had to say'.
>
> (1999: 553)

These findings confirm that victims' justice needs can be met not only through the act of submitting an impact statement, but also through the actions of the court upon receiving the statement. Effective judicial acknowledgement of the victim and their statement can meet victims' needs to be treated with respect (Payne 2009; McGlynn 2011) and their need for:

- *voice*, which includes the ability to share the story of what happened in a public setting, where the victim can receive public recognition and acknowledgement (Lievore 2005; Daly 2014);
- *validation*, which involves affirmation that the victim is believed (Bluett-Boyd & Fileborn 2014; Daly 2014); and
- *vindication*, which involves the recognition that what happened to the victim was wrong (Herman 2005; Daly 2014).

This is supported by the findings of Regehr and Alaggia (2006), whose interviews with 14 victim advocates in Canada revealed that judicial reference to victims made victims believe that the judge had understood them. Meredith and Paquette (2001) also found through their victim focus groups that, when judicial officers made explicit reference to victim impact statements in sentencing, the acknowledgement was greatly appreciated by victims. Meredith and Paquette found that this validation was beneficial to victims, 'even if they did not believe that the VIS had made any real difference in terms of the sentence imposed' (2001: 9). These findings are consistent with Tyler's (2000) theory of procedural justice, which maintains that being treated with dignity and respect is more important to victims than a particular sentence or punishment (for discussion, see also Victorian Law Reform Commission 2016; McGlynn & Westmarland 2019; Iliadis 2020; O'Connell 2020). The victims interviewed by Meredith and Paquette (2001) indicated that they would encourage judicial officers to acknowledge in sentencing both the effort that victims put into completing their statements and the content of the statements.

These findings align with those of Young and Roberts (2001), who found that victims appreciated judicial recognition of the harm they had experienced and victims being able to read sentencing remarks in which their impact statements were acknowledged could increase victim satisfaction. The Victorian Department of Justice also found that victims believed it to be 'very validating when they were able to tell that a judge had read their VIS through their judicial comments' (2014: 57). Similarly, the Victorian Victim Support Agency (2009) found a strong link between judicial recognition of victims' impact statements and their satisfaction with the process of making the statement and recommended the Judicial College of Victoria develop information for judicial officers, outlining the importance of recognising impact statements in court. At the time of our research, this recommendation had not been implemented, due to a lack of funding (Victorian Department of Justice 2014).

There already appears to be significant understanding of this issue among members of the judiciary. O'Connell (2009) found that of 21 surveyed judicial officers in South Australia, 17 reported that they always, almost always, or often referred to any impact statement in their sentencing remarks. The Victorian Victim Support Agency's (2009) survey of judicial officers also revealed that almost all of the 42 judicial officers who participated were aware of the importance of recognising the victim and their impact statement in the sentencing process. Furthermore, 81% stated that they would either always, or almost always, refer to an impact statement or its contents in their reasons for sentence. By 2012, 97% of the 41 judicial officers who were asked the same question reported that they would always refer to an impact statement in their reasons for sentence (Victorian Department of Justice 2014).

However, these findings have not previously been independently verified in terms of actual judicial practice. At the time of our research, only one Australian researcher (Booth 2014) had published research examining or quantifying actual judicial practice in acknowledging victims and their impact statements at sentencing. This research related to family victims of homicide offending. A gap therefore exists between our understanding of what judges say they do in this regard and our understanding of what they actually do in practice, especially in the context of sexual offences.

Conclusion and summary of research gaps

The initial criticism of victim impact statements has eased and fears surrounding the potential for negative outcomes have faded after these anticipated outcomes failed to materialise. Those who support the use of such statements at sentencing believe that they help to empower victims and can reduce the incidence of victims feeling ignored by the court and aggrieved by the criminal justice system (see e.g. Tyler 2000). This view is supported by research by Davis and Smith (1994b), who interviewed victims of non-sexual offences who were/were not offered the opportunity to make an impact statement. This found a strong connection between victim participation and satisfaction with the criminal justice system and suggests that an increased role in the criminal justice system assists victims with their psychological recovery; some Australian judges have described this as the 'social rehabilitation' of the victim (see e.g. *DPP v DJK* [2003] VSCA 109: [17]–[18]). Supporters of impact statements have argued that, because submitting a statement increases the victim's satisfaction and cooperation with the criminal justice system, this therefore enhances the efficacy of the justice system as a whole (Katz 2010).

Impact statements can be understood as having benefits for victims and the wider criminal justice process, whether used for instrumental or expressive purposes. When used for expressive purposes, victims can experience a number of therapeutic outcomes from completing and submitting a statement. These can stem from the therapeutic act of putting the harm experienced into words, presenting the statement to the court, and receiving acknowledgement from the judicial officer that the victim has experienced harm. As O'Connell argued:

> Many victims have an innate need to 'tell their stories', including describing the harm done to them … Many derive personal benefits, even a sense of closure, when the harm done to them is formally acknowledged in sentencing remarks.
>
> (2006: 11–12)

In contrast, when used for instrumental purposes, the information contained in an impact statement may assist judicial officers to impose a more commensurate sentence and therefore increase the effectiveness of sentencing regimes generally.

However, this chapter has identified a number of gaps in our understanding of the purposes and operation of impact statement regimes. First, there is an overarching lack of clarity around the purpose of statements, which affects the information that can be included and the way they can be used by the court. Second, research into the impact statement experiences of victims of sexual offending is sparse. This book, which involves in-depth interviews with victims of sexual offending and experienced justice professionals, is the first Australian study to begin to fill this knowledge gap.

Furthermore, although the importance of judicial acknowledgement of victim impact at sentencing has recently been recognised, nearly all previous research has consisted only of judicial officers' self-reported sentencing practices. There is a dearth of research examining actual judicial practice in respect of victim acknowledgement during the sentencing process, that is, the actual use of and reference to victim impact statements in judicial officers' sentencing remarks. This book also seeks to fill that gap by exploring judicial reference to impact statements at sentencing, with a specific focus on sexual offence cases.

The next chapter examines the legislation, case law, policies, and guidelines that guide the use of victim impact statements in Australia. This discussion identifies the unclear parameters within which victims and judges must work when preparing and receiving impact statements and frames the analysis contained throughout the remainder of the book.

References

ACT Government (2009). *A Rollercoaster Ride: Victims of Sexual Assault: Their Experiences with and Views About the Criminal Justice Process in the ACT*. Canberra.

Ashworth, A (1993). 'Victim Impact Statements and Sentencing', *Criminal Law Review*, 498–509.

Ashworth, A (2015). *Sentencing and Criminal Justice*, Cambridge University Press, 6th ed. Cambridge.

Bluett-Boyd, N & Fileborn, B (2014). *Victim/Survivor-Focused Justice Responses and Reforms to Criminal Court Practice*, Australian Institute of Family Studies. Melbourne.

Booth, T (2005). 'Restoring Victims' Voices: Victim Impact Statements in the Sentencing Process', *Reform*, 86, 59–62.

Booth, T (2011). 'Crime Victims and Sentencing: Reflections on *Borthwick*', *Alternative Law Journal*, 36, 236–239.

Booth, T (2012). '"Cooling Out" Victims of Crime: Managing Victim Participation in the Sentencing Process in a Superior Sentencing Court', *Australian and New Zealand Journal of Criminology*, 45, 214–230.

Booth, T (2014). 'The Restorative Capacities of Victim Impact Statements: Analysis of the Victim-Judge Communication Dyad in the Sentencing of Homicide Offenders', *Restorative Justice*, 2, 302–326.

Booth, T (2015). *Accommodating Justice: Victim Impact Statements in the Sentencing Process*, Federation Press. Sydney.

Booth, T, Bosma, A & Lens, K (2018). 'Accommodating the Expressive Function of Victim Impact Statements: The Scope for Victims' Voices in Dutch Courtrooms', *British Journal of Criminology*, 58, 1480–1498.

Braun, K (2013). 'Giving Victims a Voice: On the Problems of Introducing Victim Impact Statements in German Criminal Procedure', *German Law Journal*, 14, 1889–1908.

Chalmers, J, Duff, P & Leverick, F (2007). 'Victim Impact Statements: Can Work, Do Work (For Those Who Bother to Make Them)', *Criminal Law Review*, 360–379.

Christie, N (1977). 'Conflicts as Property', *British Journal of Criminology*, 17, 1–15.

Commissioner for Victims and Witnesses in England and Wales (2011). *Victims' Views of Court and Sentencing*. London.

Daly, K (2014). 'Reconceptualizing Sexual Victimization and Justice', in I Vanfraechem, A Pemberton & F Ndahinda (eds), *Justice for Victims: Perspectives on Rights, Transition and Reconciliation*, Routledge. Abindgon.

Davis, R & Smith, B (1994a). 'The Effects of Victim Impact Statements on Sentencing Decisions: A Test in an Urban Setting', *Justice Quarterly*, 11, 453–469.

Davis, R & Smith, B (1994b). 'Victim Impact Statements and Victim Satisfaction: An Unfulfilled Promise?', *Journal of Criminal Justice*, 22, 1–12.

De Mesmaecker, V (2012). 'Antidotes to Injustice? Victim Statements' Impact on Victims' Sense of Security', *International Review of Victimology*, 18, 133–153.

Doak, J (2008). *Victims' Rights, Human Rights and Criminal Justice: Reconceiving the Role of Third Parties*, Hart Publishing. Oxford.

Du Mont, J, Miller, K-L & and White, D (2008). 'Social Workers' Perspectives on the Victim Impact Statements in Cases of Sexual Assault in Canada', *Women and Criminal Justice*, 18(3), 1–23.

Duff, R (2009). 'Restoration and Retribution', in A von Hirsch, A Ashworth & J Roberts (eds), *Principled Sentencing*, Hart Publishing, 3rd ed. Oxford.

Edwards, I (2009). 'The Evidential Quality of Victim Personal Statements and Family Impact Statements', *International Journal of Evidence and Proof*, 13, 293–320.

Englebrecht, C (2011). 'The Struggle for "Ownership of Conflict": An Exploration of Victim Participation and Voice in the Criminal Justice System', *Criminal Justice Review*, 36, 129–151.

Erez, E (1990). 'Victim Participation in Sentencing: Rhetoric and Reality', *Journal of Criminal Justice*, 18, 19–31.

Erez, E (1999). 'Who's Afraid of the Big Bad Victim? Victim Impact Statements as Victim Empowerment and Enhancement of Justice', *Criminal Law Review*, 545–556.

Erez, E (2000). 'Integrating a Victim Perspective through Victim Impact Statements', in A Crawford & J Goodey (eds), *Integrating a Victim Perspective within Criminal Justice*, Routledge. Abingdon.

Erez, E (2004). 'Victim Voice, Impact Statements and Sentencing: Integrating Restorative Justice and Therapeutic Jurisprudence Principles in Adversarial Proceedings', *Criminal Law Bulletin*, 40, 483–500.

Erez, E & Rogers, L (1999). 'Victim Impact Statements and Sentencing Outcomes and Processes: The Perspectives of Legal Professionals', *British Journal of Criminology*, 39, 216–239.

Erez, E & Tontodonato, P (1990). 'The Effect of Victim Participation in Sentencing on Sentence Outcome', *Criminology*, 28, 451–474.

Erez, E, Jiang, J & Laster, K (2020). 'From Cinderella to Consumer: How Crime Victims Can Go to the Ball', in J Tapley & P Davies (eds), *Victimology*, Palgrave Macmillan. Cham.

Erez, E, Roeger, L & Morgan, F (1994). *Victim Impact Statements in South Australia: An Evaluation*, South Australian Attorney-General's Department. Adelaide.

Garkawe, S (2006). 'The Effect of Victim Impact Statements on Sentencing Decisions', Paper presented at the Sentencing Principles, Perspectives and Possibilities Conference, Canberra.

Garkawe, S (2007). 'Victim Impact Statements and Sentencing', *Monash University Law Review*, 33, 90–114.

Garland, D (2001). *The Culture of Control: Crime and Social Order in Contemporary Society*, Oxford University Press. Oxford.

Herman, J (2005). 'Justice from the Victim's Perspective', *Violence Against Women*, 11, 571–602.

Hörnle, T (1999). 'Distribution of Punishment: The Role of a Victim's Perspective', *Buffalo Criminal Law Review*, 3, 175–209.

Houlihan, L & Johnston, M (2010). 'Attorney-General Rob Hulls Weighs into Magistrate Row', *Herald Sun*, 20 June. https://www.heraldsun.com.au/news/lost-justice-for-sex-assault-victim/news-story/053f3fc7585498572d3fa4fa0315083c.

Hoyle, C & Zedner, L (2007). 'Victims, Victimization and Criminal Justice', in M Maguire, R Morgan & R Reiner (eds), *The Oxford Handbook of Criminology*, Oxford University Press, 4th ed. Oxford.

Hoyle, C, Cape, E, Morgan, R & Sanders, A (1998). *Evaluation of the 'One Stop Shop' and Victim Statement Pilot Projects*, Home Office. London.

Iliadis, M (2020). *Adversarial Justice and Victims' Rights: Reconceptualising the Role of Sexual Assault Victims*, Routledge. Abingdon.

Katz, K (2010). 'Opposing Scales of Justice: Victims' Voices in the Sentencing Process', *Canadian Criminal Law Review*, 14, 181–230.

Kearon, T & Godfrey, B (2007). 'Setting the Scene: A Question of History', in S Walklate (ed), *Handbook of Victims and Victimology*, Willan. Cullompton.

Kennedy, J, Easteal, P & Bartels, L (2012). 'How Protected is She? "Fairness" and the Rape Victim Witness in Australia', *Women's Studies International Forum*, 35, 334–342.

Konradi, A & Burger, T (2000). 'Having the Last Word: An Examination of Rape Survivors' Participation in Sentencing', *Violence Against Women*, 6, 351–395.

Lens, K, Pemberton, A & Borgaerts, S (2013). 'Heterogeneity in Victim Participation: A New Perspective on Delivering a Victim Impact Statement', *European Journal of Criminology*, 10, 479–495.

Lens, K, Pemberton, A, Brans, K, Braeken, J, Bogaerts, S & Lahlah, E (2015). 'Delivering a Victim Impact Statement: Emotionally Effective or Counterproductive?', *European Journal of Criminology*, 12, 17–34.

Leverick, F, Chalmers, J & Duff, P (2007). *An Evaluation of the Pilot Victim Statement Schemes in Scotland*, Scottish Executive Social Research. Edinburgh.

Lievore, D (2005). *No Longer Silent: A Study of Women's Help-Seeking Decisions and Service Responses to Sexual Assault*, Australian Institute of Criminology. Canberra.

Manikis, M (2015). 'Victim Impact Statements at Sentencing: Towards a Clearer Understanding of their Aims', *University of Toronto Law Journal*, 65, 85–123.

Manikis, M (2019b). 'Contrasting the Emergence of the Victims' Movements in the United States and England and Wales', *Societies*, 9(2), 35–43.

Manikis, M & Roberts, J (2011). 'Recognizing Ancillary Harm at Sentencing: A Proportionate and Balanced Response', *Canadian Criminal Law Review*, 15, 131–144.

Markin, T (2017). 'Victim Rights in Sentencing: An Examination of Victim Impact Statements', *Canadian Criminal Law Review*, 22, 95–119.

Mastrocinque, J (2014). 'Victim Personal Statements: An Analysis of Notification and Utilization', *Criminology & Criminal Justice*, 14, 216–234.

McGovern, D (2013). 'The Therapeutic Potential of Victim Impact Statements for Sexual Violence', *Sexual Abuse in Australia and New Zealand*, 5(2): 21–30.

McGlynn, C (2011). 'Feminism, Rape and the Search for Justice', *Oxford Journal of Legal Studies*, 31, 825–842.

McGlynn, C & Westmarland, N (2019). 'Kaleidoscopic Justice: Sexual Violence and Victim-Survivors' Perceptions of Justice', *Social & Legal Studies*, 28, 179–201.

Meredith, C & Paquette, C (2001). *Summary Report on Victim Impact Statement Focus Groups*, Department of Justice Canada. Ottawa.

Miller, K-L (2013). 'Purposing and Repurposing Harms: The Victim Impact Statement and Sexual Assault', *Qualitative Health Research*, 23, 1445–1458.

Miller, K-L (2014). 'Relational Caring: The Use of the Victim Impact Statement by Sexually Assaulted Women', *Violence and Victims*, 29, 797–813.

Miller, K-L (2015). *'You Can't Stop the Bell From Ringing': Protean, Unpredictable, and Persisting: The Victim Impact Statement in the Context of Sexually Assaulted Women*, Unpublished PhD Thesis, University of Toronto. Toronto.

Moffatt, L (2017). 'Victim Personal Statements in Managing Victims' Voices in Sentencing in Northern Ireland: Taking a More Procedural Justice Approach', *Northern Ireland Legal Quarterly*, 68, 555–576.

Mossman, E (2012). *Victims of Crime in the Adult Criminal Justice System: A Stocktake of the Literature*, UK Ministry of Justice. London.

O'Connell, M (2006). 'Evolving Mechanisms for Engaging Victims in the Sentencing Process: Should Victims Have a Stronger Voice in Court?', Paper presented at the Sentencing Principles Perspectives and Possibilities Conference, Canberra.

O'Connell, M (2009). 'Victims in the Sentencing Process: South Australia's Judges and Magistrates Give Their Verdict', *International Perspectives in Victimology*, 4, 50–57.

O'Connell, M (2015). 'The Evolution of Victims' Rights and Services in Australia', in D Wilson & S Ross (eds), *Crime, Victims and Policy: International Contexts, Local Experiences*, Palgrave Macmillan. Cham.

O'Connell, M (2020). 'Improving Access to Justice: Procedural Justice Through Legal Counsel for Victims of Crime', in J Joseph, & S Jergenson (eds), *Contemporary Developments in Victimology—An International Perspective: A Festschrift in Honor of Marc Groenhuijsen*, Springer. Cham.

Parliament of South Australia, Legislative Review Committee (2010). *Report of the Legislative Review Committee into Victim Impact Statements*. Adelaide.

Payne, S (2009). *Rape: The Victim Experience Review*, UK Home Office. London.

Regehr, C & Alaggia, R (2006). 'Perspectives of Justice for Victims of Sexual Violence', *Victims and Offenders*, 1, 33–46.

Roberts, J (2003). 'Victim Impact Statements and the Sentencing Process: Recent Developments and Research Findings', *Criminal Law Quarterly*, 47, 365–396.

Roberts, J (2009). 'Listening to the Crime Victim: Evaluating Victim Input at Sentencing and Parole', *Crime and Justice*, 38, 347–412.

Roberts, J & Erez, E (2010). 'Communication at Sentencing: The Expressive Function of Victim Impact Statements', in A Bottoms & J Roberts (eds), *Hearing the Victim: Adversarial Justice, Crime Victims and the State*, Willan. Cullompton.

Roberts, J & Manikis, M (2010). 'Victim Impact Statements at Sentencing: Exploring the Relevance of Ancillary Harm', *Canadian Criminal Law Review*, 15, 1–26.

Roberts, J & Manikis, M (2011). *Victim Personal Statements: A Review of the Empirical* Research, Office of the Commissioner for Victims and Witnesses in England and Wales. London.

Roberts, J & Manikis, M (2012). 'Victim Personal Statements in England and Wales: Latest (and Last) Trends from the Witness and Victim Experience Survey', *Criminology and Criminal Justice*, 13, 245–261.

Sanders, A, Hoyle, C, Morgan, R & Cape, E (2001). 'Victim Impact Statements: Don't Work, Can't Work', *Criminal Law Review*, 447–458.

Sankoff, P & Wansborough, L (2006). 'Is Three Really a Crowd? Thoughts about Victim Impact Statements and New Zealand's Revamped Sentencing Regime', Paper presented at the International Conference of the International Society for the Reform of Criminal Law, Brisbane.

Schuster M & Propen, A (2010). 'Degrees of Emotion: Judicial Responses to Victim Impact Statements', *Law, Culture and the Humanities*, 6, 77–104.

Schuster, M & Propen, A (2006). *WATCH Victim Impact Statement Study*, University of Minnesota. Minneapolis.

Shapland, J & Hall, M (2010). 'Victims at Court: Necessary Accessories or Principal Players at Centre Stage?', in A Bottoms & J Roberts (eds), *Hearing the Victim: Adversarial Justice, Crime Victims and the State*, Routledge. Abingdon.

Shapland, J, Willmore, J & Duff, P (1985). *Victims in the Criminal Justice System*, Gower. Aldershot.

Tait, F (2015). *Testaments of Transformation: The Victim Impact Statement Process in NSW as Experienced by Victims of Crime and Victim Service Professionals*, Unpublished Master's Thesis, University of Sydney. Sydney.

Tyler, T (2000). 'Social Justice: Outcome and Procedure', *International Journal of Psychology*, 35, 117–125.

UK Ministry of Justice (2013). *Code of Practice for Victims of Crime*. London.

United Nations (1985). *Declaration of Basic Principles of Justice for Victims of Crime and Abuse of Power*.

US President's Task Force on Victims of Crime (1982). *Final Report*, Department of Justice. Washington, DC.

van de Merwe, A & Mitchell, L-M (2020). 'The Use of Impact Statements, Minimum Sentences and Victims' Privacy Interests: A Therapeutic Exploration', *De Jure Law Journal*, 53, 1–18.

Victorian Department of Justice (2014). *Victim Impact Statement Reforms in Victoria—Interim Implementation Report*. Melbourne.

Victorian Law Reform Commission (2016). *The Role of Victims of Crime in the Criminal Trial Process: Report*. Melbourne.

Victorian Sentencing Advisory Council (2012). *How Much Does Imprisonment Protect the Community Through Incapacitation?* Melbourne.

Victorian Victim Support Agency (2009). *A Victim's Voice: Victim Impact Statements in Victoria*. Melbourne.

von Hirsch, A & Kazemian, L (2009). 'Predictive Sentencing and Selective Incapacitation', in A von Hirsch, A Ashworth & J Roberts (eds), *Principled Sentencing*, Hart Publishing, 3rd ed. Oxford.

von Hirsch, A, Ashworth, A & Roberts, J (eds) (2009). *Principled Sentencing*, Hart Publishing, 3rd ed. Oxford.

Walberg-Hegan, L (1997). *Voices of Victims: The Experience of Preparing a Victim Impact Statement for Use in Court, As Described by Adolescent Sexual Abuse Survivors*, Unpublished EdD Thesis, University of Toronto. Toronto.

Walklate, S (2012). 'Courting Compassion: Victims, Policy, and the Question of Justice', *The Howard Journal of Criminal Justice* 51, 109–121.

White, R, Perrone, S & Howes, L (2019). *Crime, Criminality and Criminal Justice*, Oxford University Press, 3rd ed. Oxford.

Windsor, E & Roberts, JV (2020). *Victim Personal Statements and Sentencing: Review of Policy, Operation and Research*, Sentencing Academy. London.

Young, A (2001). *The Role of the Victim in the Criminal Process: A Literature Review—1989 to 1999*, Department of Justice Canada. Ottawa.

Young, A & Roberts, J (2001). *Research on the Role of the Victim in the Criminal Process in Canada*, Department of Justice Canada. Ottawa.

RACHEL

Rachel's ex-husband pleaded guilty to two counts of aggravated sexual assault, one count of attempted rape, and three counts of assault against her. The crimes were committed during a single episode of sexual violence.

Rachel and the offender had recently separated after 11 years of marriage. The offender was upset about the separation and wanted to reconcile with Rachel. Rachel agreed to go out for dinner with him, after which they returned to the family home. The pair began to engage in sexual activity, but Rachel asked the offender to stop, which he did. Rachel went to another room and the offender followed her. She explained to him that having sex did not feel right to her. The offender followed Rachel through the house back into bedroom, where he pinned her down and assaulted her before sexually assaulting her. Rachel kicked the offender off her, but he again pushed her to the bed, choked her, and attempted to rape her. The offender then let Rachel go and she left the house and called the police. The offender admitted his offences.

Rachel did not hear anything from the authorities from that point onwards, unless she phoned to enquire about the case. She said: 'I had very little to do, because it wasn't my case. I just gave the statement and they went off and did it all … The minute I rang the police, it was taken out of my hands'.

Rachel had no previous knowledge of impact statements prior to completing one. She did online research to see what was involved and reviewed some example documents. Rachel was strongly encouraged by her witness assistance officer to complete an impact statement. Rachel viewed it as her only input into the case and took several weeks to complete the statement. She took time to write down various thoughts and feelings as they 'hit' her and then crafted these words into the statement. She considered a strong introduction and conclusion to be the most important parts of the statement, just like writing an essay. Rachel included the following information in her victim impact statement:

> What William did to me that night, the fear he instilled in me, was a fear that I have never, ever felt before. Being stripped of every ounce of control and having no idea if things were going to get worse, or if it was going to come to an end, was the most terrifying and alarming feeling. I was so scared of what would happen next. Whether he was going to continue hurting me? Whether he could actually stop? He seemed to like the fact that he could actually hurt me. This is the

same man that I once loved and shared my innermost secrets with and who I trusted frequently with my life. He was doing things to me that I hated, that I didn't want at all, and that were hurting me incredibly. I have never been faced with such physical aggression, which rendered me totally helpless and unable to defend myself.

I suffered a number of physical injuries as a result of this crime but the emotional impact has been far greater. I now go to bed very late, and wake very early, with numerous wakes during the night. I sleep minimal hours of broken sleep, which is aided by sleeping tablets and anti-depressant medication. I hate going to bed. I hate being alone. There are times when my brain goes into its own patterns of haunting me with snippets of the attack. I have needed ongoing counselling to help deal with these feelings.

William has no idea what he has put me through. His denial fits with his 'Jekyll and Hyde' persona. I tried for months prior to the attack to get away from him, but he kept using the threat of not getting the kids much, against me. Then he would get angry and unreasonable. I would then try to keep the peace by agreeing to whatever he wanted.

I am still extremely fearful of William. I can only be comfortable seeing him if I am prepared for it and in control of the situation. I cannot be surprised. I run a very fine line between being my 'normal self', and losing total control over my emotional state. I have found that certain normal, unsuspecting, daily things can trigger a totally irrational response from me which I have no control over at all. My children are great ones for 'boo-ing' you from behind a corner. The simple act can have me on the floor sobbing instantly, which is extremely upsetting for my child. I have to remain vigilant and cautious as to how and where people touch me. The simple act of innocently coming into contact with anyone – whether it be someone hugging me, or just touching me, can set off a totally irrational and unexpected reaction. I have never had personal space problems before and have always been quite comfortable with people coming into contact with me in a social setting.

William and I have had to continue working together in the same business due to financial necessity. I go day to day with every day organised so I know exactly what I am doing and who I will see, so that there is no chance of a surprise. I can see William at work and to hand over the children, because I chose the time and location that I see him and I am prepared. If he makes any movement in my direction, in any way, I find myself flinching or stepping away. I now

> need to get another job. I fear that I don't have the concentration required to do this same job any more. I find it difficult to concentrate and I suffer anxiety and panic attacks on a daily basis. The fear of accidentally running into William has me constantly looking over my shoulder and checking out my surrounds. He still scares me.
>
> I have recently been put on … sick leave from work through the stress of all these things. I have been prescribed anti-depressant tablets to help with the anxiety issues. I am not happy about taking this medication as it has side effects. But I am not sleeping and am suffering nightmares and flashbacks each night. This has made our separation procedures so much worse and more complicated. The children are now worrying about my health.
>
> I have always been a strong, intelligent working woman with a great career past. I am now doubtful of my ability and worth. William cannot see, nor does he seem to understand or care about the damage he has done within me … besides the initial physical damage. My job has gone, my career future looks damaged, my lifestyle has gone, my self-confidence has been stripped. I am still lucky to have my friends and my children.

Rachel's statement was not edited by the prosecution before submission. Rachel thought this was because she had undertaken extensive research as to what should or should not be included and that this might not have been the case if she had not undertaken this research. She also felt that the impact statement process could have been better explained to her from the beginning:

> they all know what they are talking about, and it actually needs a fresh set of eyes from outside to look at things and see how they are going … So what you're doing is filling a great void, because I didn't understand a lot, and at the time was a little bit overwhelmed. It wasn't until I got home that I thought, 'I've no idea what I've got to do', so I Googled it.

Rachel chose not to read her statement to the court or attend the sentencing hearing:

> Knowing that he was going to be in the room, there was no way I could have read it. After I wrote it, when I got the final draft, I would sit down and I would read it over and over. I figured that if I read it enough times, I would displace myself from it, so that I

> possibly could have read it in court. But reading through silently in my head is one thing. Verbalising the words is another … I thought, I can't do it.

Rachel attended one part-day of the court proceedings, but found the experience of watching the matter very distressing:

> I felt disgusting sitting there. That's something I found because the judge was speaking to the two lawyers and two lawyers only. It wouldn't have made any difference if I was there or not. I was referred to by them, but it made no difference whether I was there or not. I only went that one day and saw that one bit. I actually felt like I would have preferred to have been sitting underneath the chair than sitting there. Because it was quite humiliating, listening to it and being spoken about. I was sitting there, and they were saying all this stuff that happened to me. It was humiliating.

The judge included a lengthy paragraph about the impact of the offences on Rachel in the sentencing remarks. Rachel thought 'it was good to see that what I said was taken on board, given what [the offender] had said'. Overall, Rachel would recommend that other people in her position submit victim impact statements.

Chapter 3

Victim impact statements – Australian law and policy

Introduction

Legislation, case law, court practices, policies, guidelines, and individual judicial approaches determine how judicial officers, justice professionals, and victims apply and experience impact statement schemes. Therefore, legislation and case law should clearly establish the purpose(s) of impact statement regimes and their philosophical foundation. Related policies and guidelines should then create procedures that implement and conform to the underlying purpose(s).

This chapter analyses the legal and regulatory frameworks for impact statements in Australia. It focuses on the four jurisdictions studied in this research project and explores only the legislative principles and policies that arose as issues in the textual analysis of sentencing remarks or interviews discussed in Chapters 4 and 5, respectively (for a broader overview, see Booth 2015). It examines the relevant legislation, judicial interpretations of that legislation, policies, and guidelines. It then considers if and how they designate the purposes of the regimes they create, interpret, and/or implement and whether those purposes are consistently instituted in relevant procedures. This investigation is significant, because if the legislation fails to contain clear statements of purpose and/or if any legislated purpose is not reflected in procedures instituted by courts and prosecution agencies, then inconsistency or confusion will be replicated in judicial approaches to impact statements and victims' experiences of these statements.

Sources of impact statement law and policy

At common law, judicial officers are permitted to take into consideration, when sentencing, the effect of the crime on the victim. In *Siganto v The Queen*, Gleeson CJ, Gummow, Hayne, and Callinan JJ of the High

Court described 'the undoubted proposition that a sentencing judge is entitled to have regard to the harm done to the victim by the commission of the crime. That is the rule at common law' ((1998) 194 CLR 656: 666). In addition, sentencing legislation has been enacted in all Australian states and territories. These legislative instruments codify common law principles of sentencing and contain specific impact statement provisions (see Chapter 2). Victim participation in the sentencing process is also guided by policies and procedures implemented by agencies such as the courts and prosecution agencies (known as the Office of Public Prosecutions (OPP) in Victoria and Office of the Director of Public Prosecutions (DPP) in the other states and territories). Some procedures, such as the *Court Rules* in each jurisdiction, are legally binding. Others, such as the prosecution policies issued by prosecuting agencies, are not binding, but do appear to be closely followed by the relevant agencies (see discussion below). Therefore, as Kirchengast has explained, 'the powers that allow for victim participation are inherently diverse and fragmented. They are not consolidated within one source nor are they provided over a set of coherently organised sources' (2014: 19). This chapter consolidates these incoherently organised sources into chronologically ordered themes, from pre-trial to post-sentencing.

The definition of victim

The definition of a victim for the purpose of presenting an impact statement varies across jurisdictions (see *Criminal Law (Sentencing) Act 1988* (SA) s7A(1) (repealed); see now *Sentencing Act 2017* (SA) s14(1); see also *Sentencing Act 1991* (Vic) s3(1); *Sentencing Act 1997* (Tas) s81A; *Crimes (Sentencing) Act 2005* (ACT) ss47, 49(1)). Consequently, a person may be considered a victim of crime for the purpose of presenting an impact statement in one jurisdiction, but be ineligible in another. However, victims of sexual offending are permitted to present impact statements in all Australian jurisdictions.

Victim recognition in Australian sentencing legislation

In some jurisdictions, recognition of the victim is a specific purpose of the sentencing legislation. For example, in the ACT, one of the purposes of sentencing is 'to recognise the harm done to the victim of the crime and the community' (*Crimes (Sentencing) Act 2005* (ACT) s7(1)(g)). In addition, when sentencing an offender, the court must, when relevant, take into account the effect of the offence on the victim (s33(1)(f)). These and other relevant provisions are set out in Table 3.1. As this shows, the provisions are inconsistent in terms of how the court should recognise the victim and/or their impact statement or unclear about what weight the judicial officer can or should give to this when sentencing the offender (see also Booth 2015).

The requirement that the court must consider any injury to the victim (ACT) or 'have regard to the impact of the offence' (Vic) suggests that impact statements can or should factor into a judge's decision-making

Table 3.1 Recognition of the victim under relevant Australian sentencing legislation

Jurisdiction	*Legislation*	*Relevant provision*
ACT	*Crimes (Sentencing) Act 2005*	'A court may impose a sentence on an offender... to recognise the harm done to the victim of the crime and the community': s7(1)(g). In deciding how an offender should be sentenced ... court must consider [if relevant] ... the effect of the offence on the victim': s33(1)(f).
South Australia	*Criminal Law (Sentencing) Act 1988** *Sentencing Act 2017*	'In determining the sentence for an offence, a court must have regard to as may be relevant ... the personal circumstances of any victim of the offence [and] any injury, loss or damage resulting from the offence': ss10(1)(d), (e). 'The secondary purposes for sentencing a defendant for an offence are as follows:. to publicly recognise the harm done to the community and to any victim of the offending behaviour': s4(1)(c). In determining a sentence for an offence, a court must take into account such of the factors as are known to the court that relate to the following matters as may be relevant: ... the extent of any injury, emotional harm, loss or damage resulting from the offence: s11(1)(c).
Tasmania	*Sentencing Act 1997*	'The purpose of this Act is to recognise the interests of victims of offences': s3(h).
Victoria	*Sentencing Act 1991*	'In sentencing an offender, a court must have regard to the impact of the offence on any victim of the offence, the personal circumstances of any victim of the offence, and any injury, loss or damage resulting directly from the offence' s5(AC)(2).

* The 1988 provision applied at the time of our research, but has since been replaced by the 2017 provision.

when sentencing. These provisions are consistent with impact statements having an instrumental purpose. As set out in Table 3.1, the wording of the South Australian provision changed after our research and now makes no explicit reference to victims, but refers to 'injury, harm etc resulting from the offence' more generally. In contrast, the phrasing of the recognition of 'the interest of victims' in the Tasmanian Act is so vague that it does not explicitly or implicitly convey either an instrumental or expressive approach. Consequently, Crawford J observed in *Attorney-General for Tasmania v B* ([2010] TASCCA 6) that no provision in the Tasmanian Act specifically compels a judicial officer to consider an impact statement in sentencing. This inconsistency and lack of clarity around how the court should use impact statements influences our findings and is explored further in Chapter 5.

The content of impact statements

Victims are generally restricted, both in form and content, as to the type of information they are allowed to present to the court about the harm they have suffered as a consequence of the offending. The permissible form and content are guided by both legislation and policy documents. In Tasmania (*Sentencing Act 1997* (Tas) s81A) and South Australia (*Criminal Law (Sentencing) Act 1988* (SA) s7A at the time of our research and now *Sentencing Act 2017* (SA) s14(1)), only written statements are allowed, while Victoria and the ACT are more flexible, allowing for the inclusion of photographs, drawings, or other images, and, in Victoria, poems (*Sentencing Act 1991* (Vic) s8L(2); *Crimes (Sentencing) Act 2005* (ACT) s51(6)).

All four jurisdictions have content guidelines, which are not mandated by legislation, but rather published through each jurisdiction's victim support or witness assistance service (see Tasmanian Department of Justice nd; Victorian Government 2017; South Australian ODPP (SAODPP) 2018; ACT Government Victim Support 2020).[1] Victoria's guidelines are comprehensive where harm and injury are concerned, explaining that an impact statement can detail the following:

Emotional impacts

> You might want to describe any emotional impacts of the crime, including:
>
> - your general feelings of wellbeing or enjoyment of life
> - how the crime has affected any relationships (with your partner, family, friends, or co-workers)

- any emotions or feelings related to the crime (such as hurt, anger, fear, frustration)
- effects on your lifestyle and activities (such as trouble sleeping, eating, working)
- psychological effects of the crime, including any treatment you need (such as depression or anxiety)
- how these impacts might change your life into the future.

Physical impacts

You might include:

- injuries as a result of the crime (such as broken bones, nerve damage)
- how injuries have affected your life (such as work, sport or leisure activities)
- any long-term impacts of injuries on your life
- any ongoing medical treatment you need.

Financial impacts

You might include:

- loss of future earnings because of the crime (if a physical or psychological injury has affected your ability to work)
- general expenses caused by the crime (such as home security, replacing items)
- travel expenses because of the crime (such as court appearances)
- cost of medical treatment needed because of the crime.

Social impacts

You might describe problems the crime has caused in your daily life now and into the future, including how the crime has affected:

- work or study commitments
- family or social life (friendships, social events, sporting commitments)
- how safe you feel (Victorian Government 2017: 12–13).

The South Australian guideline offers a slightly different, but similarly comprehensive approach, by providing a list of prompt questions for victims to consider when preparing their statement:

- What was life like before the event/incident?
- What is life like now?
- Has your view of the world changed?

- What has been the emotional impact for you (i.e. distressed, ashamed, worried, overwhelmed, angry, sad, embarrassed, degraded, confused, etc.)?
- What has been the psychological impact for you (i.e. anxiety, depression, sadness, 'moody', stressed, needed counselling, feeling unsafe)?
- What has been the financial impact for you (could not go to work, stolen money, bills incurred)?
- How has this impacted on other people around you (i.e. partners, children, other family members, friends)?
- How has this impacted on your home-life and lifestyle?
- How has this impacted on work life or schooling?
- Has this had an impact on your hobbies, interests and enjoyment (i.e. I love swimming/driving/playing golf/drawing but I cannot do these things anymore)?
- Has this had an impact on your personality or character (i.e. confidence, trust in people, social ability, etc)?
- What were your feelings at the time of the event (i.e. behaviours including sleeping changed, nightmares, anger, shock, not eating)?
- What are your feelings now?
- Do you have particular feelings towards the accused (i.e. angry, not understand, disappointed, hurt)?
- What has been your experience of grief?
- Do you carry issues of trust or betrayal?
- What has been the impact of attending court and/or the Criminal Justice system for you?
- Are there positive steps you have made or ways you have managed?
- Do you have worries or fears for the future?
- Are there comments or information you would like to direct to the accused (i.e. 'You have hurt me', 'Because of what you did …', 'I want you to know …'). (SAODPP 2018: 5)

Most guidelines (Tasmanian Department of Justice nd; Victorian Government 2017; ACT Government Victim Support 2020) also provide information about what should *not* be included in a statement. These are consistent across the ACT, Tasmania, and Victoria and state that victims should not include:

- any detailed description of the crime;
- anything offensive, threatening, intimidating, or harassing;
- abuse or vilification of the offender;

- details or impacts of other offences experienced; and
- opinions on the sentence the court should give. Concentrate only on how the offence has affected you.

Victims are also told to focus on how the offence has affected them (see e.g. ACT Government 2014). Overall, the approach appears to promote an instrumental approach to impact statements in the ACT, Tasmania, and Victoria.

In contrast, the South Australian guidelines only indicate the following in relation to the information that victims should *not* include in their impact statement:

> The VIS can only focus on the impact of the charges that the defendant has admitted to, or has been found guilty of. Therefore it is not appropriate for the VIS to comment on facts or issues that the defendant has not admitted, or has not been found guilty of.
>
> (SAODPP 2018: 1)

This comparative lack of rigidity suggests a more expressive approach to impact statement content in South Australia. However, South Australia is also the only jurisdiction examined whose legislation allows a victim to express a view on the offender's sentence in an impact statement (see previously *Criminal Law (Sentencing) Act 1988* (SA) s7C(2), replicated in substance in *Sentencing Act 2017* (SA) s16(2)). This may instead imply that victims' views could have some instrumental effect on sentence, though the legislation does not actually indicate what the judge can or should do if provided with a victim's view on the offender's sentence. This again demonstrates the inconsistency in impact statement regimes within and across Australian jurisdictions.

Time frames for preparing impact statements

Neither the legislation nor prosecution policy documents in Tasmania contain suggested time frames for the preparation of impact statements, although the Tasmanian Government's Victim Support Services website (2020) indicates that victims are required to provide their statement 'to Victims Support Services at least 5 days before the expected sentencing'. In Victoria, s8N(1) of the *Sentencing Act 1991* (Vic) provides that a victim who prepares a statement 'must, a reasonable time before sentencing is to take place, provide a copy to the prosecutor'. The Victorian Government's (2017) *Guide to Victim Impact Statements* indicates that victims 'should not start preparing [their] Victim Impact Statement (VIS) straight after the crime happens' (2017: 11). Victims are also instructed that their statement 'should not be given to police or prosecutors until someone is found guilty or pleads guilty to a crime' (2017: 11). The ACT legislation provides that the statement may be given

> when the court considers appropriate after (i) the offender has pleaded guilty, (ii) the court has found the offence proved or (iii) the offender has been found guilty or convicted of the offence and before the offender is sentenced
>
> (*Crimes (Sentencing) Act 2005* (ACT) s52(2))

At the time of our research, the South Australian Prosecution Policy indicated that statements 'should be prepared prior to sentencing submissions' (SAODPP nd: Guideline 13), but the information provided to victims has since been updated and now states:

> Technically, you do not need to complete a VIS until an offender has either 1) pleaded guilty to some or all of the offences involving you, or 2) been found guilty of some or all of the offences involving you by a Judge or Jury. However you may be asked to complete a VIS soon after an offence has occurred.
>
> (SAODPP 2018: 1)

It then goes on to state that '[t]he DPP will require an original (signed and dated) copy of your finalised VIS well in advance of the Sentencing Submissions hearing date' (SAODPP 2018: 3), although what is meant by 'well in advance' is not clarified.

The sentencing legislation and court rules in some jurisdictions, including Victoria (*Sentencing Act 1991* (Vic) s8N(2)) and South Australia (see *Supreme Court Criminal Rules 2014* (SA) r 90; *District Court Criminal Rules 2014* (SA) r 90; *Magistrates Court Rules (Criminal) 1992* (SA) r 41.04), also require that a written copy of any impact statement be provided to the court and offender prior to sentencing (or 'as soon as reasonably practicable after the defendant pleads or is found guilty' in South Australia). This implies an instrumental approach in those jurisdictions, since a key aspect of the instrumental use of an impact statement is that the defence be allowed the opportunity to view and challenge the information contained within the statement.

Case law suggests that problems can arise if impact statements are completed too early in the court process. One such problem was described by Gleeson CJ in the NSW case of *R v Bakewell*:

> Where a person is charged with a certain offence and the Crown accepts a plea of guilty to a lesser offence, it is often the case that the victim of

> the crime gives an account of the circumstances which, if true, means that the offender was, in reality, guilty of the more serious offence.
>
> (Unreported, NSWCCA, 27 June 1996: 8)

Taking these circumstances into account when sentencing would also contravene the principle in *R v de Simoni*, namely, 'that no one should be punished for an offence of which he has not been convicted' ((1981) 147 CLR 383: 389). Accordingly, taking circumstances into account in relation to a more serious offence when the offender has pleaded guilty to or been convicted of a lesser offence violates this principle under Australian law. Other principles may prevail in jurisdictions where consideration of 'relevant conduct' is permitted.

The participants interviewed for this research indicated that issues around the inclusion of information about conduct for which the offender is not ultimately convicted arise regularly in practice. This would not be a problem under an expressive impact statement regime, because the judge would not take the statement into account when sentencing. Conversely, if used instrumentally, including this information is problematic because the judge might rely on it in determining the sentence. This conflict is explored further in Chapter 5.

The presentation of victim impact statements

The rules for presenting impact statements vary by jurisdiction. The ACT legislation stipulates that an impact statement may be made in writing or given orally in court and must be read aloud if the author of the statement wishes to do so (*Crimes (Sentencing) Act 2005* (ACT) s50). If not made or given by the primary victim of the offence, the impact statement may be presented only with the express consent of the victim (s51(3)). In Tasmania, the impact statement may either be read to or by the court (*Criminal Rules 2006* (Tas) r 6) and must be read out loud upon the request of the statement's author (*Sentencing Act 1997* (Tas) s81A(4)). In South Australia, the impact statement must be given to the court in writing and read out at sentencing by its author or another person (previously *Criminal Law (Sentencing) Act 1988* (SA) s7A(3)(b); see now *Sentencing Act 2017* (SA) s14(2)(b)).

The victim-focused rules for presentation in these three jurisdictions do not conform to standard procedures for presenting evidence and are therefore inconsistent with an instrumental approach to impact statements. In contrast, in Victoria, impact statements may be made in writing by statutory declaration or in writing and presented orally by sworn evidence (*Sentencing Act 1991* (Vic) s8K). The requirement for the statement to be in this form goes beyond the requirements of the other Australian jurisdictions and is consistent with an instrumental approach. However, the statement's author may request that any part of it be read aloud to the court, by the author, the prosecutor, or someone chosen by the author and approved by the court, which is more consistent with an expressive approach (s8Q). Accordingly, the requirements for the presentation of impact statements in Victoria are another example of the inconsistency of impact statement regimes within and across jurisdictions.

Alternative arrangements for verbal presentation

Victoria and the ACT provide the most flexible arrangements to support victims who read their statements aloud to the court (see e.g. *Sentencing Act 1991* (Vic) s8R(1)). These include allowing the victim to present their statement from another room via closed-circuit television (CCTV), obscuring the victim's view of the offender during presentation, allowing a support person to stand beside the victim while the statement is read, closing the court, restricting those who can be present in the courtroom while the statement is being read, and requiring lawyers not to be robed during presentation.

The ACT legislation (s52(5)) allows victims to present their impact statement via 'special requirement' provisions under the *Evidence (Miscellaneous Provisions) Act 1991* (ACT), including presenting their statement via audio-visual link (s67), or in a closed court (s50), or in court with the protection of a screen (s47), and having a support person present during their presentation (s49). The scope of the protections afforded to victims in the ACT has been expanded since we conducted our research, as a result of reforms under the *Royal Commission Criminal Justice Amendment Act 2019* (ACT), which implemented certain recommendations of the Royal Commission into Institutional Responses to Child Sexual Abuse (2017).

South Australia also allows for vulnerable witness provisions to be invoked when an impact statement is being presented to the court, although this is only available where the court considers there is good reason to do so (see *Sentencing Act 2017* (SA) s14(3)(b)). These provisions include the presentation of the statement via CCTV, in court with the protection of a screen, or in a closed court (SAODPP 2016).

In contrast to the other jurisdictions, the Tasmanian Act does not contain any provisions allowing for flexible presentation of impact statements. Instead, the *Evidence (Children and Special Witnesses) Act 2001* (Tas) may apply. This allows the court to declare witnesses to be 'special' where, among other things, the nature of the subject matter of the evidence is likely to cause the victim severe emotional trauma or 'be so intimidated or distressed as to be unable to give evidence or to give evidence satisfactorily' (s8(1)(b)(ii)). Under s8, special witnesses may be allowed to give evidence in a closed court or via audio-visual link and have a support person with them while they are giving evidence (s8(2)). Chapter 5 explores the subject of alternative arrangements for the presentation of statements and discusses the issues that arose in victim interviews around the operation of the Tasmanian legislation.

The admissibility of victim impact statements

Booth (2012) has described the process for editing impact statements in the context of homicide cases in NSW. There is some limited authority in the study jurisdictions on the admissibility requirements of impact statements. To be admissible in the ACT, an impact statement must be 'a statement made by or for a victim of the offence that contains details of any harm suffered by the victim because of the offence' (*R v Shepheard* [2008] ACTSC 116: [26] (Refshauge J)). In *R v Iacuone; R v Duffy; R v JR (No 2)*, Burns J detailed the ACT Supreme Court's approach to receiving evidence of the harm claimed in a victim's impact statement. His Honour clarified that such harm need not be proven beyond reasonable doubt. The test for admissibility was, instead, relevance:

> In deciding how an offender is to be sentenced, the court must consider any VIS. In addition, in sentencing an offender, the court must take into account any injury, loss or damage resulting from the offence as well as the effect of the offence on the victim, their family or anyone else who may make a victim impact statement. It does not follow from this requirement that the test of admissibility of details of harm in a VIS is whether the court is satisfied beyond a reasonable doubt that the harm occurred as a result of the offence. Courts frequently receive evidence which is ultimately not accepted as establishing a fact to the requisite standard. Admissibility in that regard depends on relevance, and if the proposed evidence of harm is arguably relevant it will usually be received, with the question of what it proves to be determined by the sentencing judge.
>
> ([2014] ACTSC 149: [24]; see also Skvortsova & Khazma 2017)

If there is a dispute over the contents of a statement, Redlich JJA, Coghlan JJA, and Forrest AJA of the Victorian Court of Appeal determined that any facts asserted may only be accepted if, once the judicial officer makes clear that they plan to 'make full use of relevant material … there is express or tacit acquiescence by counsel for either side' (*Arthars v The Queen; Plater v The Queen* [2013] VSCA 258: [36]). Otherwise, such statements must only be used by the court if their disputed content is established beyond reasonable doubt (*R v Olbrich* (1999) 199 CLR 270).

Dealing with inadmissible materials

Different approaches have been taken to the process for dealing with inadmissible material within impact statements. Some jurisdictions require that such material be removed from the statement prior to it being tendered. If this does not occur, the ACT Supreme Court has held that defence counsel is entitled to object to the inadmissible material in the statement (*R v Shepheard* [2008] ACTSC 116; for discussion, see Skvortsova & Khazma 2017). In another ACT case, *Grimshaw v Mann*, Refshauge J encouraged defence counsel to make such objections, citing concerns that impact statements will lose their value if defence counsel do not intervene in matters where inadmissible material is provided to the court:

> While defence counsel may be wary of exercising their rights to cross-examine a victim on a Victim Impact Statement, discussions with prosecutors should result in an appropriate response from responsible prosecutors about inadmissible material and such statements. Without that proper approach, it is likely that such statements will lose their value and that the courts will have to intervene to ensure that the legislation is respected to ensure inadmissible, and often inflammatory, material is not included in such statements.
>
> ([2013] ACTSC 189: [41]; see also Skvortsova & Khazma 2017)

As noted in Chapter 2, where an impact statement contains inadmissible material not otherwise objected to, Refshauge J explained that judicial officers 'are expected to be able to set aside material they have viewed which must be ignored because irrelevant or inadmissible' (*Welch v R* [2011] ACTCA 19: [70]).

Refshauge J has written on several occasions about perceived inadequacies of processes surrounding the preparation and presentation of victim impact statements in the ACT. For example, in *R v Schmidt,* his Honour said:

> there were some matters in the Victim Impact Statements that were not in accordance with the legislation … In order to preserve the value and acceptability of such statements, I urge those charged with helping victims to prepare them to pay close attention to the legislation and comply with it.
>
> ([2013] ACTSC 295: [74])

Further, in *R v MT*, his Honour noted that 'those who assist victims to compose such statements should take care to see that the statutory constraints are observed, else there is a danger that the value of such statements will be undermined' ([2014] ACTSC 162: [54]; see also Skvortsova & Khazma 2017).

In South Australia, the Supreme, District, and Magistrate Courts' *Criminal Rules* all stipulate that a judicial officer may direct that irrelevant material in an impact statement not be read out to the court (see Rules 90, 90, and 41.06, respectively). Similarly, under Part 2 of the Tasmanian Supreme Court *Criminal Rules*, a judicial officer may direct the victim not to read any part of the impact statement that the court considers irrelevant to the proceedings. These rules suggest an instrumental approach to impact statements' content.

In Victoria, a different approach has been adopted. The Victorian legislation does not provide guidance on how to deal with inadmissible material in impact statements. In order to circumvent both the wariness of defence counsel to object to inadmissible material and the wariness of the prosecution to edit victims' statements, a hybrid process was developed. At the time we conducted our research, the Victorian OPP Director's Policy provided that:

> It is a matter for the sentencing judge to determine the admissibility of the material in a victim impact statement. However, where a prosecutor has possession of a victim impact statement and identifies clearly inadmissible material, he or she should bring it to the attention of the court to prevent sentencing error.
>
> (Victorian OPP 2014: Rule 48)
>
> Where a victim impact statement is to be read aloud by the victim or their representative and the statement contains material likely to be regarded as inadmissible, except where the material is scandalous,

> the prosecutor should submit that the victim or their representative be allowed to read the statement out in full. It should be submitted that the court should then decide what parts of the statement it considers to be admissible. Where the prosecutor considers that parts of the victim impact statement are likely to be regarded by the court as inadmissible, the defence and the court should be put on notice of the prosecutor's view. The prosecutor should not engage in editing or vetting the victim impact statement as it is the court's role to determine the admissibility of the victim impact statement.
>
> (Victorian OPP 2014: Rule 52)

This approach, which contains elements of both expressive and instrumental approaches, has advantages for all participants in the sentencing process, as Nettle JA explained in *Swift*:

> Counsel appearing before sentencing judges have tended not to say a great deal about the admissibility of the contents of victim impact statements. In effect, they have left it to sentencing judges to work out which parts of a statement are admissible and may be relied upon. Such an approach is to some extent contrary to mainstream criminal practice, where the taking of objections tends to be punctilious. But it has considerable advantages … It also accords with the observations of Charles JA in *R v Dowlan* ([1998] 1 VR 123) and of Vincent JA in *DPP v DJK* ([2003] VSCA 109) that it would be destructive of the purpose of victim impact statements if their reception in evidence were surrounded and confined by the sorts of procedural rules which are applicable to the treatment of witness statements in commercial cases.
>
> ([2007] VSCA 52: [7])

Since we conducted our research, the material described above has been removed from the Victorian OPP Director's Policy (see now Victorian OPP 2019). We infer that this is because the Victorian legislation was amended in 2018 and now provides that the court may receive the whole of a victim impact statement, despite the statement containing inadmissible material (see now *Sentencing Act 1991* (Vic) s8L(5)(b)). However, if the court receives a victim impact statement that contains inadmissible material, in sentencing the offender, the court is not to rely on the material that it considers to be inadmissible and need not specify which of the material is not being relied on (s8L(6)). This suggests a more expressive approach to impact statement content.

Our interviews with justice professionals and with victims revealed differing opinions on the approaches to issues of statement content and admissibility. These differences appear to stem from inconsistencies in interviewees' understandings of the purpose of impact statements. This issue is explored further in Chapter 6.

The rules for cross-examination

Dealing with disputed or contested material in impact statements may involve verification of their content via cross-examination. This is allowed in both the ACT (*Crimes (Sentencing) Act 2005* (ACT) s53(3)) and Victoria (*Sentencing Act 1991* (Vic) s8O(2)). Similarly, the Tasmanian Act requires that the sentencing court ensures the offender has the opportunity to challenge the information contained in an impact statement (*Sentencing Act 1997* (Tas) ss81(2), 81A(7)). If this occurs, the court may require the information to be proved in a similar manner as if it were received at a trial (see *Attorney-General for Tasmania v B* [2010] TASCCA 6). As a result, the victim may be required to give sworn evidence and be cross-examined. However, Slicer J of the Tasmanian Supreme Court noted in the case of *Owen v R* ([2003] TASSC 53: [58]) that, in order to allow cross-examination of a victim, 'real need must be shown rather than ritualistic objection' to the content of the statement. Unlike the other research jurisdictions, South Australia has not legislated for the cross-examination of victims on the content of their impact statement. However, there is evidence that, in accordance with the common law, cross-examination does occur occasionally (see South Australian Government 2000; O'Connell 2006; 2009).

It follows from the foregoing that each of the research jurisdictions demonstrates an instrumental approach to the issue of cross-examination on victims' impact statements. However, our interviews with justice professionals reveal that the threat of cross-examination of victims on their impact statements is anti-therapeutic and can result in their re-traumatisation. This issue is explored further in Chapter 5.

The therapeutic value of impact statements

The cathartic or therapeutic value of presenting an impact statement has been recognised at common law in South Australia. In *R v Leach,* Perry J explained:

> The legislative provisions as to victim impact statements are predicated upon the view that it is in the interests of justice that the victim of a crime is entitled to have a statement as to the impact of the crime upon him or her aired publicly during the sentencing process.

> Quite apart from the evident public interest in such a procedure being part of the sentencing process, the public airing of the impact of the offending upon the victim may in some cases assist the victim to come to terms with the effect of the crime upon them.
>
> ([2003] SASC 92: [59])

In that case, Bleby J also recognised that presenting a victim impact statement 'assists in bringing some closure to the victim' (2003: [66]). Many of the justice professionals we interviewed advocated the therapeutic benefits of presenting an impact statement and, in particular, the benefits of presenting a statement verbally; this is especially important if impact statements are viewed as having an expressive purpose. This is also explored further in Chapter 5.

The absence of an impact statement

As set out earlier, there are many reasons why a victim may choose not to provide an impact statement. The absence of a statement does not invalidate a sentencing decision. Courts are often able to assess the harm caused by the offending, based on the offence type and any circumstances surrounding the offending. As Southwell, Ormiston, and McDonald JJ explained in the Victorian case of *R v Miller*, sentencing judges are 'entitled to draw reasonable inferences from the evidence before [them] of any injury, loss or damage suffered by victims and their immediate families' ([1995] 2 VR 348: 354). Similarly, in the ACT, Gray P, Refshauge and Ryan JJ noted in *R v Eisenach* that, even 'without specific evidence, a sentencing court will be aware of the destructive effects of offences' ([2011] ACTCA 2: [65]). To like effect, Refshauge J stated in *R v MT* that 'in some cases, the Court will be aware of at least the general nature of the harm suffered or, at the very least, the likely harm by offences' ([2014] ACTSC 162: [58]).

The absence of an impact statement also cannot be used to make any assumption about the effect of the offending on the victim. Section 53(1)(b) of the *Crimes (Sentencing) Act 2005* (ACT) is a reminder of this. It stipulates that, when sentencing, the judicial officer must not draw any inference about the harm suffered by a victim from the fact that an impact statement is not presented to the court. Accordingly, while an impact statement may hold weight as one of the many factors to be considered when sentencing, the lack thereof cannot be a mitigating factor. As Neave JA explained in the Victorian case of *DPP v Gerrard*, 'there are many reasons why a victim may choose not to make a victim impact statement and no authority supports the view that this should be treated as a mitigating factor in sentencing' ([2011] VSCA 200: [172]). In a recent report on impact statements, the NSW Sentencing Council recommended that a 'court must not draw any inference about the harm suffered by a victim from the fact that a VIS is not given to the court' (2018: Recommendation 4.6). This recommendation was accepted by the NSW Government (2018). The justice professionals interviewed for our research suggest several reasons why victims may choose not to submit an impact statement. These are also discussed in Chapter 5.

Conclusion

In every Australian jurisdiction, victim participation in the sentencing process is guided by a range of legislative instruments, case law, policies, and guidelines that are 'inherently diverse and fragmented' (Kirchengast 2014: 19). This chapter has consolidated an analysis of this regulatory framework around a number of organising themes, to assess whether and how the legislated procedures manifest and comply with their express or implicit statements of purpose.

This analysis has identified that there is no explicit indication as to whether instrumental or expressive purposes underlie impact statement regimes in our study jurisdictions and the implied indicators of purpose are confusing and sometimes contradictory, both within and across the jurisdictions (see also Booth 2015; NSW Sentencing Council 2018). This finding provides critical context for our research outcomes and analysis.

Note

1 The guidelines in the ACT, South Australia, and Victoria have all changed their content since our research was undertaken, while the Tasmanian guidelines have remained the same.

References

ACT Government (2014). *Victim Impact Statement Information and Form*. https://www.victimsupport.act.gov.au/__data/assets/pdf_file/0012/752889/Final-for-website-October2014.pdf.

ACT Government Victim Support (2020). *Victim Impact Statements*. http://www.victimsupport.act.gov.au/what-we-do/victim-impact-statements.

Booth, T (2012). '"Cooling Out" Victims of Crime: Managing Victim Participation in the Sentencing Process in a Superior Sentencing Court', *Australian and New Zealand Journal of Criminology*, 45, 214–230.

Booth, T (2015). *Accommodating Justice: Victim Impact Statements in the Sentencing Process*, Federation Press. Sydney.

Kirchengast, T (2014). *Participation of Victims of Crime in New South Wales Court Processes*, Victims Services NSW. Sydney.

NSW Government (2018). *Schedule of Government Response to Recommendations on Victims' Involvement in Sentencing*. http://www.sentencingcouncil.justice.nsw.gov.au/Documents/ Current-projects/Victims/Victims_gov.pdf.

NSW Sentencing Council (2018). *Victims' Involvement in Sentencing—Report*. Sydney.

O'Connell, M (2006). 'Evolving Mechanisms for Engaging Victims in the Sentencing Process: Should Victims Have a Stronger Voice in Court?', Paper presented at the Sentencing Principles Perspectives and Possibilities Conference, Canberra.

O'Connell, M (2009). 'Victims in the Sentencing Process: South Australia's Judges and Magistrates Give Their Verdict', *International Perspectives in Victimology*, 4, 50–57.

Royal Commission into Institutional Responses to Child Sexual Abuse (2017). *Criminal Justice Report*. Sydney.

Skvortsova, T & Khazma, R (2017). 'Admissability of Victim Impact Statements in the ACT', *Ethos*, 245, 26–31.

South Australian Government (2000). *Survey of Victims of Crime*, Justice Strategy Unit. Adelaide.

South Australian Office of the Director of Public Prosecutions (SAODPP) (2016). *Information/Fact Sheet—Vulnerable Witness Provisions (VWPs)*. https://www.dpp.sa.gov.au/wp-content/uploads/2015/06/VWP-Fact-Sheet-Completed.pdf.

South Australian Office of the Director of Public Prosecutions (SAODPP) (2018). *Information/Fact Sheet—Victim Impact Statement (VIS)*. https://www.dpp.sa.gov.au/wp-content/uploads/2018/06/VIS-SUGGESTIONS.pdf.

Tasmanian Department of Justice (nd). *Having Your Say; Victim Impact Statement Form*. https://www.justice.tas.gov.au/__data/assets/pdf_file/0018/161190/Victim_Impact_Statement_Brochure.pdf.

Tasmanian Government (2020). *What Happens Next?* https://www.justice.tas.gov.au/victims/vis/whatnext.

Victorian Government (2017). *Guide to Victim Impact Statements*. https://www.victimsofcrime.vic.gov.au/sites/default/files/embridge_cache/emshare/original/public/2020/07/0a/bf2cca45f/Guide-to-victim-impact-statements-JUN2017.pdf/.

Victorian Office of Public Prosecutions (OPP) (2019). *Policy of the Director of the Public Prosecutions for Victoria*. http://www.opp.vic.gov.au/getattachment/6beb7d86-d539-4443-871f-cc4165557ea4/DPP-Policy.aspx.

PHILIPPA

The offender was a stranger to Philippa, a 19-year-old student. Shortly before midnight on a night in October 1991, he broke into Philippa's home. Philippa walked into her bedroom and found the offender there. He grabbed Philippa and she screamed. The offender demanded money and Philippa told him her money was in her backpack in the lounge room. The offender told Philippa to be quiet and that he had a knife. The offender then moved Philippa into the lounge room and she got her purse. At that stage, Philippa was able to see the offender. He had a shirt wrapped around his head, concealing his face. He pushed Philippa back into the bedroom and pushed her on the bed. He pulled Philippa's clothing off, including her underwear. He placed some bedding over her face and raped her digitally and vaginally. During the incident, he also threatened to orally and anally rape her. Philippa reported the rape immediately. She could describe some of the offender's features, but not his face, because of the disguise.

In 2013, due to improvements in DNA technology, a match was found with the swab taken from the Philippa shortly after the incident. As a result, the offender was arrested in July 2013.

The offender told police that he had difficulty recalling events from in 1991 and did not recall committing the offence. The matter was committed for trial and the offender pleaded not guilty in March 2014. At that time, the judge checked whether this was a definite not guilty matter, bearing in mind that it was a case of matched DNA. The offender confirmed his not guilty plea and Philippa was then told that she would have to go through a trial. However, one day into the trial, the offender pleaded guilty, and admitted having raped Philippa.

Philippa described having been provided with little information as the court proceedings progressed; consequently, she attended each court hearing, in order to keep abreast of the matter, and felt she would not otherwise have had any knowledge of what was happening. She noted that 'you can't control the process. The next best thing to having no input is to at least know what is going on. If you're informed, it makes it bearable'.

Philippa had knowledge of victim impact statements before preparing one for this matter. She was first informed of the concept of victim impact statements when the offence happened, but was not able to prepare one at the time, because there was no arrest or proceeding against the offender. Philippa wrote her first draft notes with the assistance of a trusted friend, who helped her articulate

> the damage that sexual violence does to a person. Making the connections between sexual violence, and the damage it does to self-esteem, the sorts of relationships that you then engage in … once you've experienced being raped, that sex is no longer an intimate act. In order to have sex, it can't be intimate. Because if you have sex, and it's intimate, then the person who raped you was intimate with you.

Philippa put those notes away, but picked them up later, when the trial was scheduled. Philippa described preparing the statement as being traumatic:

> In order to write it, I had to go back into my trauma … but no more than having to go back into my original statement for the trial. It wasn't more traumatising than any other part of the process. It was just part of the process that had to be done.

Philippa's victim impact statement said the following:

> I have fought for the past 23 years to suppress the memory of his attack and subsequent rape of me. The court case and the preparation of this victim impact statement has forced me to relive the whole horrendous incident and I have found many of the old anxieties rising to the surface again … The emotional trauma I have experienced as a result of being raped by a stranger in my home at the age of 19 has been significant and ongoing. I was unable to be satisfied that the house was properly secure and the fear of my attacker returning became so great I had to move house within weeks. I endured traumatic flashbacks of the attack ever since … Seemingly innocuous tasks, for example getting into a car and driving somewhere, became exercises in overcoming the irrational but extreme fear that my newfound sense of vulnerability brought to such occasions … At the time of my attack, I had planned to travel and work overseas, however my self-confidence was so diminished I chose to cancel those plans as I felt too vulnerable even to travel with friends …
>
> Being raped severely impacted by ability to trust and openly communicate with an intimate partner … [I didn't recognise] the impact of the rape on my ability to maintain a relationship. I have only come to this knowledge since attending counselling … the sexual nature of the assault has wreaked havoc on my self-esteem, my ability to trust, and my sense of worth within intimate relationships. This, coupled with the deep and pervading sense of shame I felt, however irrational, inhibited me from honestly communicating and facing the issues it created.

Philippa's statement was edited slightly after submission. The statement had originally referred to an incident with the offender that had occurred prior to the trial. The incident involved the offender arriving late at court on one occasion. The matter was called and, in his absence, was held off for a short period of time. When the offender did arrive, he sat near Philippa in the courtroom. Philippa said that, once her hearing was over,

> I wanted to wait for 10 or 15 minutes to give him a chance to leave. We waited, but when we got outside, we were standing there talking, and he came out of the court and walked really close to me on the street. So I put something in the victim impact statement about that incident, and I think I said something like 'I felt intimidated, and I believe that he meant me to feel intimidated'.

The defence objected to Philippa's supposition about what the offender did or did not want. Consequently, Philippa redacted this part of the statement in court with a marker. Philippa chose to read her statement in court:

> I read it out because just to read it in writing, because it was well written … [this] could have taken away some of the impact of it … I only made that call on the morning of … I think I cried the whole way through it. It felt good once I had done it. In some ways it was put to bed.

Philippa felt that the judge was very receptive to her statement, which made Philippa feel comfortable reading it out loud. She noted: 'I could read it from wherever, I could take my time. That really helped'.

Philippa appreciated the judge's reference to her statement: 'the judge quoted from my victim impact statement in sentencing. She made comment on the quality of it, and continually referred to it for the rest of the sentencing process'. In spite of this, Philippa would not necessarily recommend the process of submitting an impact statement:

> I don't think it would be my place to recommend it to someone else. I might tell someone of my experience. But what I would say is that what is more important is that a person in that situation understands that at any point in the process, they have a choice. If they don't feel like that, they are back in that situation where they didn't have any choice. I would talk about it as a positive experience, afterwards. But it was horrible having to do it.

Chapter 4

Judicial use of impact statements in sentencing

Introduction

When sentencing, judicial officers speak to offenders, victims, their supporters, and the public at large about right and wrong conduct (Warner 2000; Daly & Bouhours 2008). This makes sentencing a tool for communication between the criminal justice system and society (Mackenzie 2005). Sentencing regimes in Australia (e.g. *Sentencing Act 1991* (Vic) s5(2AC)(2)) require that judicial officers use this tool to acknowledge victims and, in doing so, recognise the harm caused by the offending at an individual level (Roberts & Manikis 2011). Research has shown that this acknowledgement can be validating and therapeutically beneficial for victims (Erez 1999; King 2006), especially when judicial officers refer to 'specifics from [victim impact statements] when handing down the sentence' (Schuster & Propen 2006: 24). It is arguable that judges must, at least in some Australian jurisdictions, consider these therapeutic outcomes of sentencing upon victims, not only because of the legislative requirement to recognise the harm caused to victims as a consequence of the offending,[1] but also because of a variety of legislative instruments (e.g. *Sentencing Act 1997* (Tas) s3(h)), case law (e.g. *R v DJK* [2003] VSCA 109), and policies (see King & Auty 2006 for discussion). Accordingly, sentencing remarks are 'important and consequential speech acts' (Daly & Bouhours 2008: 502), because they allow judicial officers to facilitate what Vincent JA in *R v DJK* described as the 'social rehabilitation' of the victim (2003: [18]; see also *R v Bayley* [2015] VCC 698; *R v McLachlan* [2015] VCC 1164).

As discussed in Chapter 2, research suggests that judicial officers are aware of the therapeutic benefits of acknowledging victims in their sentencing remarks. However, actual judicial practice in relation to the use of impact statements at sentencing has rarely been empirically researched and our research was the first to quantify judicial acknowledgement of victims at sentencing, in Australia or elsewhere.

In 2018, Balfour, Du Mont, and White published their analysis of 38 Canadian sexual assault cases where a victim impact statement had been provided. The authors observed that 'the victim impact statement as a legal strategy to allow for judicial consideration of the victim's experience of sexual assault … [is] a less researched aspect of the criminal justice response to rape' (2018: 57). Their analysis focused on whether archetypes of the ideal victim continue to influence juridical discourse and what narratives of harm intersect with sentencing objectives and aggravating factors. They also called for 'the important need for further research of sentencing decisions to systemically analyze how victim impact statements are taken up in a larger sample of sexual assault cases (2018: 58).

This chapter begins to fill this knowledge gap by presenting a content analysis of the sentencing remarks in 100 sexual offence cases from the ACT, South Australia, Tasmania, and Victoria. This analysis was designed to fulfil one of the major research aims of this project, namely, exploring judicial practice in relation to the use of and reference to impact statements at sentencing in sexual offence cases. The chapter identifies both how and how often judicial officers refer to victims and their impact statements at sentencing and explores how different judicial approaches can affect the victims involved. In undertaking this analysis, we acknowledge that variation in how impact statements are used is linked with the variations in the legal and policy frameworks discussed in the previous chapter.

We begin by identifying the context in which judges operate when sentencing offenders. We then use the interview findings discussed further in Chapter 6 to explore the therapeutic benefits that victims may derive from judicial acknowledgement at sentencing. Next, the findings of the content analysis are discussed. This analysis is also informed by the interview findings and previous research about victims' justice needs. It uses excerpts from the remarks to illustrate and critique judicial practice and identify practices that may be therapeutic or anti-therapeutic from a victim-focused perspective. Finally, the chapter makes recommendations for a number of educative and legal processes to help judicial officers develop an understanding of how to effectively and therapeutically acknowledge victims when sentencing.

The wider sentencing context

While this chapter focuses on victim perspectives of judicial acknowledgement at sentencing, it would be remiss not to mention the wider sentencing context, including the parameters within which judicial officers must work (see e.g. Roach Anleu, Brewer, & Mack 2017). As discussed in Chapter 3, recognition and/or consideration of the victim is specifically required by sentencing legislation around Australia, but this does not minimise the main objectives of sentencing, which include deterrence, protection of the community, 'just' or 'adequate' punishment, denunciation, and rehabilitation. Accordingly, it is recognised that, when preparing their sentencing remarks, judges are required to balance numerous purposes of sentencing. However, because a therapeutic jurisprudence approach encourages judges to consider not only 'the substantive law and procedure, but … the way in which they interact with people in court and the potential impact of their actions on the wellbeing of those affected by them' (King 2006: 93), we encourage judicial officers to consider the effect of their sentencing remarks on victims.

The benefits of judicial acknowledgement

As detailed in Chapter 1, the justice needs of victims of sexual offending include the need for voice and participation (Shapland, Willmore, & Duff 1985; Lievore 2005). The right to present an impact statement should fulfil those two needs, at least to some extent. There are several further justice needs that could possibly be met by effective judicial acknowledgement of victims and their impact statements at sentencing. These include victims' need to be treated with respect (McGlynn 2011), their need for validation, involving affirmation that they are believed (Clark 2010; Bluett-Boyd & Fileborn 2014; Iliadis 2020), and their need for vindication, involving recognition that what has happened to them was wrong (Herman 2005).

As discussed in Chapter 5, the justice professionals interviewed for this project overwhelmingly agreed that victims can derive therapeutic benefits from judicial acknowledgement at sentencing. They identified several ways that this can meet victims' justice needs. Two witness assistance officers also explained how a victim's need for respect and voice, including public recognition and acknowledgement, can be met by the judge during sentencing:

> In the end, to have the judge say 'before you sit down, I just want to say to you that it's amazing that you just read out your victim impact statement and I admire your strength', or to have it acknowledged in sentencing remarks is so powerful. People comment on that, and you see them emotionally and physically react to it. Just to have the

> judge look them in the eye, and say 'I acknowledge your experience', it's so great for them.
>
> (Andie, WAO, Vic)

> It absolutely changes their lives. There's a really obvious sense of relief when they are referred to in the comments. I think there's nothing that gives a victim more closure than hearing a judge say 'I've heard what you've had to say about it'.
>
> (Harriet, WAO, Tas)

Two VSOs also described how a victim's need for respect and validation can be met when a judge's acknowledgement demonstrates that the victim has been believed by the court:

> That acknowledgement is very powerful for the victim and really makes a difference. It's that validation. It's about humanising them. I remember a client who said 'he really did read it, and he got it'. It was about feeling understood, and heard, and believed, and valued.
>
> (Jane, Vic)

> It is absolutely an empowering experience to see people come out the other side of [sentencing] and feel heard. They are often acknowledged by the presiding judge in very respectful ways, which is very validating and very satisfying for people … in the matters I've been involved with, victims have been quoted [by the judge]. So, they do know that they have been read and taken notice of … it's profound.
>
> (Cathy, SA)

Accordingly, our interviews confirm the significant beneficial and therapeutic effect that judicial acknowledgement at sentencing can have for victims. They also demonstrate that this meets a range of victims' justice needs.

Benefits to others

The benefits of judicial acknowledgement arguably extend beyond the individual victims. They may extend to victims' families or supporters, because judicial acknowledgement of harm may provide validation to those who have supported victims throughout their experience. Acknowledgement of harm can also benefit victims' families or supporters, insofar as they may not otherwise have understood the harm experienced by their friend or family member (Miller 2013). This may help them provide the victims with ongoing support.

The acknowledgement may also benefit the wider community, by educating them about the harm caused by the offending. In addition, it may provide an opportunity for offenders to comprehend the harm caused by their offending. This may promote their rehabilitation, by changing their views about crime or their future choices in relation to offending behaviour (Booth 2005; Hill 2005; Shapland & Hall 2010).

Content analysis findings

As set out in Chapter 1, we analysed 100 sentencing remarks from the four study jurisdictions. Impact statements were submitted in at least 79 of the cases. In 11 cases, it was not stated whether an impact statement had been submitted.

Victims and/or their impact statements were acknowledged by judicial officers in 95 cases. As shown in Table 4.1, Victoria was the only jurisdiction where the judge acknowledged the victim in all cases. In the ACT, judges acknowledged the victims in 19 of the 22 cases (86%), compared with 95% of cases in South Australia and 94% in Tasmania. This is broadly consistent with Victorian and South Australian judges' responses (see O'Connell 2009; Victorian Victim Support Agency 2009) and Booth's review of 'sentencing judgements more broadly across Australian jurisdictions [which] reveals it is rare for a sentencing judge not to refer to VISs' (2015: 150). Harm to the victim's family was also mentioned in 15 cases, most commonly in the ACT (21% of cases), followed by Tasmania (19%); this was also mentioned in 15% of cases in Victoria, but only 5% of the South Australian cases.

The degree of acknowledgement varied greatly and there was no discernible pattern according to the nature or seriousness of the offence. That is, judges did not tend to devote a greater proportion of their

Table 4.1 Harm acknowledged in sentencing remarks, by jurisdiction

	ACT (n = 22)	*SA (n = 22)*	*Tas (n = 16)*	*Vic (n = 40)*	*Total (n = 100)*
Harm to victim	19	21	15	40	95
Harm to victim's family	4	2	3	6	15
No mention of harm	3	1	1	0	5

sentencing remarks to victim harm in more serious cases, such as rape, in comparison to less serious cases, such as indecent assault. There was also no evident difference in victim acknowledgement between matters resolved by plea or at trial or on the basis of whether there was a prior relationship between the offender and the victim.

In all jurisdictions, there were examples of judicial acknowledgement that can be understood as either therapeutic or anti-therapeutic, from a victim-focused perspective. The next section identifies judicial practices that clearly fail to meet the justice needs of victims identified above. We then explore the difficulties that judicial officers may face when attempting to craft therapeutically effective sentencing remarks.

Cases with minimal reference to victim harm

It appears that the ideal extent to which judicial officers should refer to or acknowledge victims when sentencing has never been definitively identified. However, the Victorian Victim Support Agency found that victim support and witness assistance officers spoke highly of judges who acknowledged the victim in detail, in contrast to those who provided minimal acknowledgement, with a one-sentence reference described as 'tokenistic' (Victorian Department of Justice 2014: 59). The justice professionals we interviewed agreed that the extent of judicial acknowledgement varies between cases and similarly identified brief acknowledgement as problematic:

> They are all different. Some are really good and will go into a lot of detail about what a victim has said in their victim impact statement … Others will just say that they have read the victim impact statement and taken it into account.
>
> (Hannah, WAO, Vic)

> [Sometimes] they just say 'I have taken into account the victim impact statement and I note that as a consequence of your offending, the victim has suffered.' That's about the minimum that I have found.
>
> (Rose, Prosecutor, Vic)

> I think sometimes, unfortunately, [the acknowledgement] can fall flat. And the process can feel somewhat tokenistic. A bit like box ticking in terms of hearing from the victim
>
> (Trish, VSO, Vic)

> There have been some examples where the victim didn't feel like they were taken seriously. That has huge ramifications on the victim.
> (Suzanna, VSO, ACT)

We found six instances of such 'tokenistic' references in remarks from all four jurisdictions, although it appeared to be more common in South Australia. Impact statements had been submitted in five of these cases. The cases differed in terms of offence type and seriousness. Half were stranger assaults, while the other half of the offenders were well known to their victims.

In the Victorian case of *R v Johns* ([2015] VCC 840: [7]), the judge stated merely that the victim 'read her victim impact statement in court, and I have taken that into account'. With equal brevity, in *R v Kim*, an ACT judge said: 'these offences, of course, involved a gross invasion of the privacy of your victims' ([2015] ACTSC 182: [12]). In a South Australian case, *R v Pelly* (Unreported, SADC, 28 August 2014: np), the judge said 'you would have noticed from the victim impact statement the traumatic consequences for her'. Similarly, in *R v Duncan* (Unreported, SADC, 6 November 2014: np), the same judge noted: 'as you heard from the victims, [the offending was] quite alarming and devastating'. In a slightly longer comment in *R v Naiker* (Unreported, SADC, 10 October 2014: np), another judge of the South Australian District Court stated that the victim 'was shocked by what happened and has understandably suffered and been mentally and emotionally affected by your offending'. Similarly, in *R v PB* (Unreported, TasSC, 7 December 2015: np), a Tasmanian judge said '[the victim] has provided a victim impact statement. It was a very upsetting time for her, and she is still anxious about some aspects of [the offender's] conduct'.

One South Australian victim interviewed for this study recalled that the judge made only a brief and passing reference to her when sentencing the offender. According to Laura, 'it was all part of the speech; he talked about the crime and how the offender acted, and said "based on this, this is what the sentence is". It was done really quickly'. She expressed no positive views about what was said. Her recollection is confirmed by the transcript of her case, which reveals that a single sentence was the extent of the judicial acknowledgement: 'I make it clear that I take into account the impact on the victim and those close to her of this defendant's appalling treatment of her'.[2]

The Victorian Victim Support Agency's interviews with victims (Victorian Department of Justice 2014) indicated that the most important determinant of their satisfaction arising from judicial acknowledgement was whether the judicial officers made clear that they had carefully considered the victims' statements. This is consistent with victims' needs for validation and vindication. Unfortunately, the judges' fleeting acknowledgements in the foregoing cases of *R v Johns*, *R v Kim*, *R v Pelly*, *R v PB*, *R v Duncan,* and *R v Naicker,* as well as in Laura's case, fail to convey such careful consideration. This suggests that the judges in these cases either did not understand how to demonstrate their consideration of the impact statement or had not turned their minds sufficiently to this issue when crafting their remarks. This creates the risk, as identified by ACT VSO Suzanna, that victims will not 'feel like they were taken seriously' and negates the potential benefit or validation victims might obtain from more detailed acknowledgement. It also fails to pay due respect to the effort made by victims to explain the effect of the offending on them. Furthermore, it creates the risk that judicial officers may be perceived to lack understanding of the impact of sexual offending on victims, which in turn raises concerns about victims' equal treatment before the law (see Judicial Commission of NSW 2019: [7.3.3.2]).

To resolve these issues, the following section explores more therapeutically effective approaches that judges can take when acknowledging victims. Drawing on this analysis, we make recommendations below that seek to ensure that judicial officers are provided with comprehensive information about the possible therapeutic and anti-therapeutic consequences of acknowledging victims when sentencing.

The challenge of quantifying therapeutically effective levels of victim acknowledgement

As explored in the preceding section, there are clear anti-therapeutic outcomes arising from minimal judicial acknowledgement of victim harm and examples of this occurring in judicial practice. However, our sentencing remarks analysis and the victim interviews reveal that it is more difficult to definitively identify judicial practices which are likely to have therapeutic outcomes for victims. This section explores this issue by first identifying the type of acknowledgement that was found to be beneficial for some of the victims interviewed. It then examines the experiences of victims who were unsatisfied, despite receiving a similar level of acknowledgement to those victims who were satisfied. The interview findings are supplemented by the analysis of the sentencing remarks dataset.

Examples of victim satisfaction and appropriate acknowledgement

Three of the victims interviewed were extremely satisfied with the level of acknowledgement they received in their case. The judge in each case acknowledged the victims differently, but what the three cases share is that each judge implicitly met the victim's justice needs, as identified above. For example, Philippa (Victim, SA) was pleased by the following acknowledgement in her case:

> The effect upon the victim over the past 23 years has been horrendous and pervasive. As the victim has described in her victim impact statement, your arrest and the recent court proceedings have forced her to relive the whole incident again. The victim had, after much suffering, learned to deal with the effect of your crimes. She developed coping mechanisms, but still the effects of your crimes were felt in every aspect of her life. When you were arrested in 2013, the victim was forced to face the ordeal again. As she so eloquently described in her victim impact statement and I quote: 'Having spent the last 20 years trying to forget, from that moment I've been required to do nothing but remember, and remember I have. I have remembered the terror whilst I tried to work out how to best survive a situation which I instinctively knew was going to end in rape, my focus being on it not ending in death'.

In this case, the sentencing judge recognised and acknowledged the harm caused to Philippa by the offending. Philippa noted in her interview that she particularly appreciated the judge's reference to the 'impact of the offence and the impact of the process' upon her. The judge then vindicated Philippa by describing the effects of the offending as 'horrendous and pervasive'. Finally, the judge validated Philippa by making clear that the court believed her about the harm caused by the offending, through direct quotation from her impact statement.

South Australian victim August also appreciated the level of acknowledgement from the judge in her case, who validated and vindicated her by saying that it was 'abundantly clear from [her] impact statement that [the offender's] conduct has had a marked impact upon her … Hopefully time will heal the emotional and psychological impact of your behaviour'.[3] August appreciated that the judge 'referred to [the impact statement] quite a bit. And indirectly talked to me a few times, saying [things] like, "she seems like a lovely young lady and strong". It was really cool, [the judge] really listened to it'.

Rachel from Tasmania was also satisfied with the acknowledgement by the judge in her case. The following remarks validated and vindicated her experience:

> [The offender] has caused significant emotional and psychological harm. The harm is continuing and may be long-lasting … the vulnerability of [the victim] arising from her trust in [the offender], and the harm caused to her, must all be reflected in the sentence.

Rachel felt that 'it was good to see that what I said was taken on board'.[4]

Nearly a quarter of the examined remarks (n = 23; see Davies 2017) demonstrate similar levels of judicial acknowledgement. We analysed a representative sample of these remarks. To ensure that the remarks are understood in context, the comments from the sample cases relating to victim harm are extracted in Table 4.2 and analysed further below.

In *R v Ballantyne*, Murrell CJ of the ACT Supreme Court recognised the victim by detailing the harm caused to her by the offending, including the difficulties encountered by the victim's family in supporting her through the justice process. Her Honour next vindicated the victim by specifically stating that 'the Court acknowledges the suffering' of the victim. This was followed by an expression of respect and validation for the victim, through the statement that the court 'hopes that, as a consequence of the resolution of these proceedings, the victim and her family can come to terms with what has occurred and move on with their lives'. By referring to the victim's future in this way, Murrell CJ has encouraged the victim to see the resolution of the criminal proceedings as a turning point in her life.

In *R v Scrivener*, Judge McIntyre of the South Australian District Court acknowledged the victim by noting that she had read 'her very eloquent victim impact statement' in court. By describing the victim's statement as 'eloquent', McIntyre J drew attention to the way that the victim's words had moved her Honour personally. McIntyre J also honoured the victim by recognising that this had taken 'great courage'. She then vindicated the victim by explaining that the offender's actions were a 'gross breach' of trust, which would continue to affect the victim's life into the future.

Likewise, in *R v QMT*, Justice Wood of the Tasmanian Supreme Court recognised the victim by detailing the physical and emotional harm caused as a consequence of the offending. Her Honour then

Table 4.2 Examples of judicial acknowledgement that implicitly meet victims' justice needs

Case (*Jurisdiction*)	*Reference to victim harm*
R v Ballantyne (Unreported, ACTSC, 1 April 2014)	'The effects for the victim are the sorts of effects that the Court commonly sees in the case of victims of sexual assaults. The victim had been a confident, outgoing girl. She was described as a "natural leader". She engaged well at school … However, immediately after the incident, she became fearful and was very reluctant to leave her home for several weeks. She dropped out of Year 12 … She was in constant fear of encountering the offender. There was a flow-on effect to her family, who felt quite powerless in the situation … The Court acknowledges the suffering of the victim's family and hopes that, as a consequence of the resolution of these proceedings, the victim and her family can come to terms with what has occurred and move on with their lives.'
R v Barbat ([2014] VCC 42)	'I received a victim impact statement from [the victim]. In it, she eloquently describes the effect of your crimes on her. You heard that read out in court and you should feel ashamed at the impact your actions have had on her and her life. She felt sheer terror at the time of the offending … As a result of your offending, she has lost her ability to trust others, or allow others to get close to her emotionally. She has lost her innocence and bubbly personality as well as her confidence, which has reduced her circle of friends; and she feels estranged from her family. Nothing I say can make her feel safer or improve her outlook on life, and given her nightmares of seeing you out of gaol, I am conscious that the sentence I am going to impose will not seem sufficient for her. However, I assure her that I have taken the impact on her very much into account in my sentence, although it must be balanced against the other factors the law requires me to take into account. I am pleased to note that she is receiving counselling from a psychologist which is affording her some comfort and she bravely recognises that things will get better in time. I encourage her to continue to seek assistance for as long as she needs. I wish her well in the future.'
R v Kennedy (Unreported, SADC, 27 April 2016)	'I have received a victim impact statement from the complainant. It is clear your offending has had a significant impact upon her. She now feels anxious and scared when she hears unusual noises, she can't concentrate efficiently to study or work. She is desperate for her normal life back and [to] be able to function. She suffered the feelings that many people in her situation feel after an offence such as this. She felt humiliated, embarrassed, powerless, and dirty. It is not surprising that your behaviour has had such a significant impact upon her.'

(*Continued*)

Table 4.2 (Continued)

Case *(Jurisdiction)*	*Reference to victim harm*
R v McLachlan [2015] VCC 1164	'I have received a victim impact statement. In it the victim indicated that as a result of your offending she felt empty; or as she put it, "numb". She has lost trust in others. Sadly, she says she blames herself for "letting you in". Of course, the victim should not in any way blame herself for what happened in this case ... There can be no doubt that the victim suffered significant, enduring physical and psychological trauma as a result of your offending. It is to be hoped that now that this process is completed, she can successfully move on with her life, assisted by whatever psychological counselling is necessary.'
R v QMT (Unreported, TasSC, 11 May 2015)	'The complainant suffered areas of tenderness and bruising, including fingertip bruises to her thighs. The emotional consequences to her have been significant. She was extremely frightened during her ordeal. She has had difficulty sleeping and suffers from nightmares. She feels scared and anxious and also experiences outbursts of anger. The courts know very well that such adverse effects are often long-lasting, affecting wellbeing, relationships, and many facets of a complainant's life ... These are serious crimes that amounted to a complete breach of trust. The crime of rape was persistently carried out with complete disregard for the complainant's obvious distraught state, and her clear and determined refusal. The sentence must adequately reflect the nature of these crimes, the terrible ordeal experienced by the complainant and the harm you have caused to her.'
R v Scrivener (Unreported, SADC, 6 June 2014)	'Your victim read her very eloquent victim impact statement in court. This took great courage. I will not do her the disservice of paraphrasing what she said because I am sure you will remember what she told you about how your actions that night have affected her. You were a trusted friend staying in your victim's house. Your actions were a gross breach of that trust and that friendship. Your victim, her family and friends continue to live with the consequences.'
R v Stanley [2015] ACTSC 322	'The victim prepared a victim impact statement which the Crown Prosecutor read out. That can be important as it then is clear that the offender has heard what the victim has to say. It was difficult to hear that victim impact statement without experiencing some of the pain and hurt that the victim described. Courts know of the serious effects of such violence and invasions of the bodily integrity of victims but it is very valuable to hear the voices of the victims and understand how the hurt and damage can be different for each victim. The victim in this case is clearly continuing to experience serious emotional trauma and the not uncommon feelings of shame and self-doubt that are so inappropriate for the victim to feel and yet so common and so distressing. The effect that she has described also goes beyond her to the effect on her family and friends who have provided her with support and the blame they also feel for not intervening.'

acknowledged that what had happened to the victim was wrong, explaining that 'such adverse effects are often long-lasting, affecting wellbeing, relationships, and many facets of a [victim's] life'. Wood J went on to vindicate the victim, by stating that 'the sentence must adequately reflect the nature of these crimes, the terrible ordeal experienced by the complainant, and the harm [the offender had] caused to her'.

In *R v Barbat*, Judge Sexton of the Victorian County Court recognised the victim by summarising the contents of her impact statement. Her Honour then exemplified how judges can use sentencing remarks to speak to the offender, the victim, and the community about right and wrong conduct, by specifically denouncing the offender's conduct. She did so by addressing him directly, stating that he 'should feel ashamed at the impact [his] actions have had' on the victim. Later on, Judge Sexton affirmed that the victim was believed by the court and acknowledged that '[n]othing I say can make [the victim] feel safer or improve her outlook on life … However, I assure [the victim] that I have taken the impact on her very much into account in my sentence'. Her Honour concluded by further vindicating the victim through 'encourag[ing] her to continue to seek assistance for as long as she needs' and 'wish[ing] [the victim] well in the future'.

In *R v Stanley*, Refshauge J of the ACT Supreme Court recognised the victim by explaining how important it was that her statement was read aloud, so that the offender could hear what she had written. By doing this, his Honour recognised the communicative role that impact statements can play in the sentencing process. He then validated the victim, explaining how he and others present in the courtroom had empathised with her: 'it was difficult to hear that victim impact statement without experiencing some of the pain and hurt that the victim described'. He further validated and vindicated the victim by explaining that it is 'very valuable to hear the voices of the victims' and sought to comfort her by explaining that her 'feelings of shame and self-doubt … are so inappropriate for the victim to feel and yet so common and so distressing'.

Similarly, in *R v Kennedy*, Judge Davison of the South Australian District Court recognised the victim by describing the harm caused by the offending and stating that 'it is clear your offending has had a significant impact upon [the victim]'. Her Honour then validated the victim, by explaining that 'she suffered the feelings that many people in her situation feel after an offence such as this', before vindicating her: 'it is not surprising that [the offender's] behaviour has had such a significant impact upon [the victim]'. In taking this approach, Davison J used her judicial authority and experience to bring comfort to the victim, by assuring her that she was not alone in the way that the crime had affected her.

Finally, in *R v McLachlan,* Judge Howard of the Victorian County Court validated the victim by using her own words to explain that as 'a result of [the] offending she felt empty; or as she put it, "numb"'. His Honour vindicated and reassured the victim by describing her misplaced self-blame, arguing that 'of course, the victim should not in any way blame herself for what happened in this case'. He further validated the victim through his statement that 'there can be no doubt that the victim suffered significant, enduring physical and psychological trauma as a result of your offending'. He concluded the comments directed at the victim by respectfully hoping that, following resolution of the trial, and assisted by appropriate counselling, she might now 'successfully move on with her life'. In taking this approach, like Murrell CJ in *R v Ballantyne,* Judge Howard also encouraged the victim to see the finalisation of the criminal proceedings as a turning point in her life.

Examples of unsatisfactory victim acknowledgement

The cases extracted and analysed above demonstrate that a range of approaches may be used by judges to meet victims' justice needs for voice, validation, and vindication in sentencing. This involves judicial acknowledgement that the victim has been offended against, the offending was wrong, and the harm outlined by the victim in their impact statement is believed by the court. However, the interview findings reveal that this level of acknowledgement cannot be understood as being definitively therapeutic for victims. For example, Jessica (Victim, SA) was disappointed by the following acknowledgement from the judicial officer in her case:

> I had the benefit of hearing from the victim who personally read her victim impact statement ... it certainly does highlight the devastating and significant impact this offending has had upon the victim. I make it clear that the victim impact statement is but one of a number of factors I need to take into account, but it is a significant factor. It was a powerful document. That is hardly surprising — given the breach of trust and the nature of the offending in this matter.

This extract[5] does not differ in any noticeable way from the type of acknowledgement valued by the other victims. The judge's words clearly indicate that the offending was wrong and that the court believed Jessica's statement about the harm caused by the offending. However, during her interview, Jessica reported that the judicial officer only 'made reference to "having heard the victim's impact statement", and said "I know how this has affected the victim" … [but that was] pretty well it'.

While the judicial officer in Jessica's case clearly referred to the harm she had suffered in more detail than she described, Jessica's dissatisfaction with the sentencing remarks reflects her overall dissatisfaction with the way her case was managed. She was unhappy that the prosecution accepted a guilty plea for a lesser offence than what was originally charged and this had obvious and negative ramifications for Jessica's experience of the justice system generally. Jessica's example therefore reveals how difficult it can be for judges to accommodate victims' needs when sentencing, because victims' experiences of sentencing do not occur in a vacuum.

Tasmanian victim Eve was also disappointed by the level of acknowledgement in her case, but for different reasons. In this case, the judge first explained that the 'impact statement shows that the crimes had a significant impact on [Eve]. The crime made her feel humiliated and powerless. She had great difficulty reliving the event [throughout the court process]'. This extract reflects the type of validation and vindication appreciated by the other victims. However, the judge went on to describe the emotional and psychological difficulties that Eve had experienced because of earlier family tragedies, as well as her subsequent reliance on alcohol as a coping mechanism and history of self-harm and admissions to mental health facilities, as a result of suicidal ideation.[6] Eve was uncomfortable with the judge sharing this level of detail about her life, particularly because of the media interest in the trial. Eve said that wide reporting of the content of her impact statement in both print and social media 'made it hard … because that was in the paper, and it was in the news. It was horrible to hear parts of my personal victim impact statement shared to everybody'. While no other interviewed victims expressed similar concerns, WAO Robert from Tasmania confirmed that this issue is not isolated to Eve's experience. Due to concern about excessive media reporting, Robert stated that some victims 'don't want everyone to hear [the details of their impact statement], particularly the media'. Samuel (WAO, SA) also noted the problem arising in his jurisdiction and argued that limiting the level of personal information shared about a victim at sentencing is 'important in cases where there are lots of media'.

Accordingly, these findings from Eve's interview suggest that explicit and detailed reference to victims' vulnerabilities, such as mental health issues, may result in anti-therapeutic outcomes for victims, even if the judicial acknowledgement has otherwise addressed factors that victims generally find to be therapeutic.

Two of the cases we analysed contain similar levels of information about the victims' personal circumstances. In the Tasmanian case of *R v Craig* (Unreported, TasSC, 26 May 2016), the judge mentioned the victim's mental health prior to the offence, as well as discussing in great detail the harm she experienced as a consequence of the offending:

> The complainant has been severely affected by this crime. She suffers from post-traumatic stress disorder and is under the care of a psychiatrist. Her mental health was to an extent vulnerable beforehand, but she was someone who was managing well and did not require any specialist care.
>
> Since the rape was committed, the contrast in her condition is stark. The complainant has attempted to end her life and engaged in serious self-harm on multiple occasions. She nearly died on one occasion and on other occasions required surgical intervention. Her suicidality has subsisted for a lengthy period of time. In 2014 and 2015 she had 50 admissions to hospital for her self-destructive impulses. There is a risk of lasting psychiatric harm.

Likewise, in the South Australian case of *R v F,K* (Unreported, SADC, 30 June 2016), the judge discussed in detail the victim's mental health prior to and as a result of the offending:

> Eighteen months prior to the incident, the victim had been diagnosed with anxiety and fatigue for which she was receiving therapy at the time of this offence … it was a violent attack … She suffered physical injuries in the way of bruising and abrasions and … has been diagnosed with post-traumatic stress disorder.

The discussion of harm in these cases demonstrates that each judge had carefully considered the content of the impact statement received. Yet the explicit and personal information about these victims' mental health, including the detailed description in *R v Craig* of the victim's suicidal ideation, including 50 hospital admissions for 'self-destructive impulses', and the judge's reference in *R v F,K* to the 18 months of therapy the victim had received prior to the time of the offending, are similar to the level of detail that Eve found so distressing. This may consequently have diminished the therapeutic benefits that the victims in those cases might have obtained from the judicial acknowledgement.

It is quite possible that these detailed discussions of harm are examples of judicial emphasis of a number of sentencing purposes, such as denunciation, just punishment, and rehabilitation. Because denunciation 'requires that a sentence should … communicate society's condemnation of the particular offender's conduct' (*R v Ryan* (2001) 206 CLR 267: [118]), it may be that the details the judges chose to include in their remarks were what they believed made clear to the offender the exact conduct that was being denounced. Similarly, the judges may have chosen to include such explicit detail because harm caused to the victim is relevant in determining offence seriousness under a just deserts approach. It may also be that the information was included because the judges were hopeful that educating the offender on the specific consequences of their offending might assist in their rehabilitation.

These are all important sentencing considerations. However, due to the possibility of problematic outcomes for victims arising from the inclusion of such personal information, Victorian WAO Andie argued that 'boundaries' must be introduced regarding the information that judicial officers are allowed to share about victims when sentencing. Recommendations for the introduction of such boundaries are explored further below. We also note recent research from South Africa examining a homicide case in which the prosecution indicated that, in order to protect the right to privacy of the surviving victim, no impact statement would be presented during sentencing (see *S v van Breda* (SS17/16) [2018] ZAWCHC 87). In their analysis of this case, van de Merwe and Mitchell considered the importance of privacy and the victim's privacy needs, before concluding that:

> victims should have control of what information about themselves and their lives are made public, and that they should have a reasonable expectation of privacy within the public sphere. It is recommended that an individualised approach should be followed where victims are first properly informed of the consequences of making an impact statement and then allowed to make an informed decision.
> (2020: 18)

Cases with no impact statement

Our analysis of the sentencing remarks reveals that therapeutically effective judicial acknowledgement of victim harm is possible even in cases where a victim impact statement has not been submitted. The court is usually aware of the type of harm that may have been experienced by the victim. This is informed by the offence type and the circumstances surrounding the offending outlined in the evidence or agreed facts. As Southwell, Ormiston, and McDonald JJ explained in *R v Miller*, sentencing judges may draw 'reasonable inferences' from the evidence before them 'of any injury, loss or damage suffered by victims and their immediate families' ([1995] 2 VR 348: 354). In the absence of an impact statement, it is unlikely that a judge will be able to meet a victim's need for validation, which requires affirmation that the victim's statement is believed by the court. However, it is still possible to ensure the victim's need for acknowledgement and vindication are met. The analysed remarks contain seven examples where harm to the victim was identified as being effectively acknowledged, even in the absence of an impact statement (for further details, see Davies 2017). In *R v Agresti* ([2016] ACTSC 9: [8]), Murrell CJ of the ACT Supreme Court noted that the court did not receive an impact statement, but she acknowledged and vindicated the victim by explaining that she had 'no doubt that the offence had a very significant impact on the victim's psychological wellbeing'.

In *R v Kubsch*, Judge Rice of the South Australian District Court acknowledged the victim by saying that, although no impact statement had been submitted, 'that is not to say your offending was without a significant impact upon her' (Unreported, SADC, 6 February 2015: np). His Honour further vindicated the victim by recognising the harm caused to her, explaining that she was 'unwilling to give a statement because to do so would revive memories of [the] offending' (2015: np). Likewise, in *R v Daglas* ([2015] VCC 1038: 5), Judge Murphy of the Victorian County Court vindicated the victim by explaining that, while she did not submit a statement, 'her demeanour when giving evidence in the trial was a graphic indication of the impact of [the offender's] crimes on her'. His Honour further acknowledged and vindicated the victim by saying that 'this must have been a traumatic, humiliating experience for a defenceless woman'.

Because of the absence of an impact statement, acknowledgement of victim harm in these cases cannot match what is possible in cases where an impact statement has been submitted. Nevertheless, the judges who delivered these remarks clearly made an effort to meet the victims' justice needs, by demonstrating that they understood that the victims had suffered as a consequence of the offending. In such cases, this approach should be encouraged.

In contrast, in only one case in the dataset did the judicial officer note the lack of impact statement and then fail to consider the harm that may have been caused to the victim. This occurred in *R v AGB* (Unreported, TasSC, 28 January 2015), where the judge said: 'I have no victim impact statement and therefore have no information as to what, if any impact, your behaviour has had on [the victim]'. This is inconsistent with the usual approach to the absence of a victim impact statement and is contrary to the guidance in *R v Eisenach* that, even 'without specific evidence, a sentencing court will be aware of the destructive effects of offences' ([2011] ACTCA 2: [65]). Accordingly, the judge's approach in *R v AGB* should not be followed, as it is likely to cause anti-therapeutic effects for victims and the criminal justice system more broadly.

Judicial reference to impact statements' instrumental and expressive purposes

As discussed in Chapter 3, while the relevant legislation requires a sentencing court to recognise the victim or have regard to the impact of the offence on the victim, current Australian impact statement regimes give no indication 'as to how the court will use such statements and what weight [they] will be afforded' (Booth 2015: 36). In many of the cases we examined, the harm outlined in the victim's statement was simply repeated or summarised by the judge. Some judges also mentioned that the victim's statement was 'taken into account', without specifying how they had done so (see e.g. *R v Barbat*, *R v Daglas*, and *R v Taylor* [2015] ACTSC 43). When a judge states that they have 'taken into account' an impact statement, this could demonstrate that the judge has recognised or had regard to the victim in accordance with the relevant sentencing legislation. Additionally or alternatively, it could mean that the judge relied upon the statement in determining the offender's sentence. However, these brief references do not assist with any analysis seeking to determine how the judge used the statement, and what, if any, weight was given to it.

The findings of our analysis therefore do little to alleviate the existing confusion over instrumental and expressive uses of impact statements in practice. This is not unexpected, because, as Light (2014: 473) has argued, an analysis of sentencing remarks alone cannot 'definitively determine the mechanisms' that drive judges when sentencing. We recognise that one of the limitations of this research is the fact that no judicial officers were interviewed about their choices around incorporating victim acknowledgement in their sentencing remarks. Future research would benefit greatly from judicial interviews on this subject.

Educating judges on the therapeutic outcomes of acknowledging victims at sentencing

The results of our analysis of the sentencing remarks, as well as the interviews with victims and justice professionals, have revealed that judicial acknowledgement consisting of merely one sentence is anti-therapeutic for victims. Our findings also indicate that victims respond differently and unpredictably to more detailed remarks. While some victims were very satisfied with judicial acknowledgement that implicitly met their needs for vindication, validation, and voice, other victims felt that the detailed acknowledgement in their case was either too little or too much.

These findings demonstrate the significant challenges that judicial officers encounter in crafting therapeutically effective remarks. This section recommends a number of practical strategies to help judges develop an understanding of how to effectively and therapeutically acknowledge victims when sentencing, while still balancing other requirements under Australian sentencing regimes. These recommendations are designed to achieve the therapeutic jurisprudence goal of minimising the unintended anti-therapeutic effects of impact statement processes and maximising the potential for healing for victims (Winick 2009).

Recommendation 1: the publication of a victim-focused benchbook

The Victorian Victim Support Agency (2009) recommended that judicial education courses throughout Australia should inform judicial officers of the benefits of acknowledging the harm suffered by the victim at sentencing. The findings of this chapter suggest that this recommendation does not go far enough. Instead, we suggest that judicial officers would be better assisted by the publication of a victim-focused benchbook to provide detailed information about the potential for both therapeutic and anti-therapeutic outcomes for victims, based on different levels of judicial acknowledgement.[7]

This benchbook, which should be jointly developed with justice professionals experienced in working with victims, must be designed to guide judges concisely and clearly through the 'dos and don'ts' of victim acknowledgement at sentencing. It should contain real-life examples, like those included in this chapter, to illustrate particular judicial approaches that appear to effectively and therapeutically meet victims' needs. It should also flag matters of particular sensitivity to victims, such as sharing details about their mental health, which should not be published too explicitly in sentencing remarks. The benchbook could suggest alternative ways to handle this sort of information, based on the findings of this chapter around the style of remarks identified as being most likely to have therapeutic outcomes for victims.

The benchbook should be introduced to judicial officers and justice professionals at judicial or other professional conferences across Australia and via the Australasian Institute of Judicial Administration, National Judicial College of Australia, Judicial Commission of NSW, and Judicial College of Victoria. This should be accompanied by professional development sessions, to enable judicial officers and justice professionals to share their experiences and examples of 'what works' and 'what doesn't work' from a victim-focused perspective.

Recommendation 2: the introduction of victim-focused pre-sentencing hearings

As explored throughout this chapter, victims may experience anti-therapeutic outcomes when judges' sentencing remarks are very explicit about victims' personal issues. In her interview, Andie (WAO, Vic) argued that 'boundaries' must be introduced regarding the information that judicial officers are allowed to share about victims when sentencing. Consequently, we recommend the introduction of a mechanism that will allow judges to be informed, prior to sentencing, if there is material within a victim impact statement that is particularly sensitive and should not be outlined in explicit detail in the judge's sentencing remarks. This would require the judicial officer to convene a short pre-sentence hearing with prosecution and defence counsel, where any particularly sensitive material could be identified by the prosecutor.

The proposed hearing would also benefit the defence, by allowing the judicial officer to make clear what information from the impact statement would be relied on in passing sentence. As will be discussed further in Chapter 5, this approach would allow the defence to raise any relevant issues they may have with the content of the impact statement, prior to the submission of the statement at the sentencing hearing.

Our suggestion predates (Davies 2017), but is broadly consistent with, the model proposed by the NSW Sentencing Council (2018: Recommendation 4.7), which was supported by the NSW Government (2018). Specifically, the Council recommended that the prosecution and courts adopt 'non-mandatory guidelines', which would include:

- the prosecution providing the defence with a copy of the statement at least four working days before the hearing;
- the defence advising the prosecution of the basis of any objections to the content of the statement and whether it intends to cross-examine the victim at least two working days before the hearing; and
- the court hearing any submissions as to any unresolved objections on the content of the statement.

Our recommendation also aligns with existing processes for 'ground rules' hearings, which bring the parties and judge together before a proceeding commences, to ventilate a range of issues, including settling cross-examination questions. Ground rules hearings were first piloted across a number of UK courts in 2014 (see Scottish Court Service 2015) and then rolled out across the UK (Shipman & Harper 2017). They have since been introduced in several Australian jurisdictions, albeit only in limited circumstances. For example, in the ACT, ground rules hearings may be directed for witnesses if a court is satisfied it is in the interests of justice (*Evidence (Miscellaneous Provisions) Act 1991* (ACT) s4AB(1)). In Victoria, ground rules hearings were piloted from 1 July 2018 until 30 June 2020, though the provisions for such hearings applied only to victims aged under 18 or adult victims with a cognitive impairment (*Criminal Procedure Act 2009* (Vic) s389A(3)). There are no provisions for ground rules hearings in Tasmania or South Australia, though a 'pre-trial special hearing' can be ordered in South Australia where the victim has a physical disability or cognitive impairment (see *Evidence Act 1929* (SA) s12AB(2)). We recommend that impact statement-focused 'ground rules' pre-sentencing hearings be introduced in all relevant jurisdictions. In order to ensure that the benefit to victims is maximised, such hearings should be allowed in relation to all victims who provide impact statements, not just those who are under 18 or who have a cognitive or physical impairment.

It is conceded that such an approach will not be compatible with all legislative frameworks; in some jurisdictions, it would violate a defendant's procedural rights in relation to questioning witnesses. However, it should be borne in mind that the protections that are (properly) in place during a trial are different from the sentencing stage, where there has already been a determination of guilt. Accordingly, a balance must be struck between a defendant's rights and those of his or her victim. In such circumstances, our proposal is designed to minimise trauma to victims, while still respecting defendants' legitimate rights.

Conclusion

Sentencing remarks are a communication tool that can be used by judges to acknowledge victims and, in doing so, recognise the harm caused to them by the offending. Yet actual judicial practice in relation to the use of impact statements at sentencing has rarely been empirically researched and no previous research had sought to quantify judicial acknowledgement of victims at sentencing. Consequently, this chapter sought to determine exactly how and how often judicial officers refer to and acknowledge victims and their impact statements in practice. It also sought to make recommendations to improve judicial practice in acknowledging victims, from a victim-focused perspective.

The findings from this chapter have identified that judicial acknowledgement at sentencing can meet a number of victims' justice needs, including voice, validation, and vindication. Although this cannot be achieved through a one-line reference to victims or their statements, we were unable to definitively identify an ideal approach. Some victims were satisfied with clear and specific articulation that the judge, and therefore the court, understood, acknowledged, and believed the harm caused to them. However, this approach does not guarantee victim satisfaction in all cases, as was demonstrated by the examples of Jessica and Eve.

We therefore recommended the implementation of two particular mechanisms to assist judges in understanding how best to therapeutically and effectively acknowledge victims at sentencing, namely, the publication of a victim-focused benchbook, with supplementary judicial training, and the introduction of a short, victim-focused pre-sentence hearing. These recommendations should, in conjunction with the recommendations contained in the following two chapters, assist in increasing therapeutic outcomes for victims.

Notes

1 It should be noted that we do not argue that judges should impose sentences for the purpose of facilitating therapeutic outcomes for victims. Instead, we argue that it is possible to shape the process in which the sentence is imposed to collaterally benefit victims. This requires no express statutory authority, because it is not inconsistent with and does not detract from the purposes of sentencing.

2 The judgment in each victim's case is on file with the authors. The citations for these judgements have been withheld to protect the victim's anonymity.

3 The judge spoke about August and her impact statement for one paragraph of the remarks. The authors have a copy of the remarks on file, but they are also archived on a searchable website. Accordingly, they have not been fully transcribed here, to protect August's anonymity.

4 The remarks in Rachel's case, like all Tasmanian remarks, are permanently available online. Accordingly, they have not been fully transcribed here, to protect Rachel's anonymity.

5 Some information has been removed to avoid identifying the victim.

6 The sentencing remarks in Eve's case, like all Tasmanian remarks, are permanently available online and have not been fully transcribed here, to protect Eve's anonymity.

7 We note that, since the completion of the research for this project, the Australasian Institute of Judicial Administration (2018) has released the *National Domestic and Family Violence Benchbook*. This is commendable and supplements, but does not obviate, the need for a victim-focused benchbook.

References

Balfour, G, Du Mont, J & White, D (2018). '"To This Day She Continues to Struggle with the Terror Imposed upon Her": Rape Narratives in Victim Impact Statements', *Women & Criminal Justice*, 28, 43–62.

Bluett-Boyd, N & Fileborn, B (2014). *Victim/Survivor-Focused Justice Responses and Reforms to Criminal Court Practice*, Australian Institute of Family Studies. Melbourne.

Booth, T (2005). 'Restoring Victims' Voices: Victim Impact Statements in the Sentencing Process', *Reform*, 86, 59–62.

Booth, T (2015). *Accommodating Justice: Victim Impact Statements in the Sentencing Process*, Federation Press. Sydney.

Clark, H (2010). *'What Is the Justice System Willing to Offer?' Understanding Sexual Assault Victim/Survivors' Criminal Justice Needs*, Australian Institute of Family Studies. Melbourne.

Daly, K & Bouhours, B (2008). 'Judicial Censure and Moral Communication to Youth Sex Offenders', *Justice Quarterly*, 25, 498–522.

Davies, R (2017). *Stories of Pervasive Uncertainty: A Victim-focused Analysis of Victim Impact Statements and Sentencing in Sexual Offence Cases*, Unpublished PhD Thesis, University of Tasmania. Hobart.

Erez, E (1999). 'Who's Afraid of the Big Bad Victim? Victim Impact Statements as Victim Empowerment and Enhancement of Justice', *Criminal Law Review*, 545–556.

Herman, J (2005). 'Justice from the Victim's Perspective', *Violence Against Women*, 11, 571–602.

Hill, T (2005). 'Victim Impact Statements: A Modified Perspective', *Law and Psychology Review*, 29, 211–221.

Iliadis, M (2020). *Adversarial Justice and Victims' Rights: Reconceptualising the Role of Sexual Assault Victims*, Routledge. Abingdon.

Judicial Commission of NSW (2019). *Equality Before the Law Bench Book*. Sydney.

King, M (2006). 'The Therapeutic Dimension of Judging: The Example of Sentencing', *Journal of Judicial Administration*, 16, 92–105.

King, M & Auty, K (2006). 'Therapeutic Jurisprudence: An Emerging Trend in Courts of Summary Jurisdiction', *Alternative Law Journal*, 30(2), 69–74.

Lievore, D (2005). *No Longer Silent: A Study of Women's Help-Seeking Decisions and Service Responses to Sexual Assault*, Australian Institute of Criminology. Canberra.

Light, M (2014). 'The New Face of Legal Inequality: Noncitizens and the Long-term Trends in Sentencing Disparities across US District Courts, 1992–2009', *Law and Society Review*, 48, 447–478.

Mackenzie, G (2005). *How Judges Sentence*, Federation Press. Sydney.

McGlynn, C (2011). 'Feminism, Rape and the Search for Justice', *Oxford Journal of Legal Studies*, 31, 825–842.

Miller, K-L (2013). 'Purposing and Repurposing Harms: The Victim Impact Statement and Sexual Assault', *Qualitative Health Research*, 23, 1445–1458.

NSW Government (2018). *Schedule of Government Response to Recommendations on Victims' Involvement in Sentencing*. http://www.sentencingcouncil.justice.nsw.gov.au/Documents/ Current-projects/Victims/Victims_gov.pdf.

NSW Sentencing Council (2018). *Victims' Involvement in Sentencing—Report*. Sydney.

O'Connell, M (2009). 'Victims in the Sentencing Process: South Australia's Judges and Magistrates Give Their Verdict', *International Perspectives in Victimology*, 4, 50–57.

Roach Anleu, S, Brewer, R & Mack, K (2017). 'Locating the Judge within Sentencing Research', *International Journal for Crime, Justice and Social Democracy*, 6, 46–63.

Roberts, J & Manikis, M (2011). *Victim Personal Statements: A Review of the Empirical* Research, Office of the Commissioner for Victims and Witnesses in England and Wales. London.

Schuster, M & Propen, A (2006). *WATCH Victim Impact Statement Study*, University of Minnesota. Minneapolis.

Scottish Court Service (2015). *Evidence and Procedure Review Report*. Edinburgh.

Shapland, J & Matthew Hall, M (2010). 'Victims at Court: Necessary Accessories or Principal Players at Centre Stage?', in A Bottoms & J Roberts (eds), *Hearing the Victim: Adversarial Justice, Crime Victims and the State*, Routledge. Abingdon.

Shapland, J, Willmore, J & Duff, P (1985). *Victims in the Criminal Justice System*, Gower. Aldershot.

Shipman, T & Harper, T (2017). 'Rape Victims to be Spared Court Ordeal', *The Times*, 19 March. https://www.thetimes.co.uk/edition/news/rape-victims-to-be-spared-court-ordeal-q2nd8d29t.

van de Merwe, A & Mitchell, L-M (2020). 'The Use of Impact Statements, Minimum Sentences and Victims' Privacy Interests: A Therapeutic Exploration', *De Jure Law Journal*, 53, 1–18.

Victorian Department of Justice (2014). *Victim Impact Statement Reforms in Victoria—Interim Implementation Report*. Melbourne.

Victorian Victim Support Agency (2009). *A Victim's Voice: Victim Impact Statements in Victoria*. Melbourne.

Warner, K (2000). 'Sentencing in Cases of Marital Rape: Towards Changing the Male Imagination', *Legal Studies*, 20, 592–611.

Winick, B (2009). 'Therapeutic Jurisprudence Perspectives on Dealing with Victims of Crime', *Nova Law Review*, 33, 535–543.

JESSICA

The offender was Jessica's ex-husband and they had an amicable relationship. He would visit her house from time to time, to assist with handyman tasks. In relation to the time period for which the offender was convicted, he stayed at her home for about a week to undertake these tasks. Each night, Jessica was drugged and orally raped by the offender, which Jessica filmed using a hidden camera. She filmed this, because on other occasions that he had stayed at her house, she had woken groggy and with suspicous substances on her body. She explained:

> On the first night, he saw the camera and he questioned me about it. I lied and said: 'it shouldn't be turned on, it's not set up properly, thanks for pointing it out to me'. We went outside and laid some pavers. At the end of the day, I said 'I'll make us something to eat', and I went inside and turned it on again.
>
> I couldn't check it to see what had happened until he left, but I cut out gaffer-tape and hid the lights that showed it was on. I thought he would err on the side of caution. But he fell for it and went about his routine, with no reason for me to suspect that anything had happened. He stayed each night and said he would get a bit more work done each day. At the end of the week, he wanted to go home. We went back to his place and he said: 'I could come back for one more day if you want'. I think now he had run out of whatever [drug] it was and he must have needed to go home and get some more.

When Jessica told her ex-husband that she had recorded the offending acts, he reported himself to the police. He was charged with 12 counts of rape, but ultimately pleaded guilty to 12 counts of aggravated indecent assault, which were representative of a total of 49 separate acts. She explained:

> What didn't come into it at all is that it wasn't just over those six nights. Since setting up the camera, I have now seen and realise I was obviously drugged and subjected to what is tantamount to rape … over numerous years – and all my previous doubts, confusion, and flashbacks suddenly made extreme sense.
>
> He had been doing it to me for years, yet his offending all came down to a block of six nights, but twice during sentencing remarks the magistrate referred to it as only three nights and had to be

> corrected by the prosecutor. He also referred to the then combined charge as 'indecent assault', when it was actually plea-bargained down to 12 counts of aggravated indecent assault.
>
> By their definition, it was rape, but the police said they couldn't take the chance of him getting off [on] any technicality, because on the footage, you can't actually see that 'it's in your mouth'. After sentencing, they informed me of the forensic results, that proved the white stuff, which had dribbled from my mouth and dried on my face, was in fact semen and a match to the defendant's DNA, but that police were unable to present it as evidence again, because of the break in its chain of custody.

Jessica chose to attend as much of the court proceedings as she could, as a means of keeping aware of what was happening. She said she felt like a nuisance having to regularly contact the DPP to ask what was happening:

> I chose to attend on the final four occasions because waiting a month, two months, three months between hearings, and wondering when they are going to ring me, or wondering if I am a nuisance ringing them, did lead me to feel I had become a passenger on someone else's journey.

Jessica's victim impact statement was very lengthy, which is understandable in the context of the offending. She struggled with the limitations of what could be included in the statement, given that the offender had pleaded guilty to offences significantly less serious than those with which he had originally been charged. Jessica explained her process of writing the statement:

> I began to write the victim impact statements so many times. It was doing my head in, there was so much I wanted to say. Each time I began, it included more than I was technically permitted to say. So, I wrote it all and tried to keep it in some order. My friend who came to court with me, to support me through this, is a retired schoolteacher. I emailed her my great long attempt in full and she printed it out and we met for lunch. She brought a writing pad, scissors, and a glue-stick, and literally cut and pasted from what she had printed off. I could have done it myself – but, by that stage, I was so short of time, and stressed about it; I was worried about not getting to say all the things I wanted to include, not even knowing at that stage that the magistrate would refuse to view the footage.

Some of the text included:

> No matter how tired I am, I have trouble getting to sleep and staying asleep due to an irrational fear that he might still somehow gain entry and sneak up on me. And this, despite me having rekeyed my locks. When I do sleep and waken, it is to immediate self-questioning of whether anything of which I have absolutely no memory could possibly have occurred.
>
> It is not uncommon for me to have nightmares where I am terrified, gagging, unable to breathe. My throat, my airway, is blocked and try as I might, I cannot move to break free. I am paralysed in total blackness, with intense fear. I have no vision. I cannot see. My attempts to call out for help, emit no sound. I am completely paralysed, and panic stricken. When I am finally able to produce a sound, I actually hear it. It wakens me to my reality, and I waken sobbing …
>
> Once abundant, there has been a steady decline in former friendships, including some of my most solid friendships, and a recent further breakdown of my remaining friendships which has resulted in virtual total isolation. I am no longer any fun, or good company. I have lost so many friends, my confidence and ability to trust. And now my family also avoid me like the plague. It has affected me very badly.
>
> I have lost my family as a result of either their total denial, their minimization of events, or their complete failure to recognise and accept my reactions as being normal responses to the trauma of extreme violation. I have lost my family and friends, some of whom are undoubtedly secondary victims of this trauma.

Jessica read her statement aloud:

> I wanted to do it. I know what happened. It was written by me. I want it expressed by me, the way that it should be expressed, not read out by someone else, who might be monotone. I made it dramatic, I delivered it dramatically, but honestly. It wasn't acting.
>
> … The witness assistance officer said: 'you don't get any points for reading it yourself'. I felt like maybe they wanted to keep me out of it, but I needed to make sure it was read the way it was intended to be delivered, the way it was written. I said 'it's my story, it's my life and it's how it's affected me and I would like for him to hear me read it'.

> The thought of my ex being in the dock and of me being in the courtroom for my own matter was very distressing. The witness assistance officer reiterated, 'you know, you don't have to do this yourself', but I told her that I really should do it, because it was written by me and I know what happened.

The magistrate in Jessica's case made the following reference to her in the sentencing remarks:

> I had the benefit of hearing from the victim who personally read her victim impact statement. I make it clear that I put that statement into the context of the overall circumstances of this matter, and that is a reference to the previous relationship, obviously, between the victim and the defendant, but it certainly does highlight the devastating and significant impact this offending has had upon the victim. I make it clear that the victim impact statement is but one of a number of factors I need to take into account, but it is a significant factor. It was a powerful document. That is hardly surprising – given the breach of trust and the nature of the offending in this matter.

Jessica recalled the magistrate's reference to her as being more limited: 'During his sentencing remarks, he made reference to "having heard the victim's impact statement" and said "I know how this has affected the victim"'. Despite her negative perception of how her statement was taken into account, she would recommend that others complete such statements:

> Every victim and each story is different and, if nothing else, it will help them to summarise and assess their personal losses … It's one's opportunity to put it into their own perspective, and to say 'these are the consequences I suffer as a result of what you did to me'. And then for it to ultimately become an official court document.

Chapter 5

Balancing the expressive and instrumental purposes of victim impact statements

Introduction

In 2015 and 2016, we conducted interviews with six victims of sexual offending and 15 justice professionals: 12 victim support and witness assistance officers and three prosecutors experienced in working on sexual offence cases. The interviews were designed to help us achieve a better understanding of sexual offence victims' perspectives of impact statement and sentencing processes and procedures in the four study jurisdictions.

The interviews revealed two overarching problems around impact statements and sentencing. The first is the subject of this chapter, while the second is the subject of Chapter 6. The first problem is the significant effect that pervasive uncertainty around the purpose of impact statements has on victims' and justice professionals' understanding and experiences of these statements. This lack of clarity has ramifications both for victims and the justice professionals who work with victims in preparing and submitting impact statements. Due to this lack of clarity, issues can arise at every stage of the statement process, starting with the initial information that justice professionals provide to victims about their right to submit a statement, the support and guidance provided to victims in preparing their statement, the process of submitting the statement to the court, and finally, as explored in Chapter 4, the receipt and acknowledgement of these statements by judicial officers in court.

This chapter explores the consequences of this uncertainty through a victim-focused, therapeutic jurisprudence lens. It proposes a solution to the lack of clarity and consistency by developing a modified version of Manikis' (2015) *Canadian Multi-Functional Model for Victim Impact Statements* for the Australian context. The proposed model combines instrumental and expressive approaches to impact statements; however, where these are inconsistent, it prioritises a victim focus, without subordinating due process for the offender (Wexler 2000). Our approach therefore achieves the therapeutic jurisprudence goal of minimising the unintended anti-therapeutic effects of impact statement processes, while maximising the potential for healing for the victim (Winick 2009).

The purpose of impact statements

Chapter 3 explored the inconsistent messages provided by Australian sentencing legislation as to the purpose and permissible content of impact statements. Some legislative provisions indicate that judges can use such statements instrumentally, while others imply that they are instead to be used for the expressive benefits they may provide victims. We also identified the consequential inconsistency in impact statement policies and guidelines across the research jurisdictions.

These inconsistencies were cause for lengthy discussion during interviews with both victims and justice professionals. There was no consensus from the justice professionals as to their understanding of the purpose of impact statements. Several interviewees viewed them as having at least some instrumental effect on sentencing:

> I would explain that the victim impact statement makes up a part of a plea hearing and that the judge will take it into account when forming a sentence.
>
> (Andie, WAO, Vic)

> I don't think it's true to say that [impact statements are] not supposed to have any impact on the sentence … the fact that [victims] might have nightmares, or can't sleep, or feel revolted, or it's affected their sex life, of course the judge can take that into account.
>
> (Michael, Prosecutor, Tas)

> If the offender has been found guilty, then the victim impact statement can definitely inform the judge's decision around sentencing.
>
> (Alisa, VSO, Vic)

In contrast, only one justice professional held the belief that statements do not have any instrumental purpose, with Harriet (WAO, Tas) noting: 'we are very clear to let them know that it's a therapeutic process for them as opposed to be[ing] something that is intended to affect the sentence'. Two other WAOs explained the complex discussions they have with victims when trying to clarify the purpose of these statements:

> Different stakeholders will use [the impact statement] for different purposes and that's a thing that can cause issues. It's not just about what the victims want to say. It's about what the prosecution can present. It's about what the defence won't allow. It's about what the judge can receive. I think what is very difficult for victims, is that they think it's their opportunity to speak, when in fact a whole lot of people have a lot to say about what is presented in that victim impact statement.
>
> (Samuel, SA)

> A lot of people ask me if it will make any difference to sentence and I say I don't know … I always say to people that I don't think it will necessarily result in a higher sentence and that essentially that's not the purpose of it. I always say to people it's important that [the court] hears the specific details of how it has affected you … I also say that for a lot of people I deal with it seems to have a therapeutic effect.
>
> (Robert, Tas)

These findings confirm the complicated reality of working within a system that does not prescribe how the court should use these statements (Booth 2015). Given the lack of consistency in legislative instruments, policies, and guidelines, both within and across jurisdictions, these findings are not surprising. They are, however, problematic and prevent justice professionals from providing victims with accurate information about how the court may use the information contained in impact statements.

Notably, each of the interviewed victims viewed their impact statement solely as an expressive tool:

> [I did it because] I could let the judge know [about the harm I experienced], because otherwise nobody would know. It was also a chance to have a bit of power and stand up and have my say and be listened to, which I really liked the idea of.
>
> (August, SA)

> It's one's opportunity to put it into [my] own perspective, and to say 'these are the consequences I suffer as a result of what you did to me'.
>
> (Jessica, SA)

> You never have an opportunity to say anything to [the offender or the court] … so, that was the most important part, for me.
>
> (Laura, SA)

> The victim impact statement became the avenue for me to have some sort of voice in the process.
>
> (Philippa, SA)

> It was predominantly …, because he pleaded guilty, my chance to say my piece … it served that purpose, and that's why I chose to do it.
>
> (Rachel, Tas)

> I wanted to do it … because I felt that I didn't have a voice through the process. There was nothing that I was allowed to say through free will without being cut off in the courtroom … For me, the purpose of it was that I got a voice, and I got to tell [the judge] how I was feeling, rather than just the facts of what happened that night.
>
> (Eve, Tas)

This finding is significant, because one of the early criticisms of impact statement schemes, discussed in Chapter 2, was victims' reported level of dissatisfaction with the impact statement process, once they realised that their statement had not increased or would not increase the sentence imposed on the offender. However, no victim we interviewed believed that the role of their statement was to increase the offender's sentence; accordingly, there was no lack of satisfaction reported by any victim on the basis of such misunderstanding. However, we recognise that, because the sample of victims was self-selected, the reported understanding of the purpose of their impact statement cannot be assumed to be representative of all victims' experiences.

While no victim was dissatisfied on the basis of a misunderstanding about the impact statement's purpose, the potential remains for victim disappointment arising from other unmet expectations, which may stem from confusion over the purpose of impact statements. If, like the victims we interviewed, other victims view their statements solely as an expressive tool, they may not understand that, under current sentencing regimes, statements can be used instrumentally. As explored in Chapter 5, this involves the possibility that the defence could object to all or parts of the statement, which could lead to cross-examination of the victim and/or the impact statement being edited by the court. While research suggests that this rarely happens in Australia (O'Connell 2006; 2009;

Victorian Victim Support Agency 2009), it can cause problems when it does occur. As South Australian WAO Samuel explained, 'it's very distressing … I think it's the one time that victims feel like they're getting a voice, only to have that voice taken away' (see also Booth 2015). Accordingly, it is vital that all Australian jurisdictions clarify the specific purposes for which impact statements can be used. This would enable justice professionals to provide clearer guidance to victims who prepare these statements and would prevent the potential for victim disappointment arising from unmet or incorrect expectations.

The Manikis model

Manikis has discussed the same problem of confusion over the role and purpose of impact statements in Canada, due to the inconsistency between instrumental and expressive approaches. In response, she developed a 'multi-functional model justified by a principled analysis and evidence-based findings' (2015: 109). According to Manikis, this model, which is outlined in Table 5.1, embraces both the instrumental and expressive purposes of impact statements. The instrumental function is valued because it enables judges to 'facilitate a more accurate and informed assessment of harm' (2015: 110). Bearing in mind that judges believe that the content of an impact statement may help them to impose 'a more commensurate sentence' (O'Connell 2006: 6; see also Erez 1999), Manikis' model recognises that an instrumental approach 'can serve retributive purposes, including denunciation, while also according with the fundamental principle of proportionality' (2015: 110). However, the model also embraces the expressive role of impact statements, recognising that statements can offer a therapeutic experience for victims, and can assist the court to appropriately acknowledge the harm caused by the offending. Furthermore, the model recognises that, when used expressively, information about the harm experienced by the victim may educate and assist offenders in their rehabilitation. Table 5.1 schematises the model, by framing it in Manikis' (2015: 92–115) understanding of the rules required by instrumental and expressive impact statement regimes.

Because it was created to address problems similar to those that arise in Australia, the Canadian model developed by Manikis is also relevant to the Australian context. This chapter undertakes a critical evaluation of the model and explores its applicability and transferability to the Australian jurisdictions covered by our research. In contrast to the Manikis model, which is largely guided by findings from Canadian case law and previous impact statement research, this chapter is guided by a combination of

Table 5.1 Manikis' model for impact statements

Issue	*Instrumental approach*	*Expressive approach*	*Manikis' model*
1. Purpose Lack of clarity around the function and purpose of impact statements	Impact statements are used by the judge to assess harm to the victim and therefore determine a proportionate sentence.	Impact statements are a cathartic tool for the victim, who is allowed to express the harm caused to them by whichever means they choose. It has no bearing on the offender's sentence.	Both the instrumental and expressive functions of impact statements are valued.
2. Content The permissible content of impact statements	Impact statements should only contain information about the actual harm caused to the victim by the offending for which offenders are convicted. This is the only information considered relevant to the determination of sentence.	Impact statements can contain any information the victim wishes to include, because the impact statement is not relied upon by the judge in sentencing.	Impact statements can contain any information the victim wishes to include, but only the actual harm caused to the victim will be considered relevant to the determination of sentence. It is the responsibility of the judicial officer to discard irrelevant information when sentencing the offender.

3. Form The permissible form of the impact statement	Victims can present their statements only in writing.	Victims can present their statements in a variety of forms, including prose, poems, drawings, and songs.	Victims can present their statements only in writing.
4. Cross-examination The permissibility of cross-examining victims on their impact statement	Victims can be cross-examined on the content of their impact statement.	Victims cannot be cross-examined on the content of their impact statement.	Victims can be cross-examined on the content of their impact statement, but victims with specific needs can only be cross-examined under vulnerable witness provisions.
5. Time frames The time frames for preparation and disclosure of the impact statement	'Adequate' disclosure of the statement to the defence is required.	N/A – Manikis did not identify parameters for disclosure under an expressive approach.	Early disclosure of the impact statement to the defence is required.
6. Presentation The permissible methods for impact statement presentation	Victims may not personally read their statement to the court. It can be presented in writing or read aloud by the prosecutor.	Victims or another person of their choosing may present their statements verbally to the court.	Victims may present their statements verbally to the court.

Manikis' model, Australian law and policy, the implications of fundamental criminal justice principles discussed in Chapter 2, and the insights gained from the empirical research conducted for this project. Manikis' model focuses primarily on the content, reliability, and presentation of impact statements. These themes guide much of the remaining discussion in this chapter.

The content and reliability of impact statements

Content

A lack of certainty about the purpose of impact statements has significant ramifications for their permissible content. When viewed expressively, impact statements have no effect on the sentence imposed and are instead seen as a therapeutic tool for victims. Accordingly, an expressive impact statement regime allows victims to write or say whatever they want in their statement and present their statement in a variety of forms, without being constrained by rules of evidence or fear of the content being verified via cross-examination or removed in court. Some authors believe that impact statements were always intended to be solely expressive. Erez (2004) has argued that emphasising impact statements' instrumental function to inform judicial sentencing has derailed their original purpose, namely, as a vehicle for victim voice. She also suggested that impact statements were never intended to 'restructure sentencing priorities' (1999: 555). On the other hand, it has been suggested that, if impact statements do not influence the offender's sentence, then they fail to give real effect to the victim's voice, and can only be viewed as 'symbolic rather than meaningful' (Booth 2005: 61; see also Englebrecht 2011).

In contrast, an instrumental approach views an impact statement as a tool for the judicial officer to assess the actual harm caused by the offending. This information could enhance the retributive aims of sentencing and assist the judicial officer to address relevant aggravating factors when sentencing. Under an instrumental approach, the content of an impact statement is treated as evidence and so must be limited to that which is both relevant and meets the standard of proof in the event of a challenge from the defence. McGovern (2013) has noted that being required to exclude certain content, in line with the requirements of New Zealand case law, could limit the therapeutic benefits of making a statement, by preventing full acknowledgement of the harm experienced by the victim and hindering victims' ability to develop insight into the effects of the offending. According to Manikis, this approach may also limit the form in which the statement is presented; she has argued that, to prevent the 'injection' of emotion into the sentencing process, an instrumental approach may require victims to present their statement only in text or spoken word, rather than through alternative creative options (2015: 105).

While still offering victims the opportunity to share the harm caused to them, instrumental rules that restrict the type of information that can be included in a statement and allow for cross-examination of the victim at sentencing can be seen as anti-therapeutic from the victim's perspective. Several justice professionals interviewed for this study also identified an additional anti-therapeutic problem that can arise when impact statements are approached instrumentally. This occurs when victims are asked to separate the harm caused by the acts for which the offender was convicted from the harm caused by uncharged or unproven acts. Prosecutor Michael from Tasmania explained that this problem often occurs where, 'for example, there might be an acquittal for rape, but a conviction for indecent assault'. Under an instrumental approach, the information in an impact statement should address only those matters the judge is able to take into account in sentencing. Accordingly, information about uncharged or unproven acts should not be included. However, many of the justice professionals interviewed shared stories of the problems that can be caused by this issue:

> For example, someone is charged with a number of counts of sexual intercourse against a child across the course of a number of year, and then they offer to plead guilty and we might take out some of the counts and have representative counts, [but] then there may have to be some limitation in what the victim can and can't refer to in terms of the criminal acts.
>
> (Jacqui, Prosecutor, ACT)

> Often an offence occurs within the context of uncharged acts. So, it can be a really awkward conversation to have with someone, because you want them to be able to express what they need to say, but there are really tight guidelines.
>
> (Suzanna, VSO, ACT)

> The worst example I had was that we dealt with a situation where we did a rape trial with a young complainant and she had prepared her own victim impact statement … It was quite traumatic. In the end, it was a not guilty verdict [for rape], but because of her age, it was a

> guilty verdict for unlawful sexual intercourse. She said, 'I don't want to submit [the impact statement regarding unlawful sexual intercourse] because in doing that, it's assuming that I consented, which I didn't do'. We had to say to the court that we had a victim impact statement, but that we weren't going to present it because of the nature of the charges changing … So, she never really got to say how that affected her.
>
> (Robert, WAO, Tas)

These quotes illustrate the significant difficulties victims may experience when asked to distinguish between the harm caused by uncharged or unproven acts and the harm caused by acts for which the offender has been convicted. The Royal Commission into Institutional Responses to Child Sexual Abuse (2017) also identified this issue as problematic (see also NSW Sentencing Council 2018).

One of the victims we interviewed shared the frustration she felt because of her inability to convey the whole circumstances of the offending. In Jessica's case, the offender pleaded guilty to lesser offences than those with which he was originally charged. As Jessica explained: 'You're not allowed to mention the crime and you can't mention the judicial system. The plea-bargained charges … do not portray the crime as it should be … [but] of course, they don't want to hear that' (for discussion of the issues that can arise in the context of plea-bargaining, see e.g. Flynn 2012; Iliadis 2020).

As a solution to this problem, two justice professionals described their preference for a largely expressive approach to the content of impact statements:

> I personally think that they should be able to say what they want … I think it's one part of the process where victims should get to have a say in the words and the way that they want to. And judges, surely, are smart enough to use their discretion to determine what is appropriate [in relation] to sentence, and what you can just take as comment.
>
> (Samuel, WAO, SA)

> I wish they were allowed to say whatever they wanted. I wish they could just vent. Because the … judge [has] the discretion to ignore certain things anyway, so I don't quite see why we need to be so strict with rules of evidence when it comes to them.
>
> (Harriet, WAO, Tas)

Viewing statements only as expressive, and removing rules governing their content, may at first glance appear to maximise their therapeutic benefit for the victim. However, as discussed in Chapter 2, a solely expressive approach is disadvantageous to both the victim and the justice system more generally, because it means the sentencing judge has no power to use the statement when sentencing the offender, even if it brings relevant aggravating factors to light. It might also prevent fulfilment of the goal of 'just' or 'adequate' punishment, which is legislated for under all Australian sentencing regimes. Accordingly, under a solely expressive approach, the victim's potential for therapeutic outcomes may be limited by the fact that the judge cannot take the impact statement into account when sentencing.

Manikis' model goes some way to resolving this conflict. It promotes the therapeutic benefits of impact statements, by advocating for a largely expressive approach to their content, while still providing certain restrictions to ensure that statements can also be used instrumentally without disadvantaging the offender. Under this model's content rules, victims are offered significant flexibility in their expression and can include any information about the harm they have experienced, without being limited to the harm caused by offences for which the offenders were convicted. However,

> only the actual harm suffered by the victim [in respect of the offences for which the offender is convicted] will be considered relevant to the determination of the sentence or be taken into account by the judge in crafting the sentence
>
> (Manikis 2015: 112)

Because of this flexibility of expression, prosecutors and victim support and witness assistance officers are not responsible for editing impact statements to remove information 'considered irrelevant to the determination of harm or the determination of the sentence' (2015: 112), as is common practice in the ACT. Instead, the judge is responsible for determining which, if any, part is relevant to the offender's sentence. This aligns with the Victorian Law Reform Commission's suggestion that:

> strict rules about the contents of victim impact statements limit victims' autonomy and voice. Allowing victims more freedom in what they can include in victim impact statements, and then relying on judges to take only admissible content into account, may allow victims to convey the impact of the offending more authentically.
>
> (2016: 154)

Under Manikis' model, 'the judge's role [is] paramount and judges … need to be very careful to discard the parts unrelated to [relevant] harm when crafting and deciding the severity of a sentence' (2015: 113). This approach is very similar to the Victorian OPP Prosecution Guidelines in place at the time of our research, which stated that 'it is a matter for the sentencing judge to determine the admissibility of the material in a victim impact statement' (2015: Rule 44). As noted above, presumably as a result of recent legislative reforms, this aspect has regrettably been removed from the current Victorian guidelines (Victorian OPP 2019).

This approach accords with the recommendations of a recent article in the journal for ACT legal practitioners, which set out the following 'takeaway messages' in relation to impact statements:

> - It is open to the court to approach the admission of the contents of a VIS with a degree of flexibility.
> - Defence practitioners and prosecutors are encouraged to engage in discussions about potentially inadmissible portions of a VIS ahead of the sentencing proceedings.
> - Defence practitioners should start by identifying and, where appropriate, objecting to inadmissible material in a VIS by reference to the constraints of sections 48, 49 and 51(7) [of the *Crimes (Sentencing) Act 2005* (ACT)].
> - While counsel can expect courts to approach VISs with a degree of flexibility, it is important for counsel to identify explicitly what material is objected to and the grounds for the objection.
> - Similarly, where part of a statement is challenged, it is counsel's responsibility to identify the use to which the remaining parts of the statement should be put, and the weight that can be given by the court to the material.
>
> (Skvortsova & Khazma 2017: 31)

As discussed in Chapter 3, this approach is also reflected in judicial practice in Victoria, as outlined in the case of *R v Swift* ([2007] VSCA 52: [7]). Two examples of the way that Victorian judges have applied this approach in practice are the cases of *R v Mulhall* and *R v Panckow*. In *R v Mulhall*, King J acknowledged that there was extraneous information contained in the submitted victim impact statements, but still allowed the victims to read them in their entirety:

> Despite the inadmissible material, four of the statements were read in their entirety and all of the documents were in fact tendered and

> I have read them. I have taken into account the relevant and admissible material contained therein. I have put to one side the material that is not admissible and not of any assistance for the process of assisting me in determining the appropriate sentence.
>
> ([2012] VSC 471: [8])

Similarly, in *R v Panckow*, Judge Cannon explained:

> In taking into account the relevant parts of the Victim Impact Statement I have also had to temper the degree of impact described, because more serious allegations are made in the course of [the impact statement] which are not the subject of any charge.
>
> ([2014] VCC 163: [17])

Of these two examples, Judge Cannon's is perhaps more consistent with the principles of procedural fairness (Tyler 2007). While both judges explained that they had taken into account only the relevant and admissible materials, only Judge Cannon was explicit about the type of information she was not able to take into account. In contrast, Justice King was less specific, and therefore less transparent, in this regard. Accordingly, Judge Cannon's approach should be preferred.

Jane (VSO, Vic) particularly noted the positive outcome of the flexible Victorian approach in place at the time that we interviewed her, especially when compared with the more restrictive approach of the past:

> In the last couple of years, there has been a change with victim impact statements. They have become less rigid. There used to be a lot of clients who had been distraught because they had written their statements but had to change them because the rules said that they didn't look right. But in the last two or three years, I haven't had anyone come back and say that they had to change what they wrote.

Based on the clear benefit to victims arising from this practice, we recommend that all jurisdictions adopt this approach. We recognise that there is a risk that a victim may not feel supported and may in fact be retraumatised where a judge highlights that sections of their impact statement were not relevant and were therefore not considered in the sentencing process. However, our proposal is designed to minimise this risk, by providing guidance for a judge to explain why they cannot consider it.

This approach will require reform of the relevant court rules in each jurisdiction. As discussed in Chapter 3, judges in the ACT have sought to rely upon prosecutors to remove extraneous information from impact statements prior to their submission (see *R v MT* [2014] ACTSC 162). In contrast, but to similar effect, South Australia and Tasmania stipulate that a judicial officer may direct that irrelevant material in an impact statement not be read out to the court (see Rule 90 of the Supreme Court Rules and District Court Rules and Rule 41.06 of the Magistrates Court Rules). Similarly, under Rule 10 of the *Criminal Rules 2006* (Tas), judges may direct the victim not to read any part of the impact statement that the court considers irrelevant to the proceedings.

Accordingly, to apply Manikis' model and the previous Victorian approach to these jurisdictions, changes are required in all jurisdictions. For example, Rule 90(7) of the *Supreme Court Criminal Rules 2014* (SA) states that 'the Court may direct that irrelevant material in the statement not be read or played to or taken into account'. To ensure consistency with the Manikis model, this rule, and the equivalent rules in the other South Australian courts, should be amended to reflect the previous Victorian OPP Prosecution Guidelines. The Tasmanian rules should also be amended to reflect the same principles. The ACT *Court Procedures Rules 2006*, which are otherwise silent on this issue, should be amended to insert an equivalent rule.

As discussed above, the Victorian sentencing legislation was amended in 2018 and now provides that 'the court need not specify the impact statement material that is not being relied on in sentencing' (s8L(6)). When this provision was introduced, the then Attorney-General noted that

> this would minimise the distress experienced by victims when a sentencing judge edits their statement in open court. This reflects a common practice often adopted by the courts which parties are generally prepared to accept
>
> (Pakula 2018: 2325)

We recognise that the 2018 reforms were informed by the recommendations of the Victorian Law Reform Commission's (2016) inquiry on victims. However, we suggest that the previous Victorian approach should be reinstated. Coupled with the proposed pre-sentence hearing, this would minimise distress to victims, as well as providing clarity about what aspects of the impact statement are not being relied on in sentencing, thereby providing greater clarity to the sentencing process.

Judicial training may also be required to ensure that judicial officers are aware of the new rules, so they apply them correctly in practice. The impact statement guidelines in all jurisdictions will also need to be updated accordingly.

Reliability

Applying Manikis' model to the Australian context requires consideration of how an expressive approach can be reconciled with the instrumental use of statements when issues of statement reliability and fairness to the offender arise. If the judge is able to draw adverse inferences against the offender because of the content of a statement, particularly if those adverse inferences lead to an increased sentence, it is vital that the statement be verifiable by the defence. Yet Hannah (WAO, Vic) described cross-examination of the victim at the sentencing stage as 'traumatic', while South Australian WAO Samuel said it was 'distressing' and 'difficult'. Under a therapeutic jurisprudence approach, it is crucial that steps be taken to limit the possibility that victims become re-traumatised by the justice process, including through cross-examination on the content of their impact statement.

Manikis described the balance between expressive and instrumental approaches to statement reliability as an equilibrium. Her model allows for cross-examination of victims on their statements, but introduces certain rules to reduce the likelihood of victims being re-traumatised, because 'an offender's "right" to cross-examination should not justify using methods and techniques known to confuse or mislead' victims (Bowden, Henning, & Plater 2014). These rules stipulate that 'if cross-examination takes place, victims would need to be treated with courtesy and respect', while victims 'with specific needs should also benefit' from vulnerable witness provisions (Manikis 2015: 115).

Once again, Victorian practice is largely consistent with Manikis' model. Under s8S of the *Sentencing Act 1991* (Vic), if the victim is to be cross-examined on their statement, arrangements can be made for this to occur under vulnerable witness provisions. In addition, s8R provides that victims may use vulnerable witness provisions when presenting their statements. Victorian legislation therefore leaves no doubt as to the victim's right to be protected via vulnerable witness provisions at all points during the impact statement process. However, unlike Manikis' model, the Victorian rules adhere more closely to a therapeutic jurisprudence approach, because they apply to all victims who present statements, not just those with 'specific needs'. In contrast, the sentencing legislation in the other jurisdictions does not make clear that vulnerable witness provisions apply in this situation. This is not to say that vulnerable witness provisions cannot be invoked during cross-examination of victims about their impact statements in the ACT, South Australia, and Tasmania, but rather that their legislation is not as clear in specifying the existence of this right. In order to achieve consistency with the more therapeutic Victorian approach, these jurisdictions should introduce similar legislative provisions. Further, all jurisdictions should amend their legislation or policies to ensure that victims are only ever cross-examined on their impact statement under vulnerable witness provisions, rather than this being merely an option that can be applied for, as is the case in Victoria.

All four research jurisdictions go beyond the Manikis model in relation to aspects of cross-examining victims on their impact statement. First, all jurisdictions prevent unrepresented offenders from cross-examining victims (see *Crimes (Sentencing) Act 2005* (ACT) s53(4); *Evidence Act 1929* (SA) s13B; *Evidence (Children and Special Witnesses) Act 2001* (Tas) s8A and *Criminal Procedure Act 2009* (Vic) s356). This should ensure that, when cross-examination does occur, it is undertaken only by legal practitioners, whose duty to the court prohibits the use of aggressive tactics (Ipp 1998). Second, in order to further minimise the possibility of aggressive or upsetting cross-examination, all four jurisdictions require the court to disallow 'improper' or 'inappropriate' questions, including questions that are confusing, offensive, intimidating, humiliating, insulting, or repetitive, under the 'section 41 rules' (see s25 of the *Evidence Act 1929* (SA) and s41 of the *Evidence Act 2001* (Tas), *Evidence Act 2008* (Vic) and *Evidence Act 2011* (ACT); for discussion, see Kennedy, Easteal, & Bartels 2012).

However, it appears that the existing protective provisions and measures may not go far enough. Several researchers have identified that the section 41 rules are difficult to apply in practice, and consequently provide only weak protection from inappropriate cross-examination (see e.g. Wood 2004; Cashmore & Trimboli 2005; Boyd & Hopkins 2010; Henning 2013). Accordingly, we contend that further protections are required and that these should be incorporated into the victim-focused pre-sentence 'ground rules' type of hearing proposed in Chapter 4. As we argued there, this type of hearing would allow judicial officers to clarify what information from the impact statement would be relied on in passing sentence and enable the prosecution to make submissions about any matters in the statement that the victim would prefer not to be expressly mentioned in the sentencing remarks. Such a hearing would also, in accordance with the findings of this chapter, enable the defence to raise relevant issues with the content of the impact statement and consequently identify any intention to cross-examine the victim on their statement. If such an intention were expressed, the proposed hearing would help to settle the questions to be asked in cross-examination and act as an additional safeguard to ensure that the section 41 rules are not breached. This proposal is not without precedent: pilot testing of 'ground rules' hearings commenced across a number of UK courts in 2014 (see Scottish Court Service 2015) and it was subsequently announced that these arrangements would be rolled out nationwide (Shipman & Harper 2017). It is also consistent with the recommendations by the NSW Sentencing Council (2018) and supported by the NSW Government (2018). Specifically, the Council recommended that there be limits on when the defence can cross-examine a victim on the content of their statement (2018: Recommendation 4.8) and the court, in allowing cross-examination, 'should make such orders … as are considered necessary in the interests of the victim' (2018: Recommendation 4.9).

Timeframes for preparing impact statements

The legislation and policy requirements in relation to the time frame for preparing statements were discussed in Chapter 3. Problems around these time frames were raised by a number of justice professionals interviewed in South Australia and Tasmania. Prosecutor Michael and WAO Robert explained that, in Tasmania, sentencing of the offender usually occurs very quickly after conviction, 'sometimes on the same day'. Further, in South Australia, the recently superseded ODPP Prosecution Policy indicated that impact statements should be prepared before arraignment.[1] Accordingly, South Australian victims were previously required to prepare their statements very early in the justice process, while Tasmanian victims are currently required to prepare them prior to the offender's conviction.

This approach is actually consistent with Manikis' (2015) model, which promotes early disclosure of the impact statement to allow offenders time to assess the statement's reliability. However, the justice professionals we interviewed revealed that this practice can cause problems. First, it can be problematic if a statement of harm is requested before the victim has had the chance to reflect on the harm caused. As WAO Samuel explained in relation to the earlier South Australian policy, 'I don't think people know what the impact is straight after an offence. I think [impact statements] are requested too early in the process'. Second, if an early statement is requested prior to conviction, it is possible that the statement may be redundant in the event of a complete acquittal. Samuel found this idea particularly worrying, arguing that 'it's disrespectful to ask for victim impact statements from people if [they] may not be used'. Hannah (WAO, Vic) likewise stated: 'if there is a not guilty verdict, it would be pretty horrible to have poured out your heart into a victim impact statement, but not be able to submit it'.

Accordingly, we do not recommend that this aspect of Manikis' model be adopted in the Australian context. Instead, we suggest that it is appropriate that victims submit their statement only once they have had time to process the harms caused by the offending and have been made aware that the offender has actually been convicted. This requires a change to current Tasmanian court practice. To allow victims time to complete their statement and then disclose the statement to defence prior to the sentencing hearing, it is recommended that sentencing hearings in Tasmania be scheduled within a few days, rather than a few hours, of the offender being found guilty. This is consistent with sentencing practices in other jurisdictions, and should not cause a protracted period of delay that could interfere with the rights of any offender who may be in custody.

The presentation of victim impact statements

Impact statement form

The Manikis model emphasises the expressive purpose of impact statements, but does not extend this beyond the content of these statements. It rejects the current approach to impact statement submission in the ACT and Victoria, where victims are allowed to present their statement in a number of ways, including through poems, drawings, and/or songs (see Chapter 3). As mentioned previously, Manikis has argued that restrictions in form may be required to prevent the 'injection' of emotion into the sentencing process (2015: 94; 105). However, this restriction is not actually required by the fundamental principles of criminal justice explored in Chapter 2. Furthermore, Victorian VSO Jane has explained the therapeutic benefits of offering presentation flexibility to victims: 'we know that people don't always express verbally. They could express through a piece of artwork. I know for a lot of people, that is how they communicate, and that's really powerful'. The accessibility of victim impact statements for victims with low literacy levels was also identified as an issue by Meredith and Paquette (2001). Accordingly, this is another aspect of Manikis' model that should not be adopted by any Australian jurisdiction. It is instead recommended that the South Australian and Tasmanian sentencing legislation, which allow only for written statements, be amended to conform with the current approach in the ACT and Victoria.

Verbal submission of statements

Under the Manikis model, victims are allowed to read their written statement aloud if they wish. Previous research has found that this provides some victims with a sense of power or strength (Victorian Victim Support Agency 2009), which demonstrates the benefits of this approach from a therapeutic jurisprudence perspective. Several of the justice professionals interviewed agreed, arguing that statements are most powerful when read by victims personally. This notion of power can be understood within the context of victims' identified justice needs. Three justice professionals particularly identified that the needs for participation and voice, including the need to share their experience in a public setting, can be met by verbal presentation of their statement:

> [Victims] have all reported that they have found that a therapeutically useful thing … to tell their truth publicly about something they have had to be silent about for many years of their life.
>
> (Alisa, VSO, Vic)

> [Reading their statement out loud is] validating for the victim. No matter what the outcome, they have had their opportunity to tell people [about the harm caused by the offending] … So, I think it is more powerful in that way for clients.
>
> (Jane, VSO, Vic)

> It's a very therapeutic thing to do … Up until that point, the whole court is focused on finding someone accountable for breaking the law … whether it be driving down the street too fast, or whether it be the rape of a child, the matter is focused on holding an offender accountable. It's not until that point that the whole court and the whole system becomes focused on 'who is this person?'
>
> (Clare, VSO, Tas)

Some justice professionals also identified that, in addition to meeting victims' needs for participation and voice, victims' need for control over their experience of the justice process can be met through verbal presentation:

> There's always something very powerful and cathartic to see people go into court, stare at the accused and say in their own authentic words what the impact is.
>
> (Samuel, WAO, SA)

> Some people feel really empowered reading out their victim impact statement ... some people feel like they are regaining control in facing their offender, that the power is reversed. They are telling the accused how it has affected their life, and it can be really powerful for them in their healing and recovery.
>
> (Hannah, WAO, Vic)

Several of the victims interviewed gained benefits from reading their statement aloud. Eve's and Philippa's experiences are presented elsewhere in this book. In addition, August stated:

> I was so, so nervous. I got up there and I was confident in my brain but my body was just freaking out. I did get my wits about me as I got to the second paragraph. And did it exactly how I wanted to. And because I was able to do it how I wanted to, I felt so good after. I think I felt better after reading that out than when being at sentencing and getting the end result. It was so empowering.
>
> (August Victim, SA)

August described the power she felt as a result of reading the statement aloud, which clearly met her needs for participation, voice, and control. These needs were achieved because she was allowed to present her statement 'how [she] wanted to'.

Jessica had a similar experience. In addition to fulfilling her needs for participation and voice, she explained the sense of control she gained by presenting her own statement to the court:

> I wanted to do it. I know what happened. It was written by me. I wanted it to be expressed by me, the way that it should be expressed, not read out by someone else ... I am [glad I read it out loud] ... I paced myself as I read it aloud, and I got through it without a hitch, although I did begin to cry at one point and stopped momentarily to blow my nose and compose myself before continuing. Other than my voice, you could have heard a pin drop in that room. I felt in total control and was told later by my team that the delivery of my victim impact statement was extremely powerful.
>
> (Jessica, Victim, SA)

These findings confirm the therapeutic benefits of offering victims the choice to present their statements verbally (see also ACT Government 2009). Significantly, no legislative amendments are required in most of the research jurisdictions, as the choice to do this is already allowed under their regimes. However, one change is required in Victoria, where only the admissible parts of a victim impact statement may now be read aloud in open court (*Sentencing Act 1991* (Vic) s8Q). This should be amended to allow victims to read the totality of their impact statements aloud.

Written submission of statements

Not all victims choose to present their statement verbally. Samuel (WAO, SA) explained that 'some people just want the impact known, but they don't want to go to court for the submissions on sentence'. Andie (VSO, Vic) similarly noted that, 'for some victims … there is no physical way they could read a single word out, but they do want their feelings heard. So, it's empowering for them [to submit it in writing]'. Accordingly, as Andie explained, it is possible for victims' needs for participation, voice, and control to be met by written submission of their statement, as well as by verbal presentation.

However, the two victims we interviewed who chose not to read their statements aloud did not categorise this choice as empowering. Laura, from South Australia, and Rachel, from Tasmania, made this choice because the idea of reading their statement in front of the offender was too overwhelming. Laura explained that 'I didn't really want to read it out in court; I didn't want him to look at me. So, I asked for it to be read out for me'. Laura's experience demonstrates the benefits of arrangements allowing the statement to be read aloud by a person other than the victim, as is current practice in all of the research jurisdictions (see *Crimes (Sentencing) Act 2005* (ACT) s51(3); *Criminal Law (Sentencing) Act 1988* (SA) s7A; *Sentencing Act 1991* (Vic) s8Q; *Criminal Rules 2006* (Tas) r 6; *Sentencing Act 2017* (SA) s14(2)). In contrast, Rachel chose to submit her statement in writing, after finding that: 'I tried one night to read it out loud, and I think I got half way through the first paragraph and it was just tears. I couldn't speak at all'.

Presentation using vulnerable witness provisions

Manikis' model does not address the problem of victim concern about presenting their statement in the presence of the offender. A solution is to ensure that all victims are given the option to present their statement, using the entire range of vulnerable witness provisions. As discussed in Chapter 3, these provisions are already available to some extent in each of the research jurisdictions.

ACT prosecutor Jacqui particularly emphasised that remote facility CCTV arrangements 'work well'. WAO Hannah from Victoria explained their usefulness in sexual offence cases specifically:

> [Remote facilities] are great because … most accused for sexual offences are on bail. So, on breaks, or walking through the front door of the court, there is the risk of bumping into them, which defeats the purpose. So, having the offsite ones is great. Just for [the victim] not to have to see the accused, and just see the judge and the barristers. Most victims choose that option.

The Victorian legislation provides the most extensive range of options for vulnerable witnesses. In accordance with a therapeutic jurisprudence approach, the full range of vulnerable witness arrangements should also be provided to victims in the other jurisdictions. These should be offered to all victims who wish to present their impact statements verbally, not only where the court determines that there is 'good reason to do so' or the victim might suffer severe emotional trauma by reading the statement aloud.

The need to amend these arrangements can be demonstrated by the case of Tasmanian victim Eve. She was the only victim interviewed for this research who had a negative experience of presenting her impact statement verbally and it is clear that this experience occurred because vulnerable witness provisions were not invoked for the presentation of her statement. While Eve 'liked doing [her statement] to [the offender's] face', she was perturbed by the presence of the media in the courtroom, stating: 'I didn't want the media and other unnecessary people. There was just no benefit to the community [for the media to be present]'. Robert (WAO, Tas) agreed that 'some people like [to have their statement handed up to the judge and not read out], because they don't want everyone to hear it, particularly the media'.

In these circumstances, the victims' concerns could have been easily resolved if the courtroom had been closed while the impact statements were read, but this would have only been available if it was considered likely that the victim may experience 'emotional trauma' because of the subject matter of the evidence given or be 'so distressed as to be unable to give evidence satisfactorily'. It may well be that the prosecutor responsible for Eve's case did not believe she met the threshold to access the vulnerable witness provisions under s8 of the *Special Witnesses Act 2001* (Tas). Under our proposed model, vulnerable witness provisions should always be offered to victims who wish to read their statement aloud, so victims such as Eve are not affected by the unwanted presence of the media or others in the courtroom while presenting their statements. This may not be required for all victims, but we suggest a model which supports individual victims' agency and choice. We note that our recommendations align with the recent recommendation of the NSW Sentencing Council that '[a]ll special arrangements that are available for victims of prescribed sexual assault offences in a court should be made available, upon request and with the leave of the court, to victims reading a VIS' (2018: Recommendation 3.7(1)). The NSW Government (2018) supported this recommendation and acknowledged 'the stressful and difficult experience delivering a VIS can be for victims and their family members' (2018: 7).

Summary of the proposed Australian model

This chapter has proposed a number of solutions to resolve the pervasive uncertainty in Australia around the purpose and function of victim impact statements. These solutions modify and expand on the Canadian model developed by Manikis. Table 5.2 compares and contrasts the Manikis model with the model proposed in this chapter and clarifies the required changes to policy and legislation across the research jurisdictions as a consequence of our findings.

Choosing not to submit an impact statement

As discussed in Chapters 2 and 4, the absence of a victim impact statement does not prevent a judicial officer from taking into account the effects of the crime on the victim. Furthermore, there are various reasons why victims do or do not choose to submit a statement (see e.g. Lens, Pemberton, & Bogaerts 2013; Mastrocinque 2014). Some of the reasons victims may be reluctant to make an impact statement include a fear that this would provoke retaliation, make the victim vulnerable to pressure to revise the content of their statement, or provide the offender or others with information to use against the victim in the future (see De Mesmaecker 2012).

Even without a statement, a judicial officer will usually be aware of the possible effects of the offending upon the victim. Because only victims who had completed statements were interviewed for this research, we did not obtain empirical data from victims on the possible reasons why they chose not to engage in this process. However, previous research suggests that impact statements are generally submitted only in a minority

Table 5.2 The Manikis and proposed Australian models and reforms required to achieve this

Issue	*Manikis' Canadian model*	*The proposed Australian model*	*Required reforms*
1. Purpose Lack of clarity around the function and purpose of impact statements	Both the instrumental and expressive functions of impact statements are valued.	Both the instrumental and expressive functions of impact statements are valued.	N/A
2. Content The permissible content of impact statements	Impact statements can contain any information the victim wishes to include, but only the actual harm caused to the victim will be considered relevant to the determination of sentence. It is the responsibility of the judicial officer to discard irrelevant information when sentencing the offender.	Impact statements can contain any information the victim wishes to include, but only the actual harm caused to the victim **as a consequence of the offending** will be considered relevant to the determination of sentence. It is the responsibility of the judicial officer to discard irrelevant information when sentencing the offender **and make it clear in the sentencing remarks that this has been done**.	The South Australian, Tasmanian, and ACT rules require amendments to introduce this rule. Some changes are also required in Victoria, as the proposal is not entirely consistent with the current approach there (see eg s8L(6), discussed above). All four jurisdictions' impact statement guidelines need to be updated.

3. Form The permissible form of the impact statement	Victims can present their statements only in writing.	**Victims can present their statement in a variety of forms, including in writing, verbally, in poems, drawings, and/or songs.**	No changes are required in Victoria, as the proposal is consistent with their current approach. A minor change is required in the ACT, to allow victims to present their statements via poetry. The South Australian and Tasmanian sentencing legislation only allows victims to present statements in prose. Amendments are therefore required to reflect the more expansive ACT and Victorian approach.
4. Cross-examination The permissibility of cross-examining victims on their impact statement	Victims can be cross-examined on the content of their impact statement. However, those with specific needs can only be cross-examined under vulnerable witness provisions.	**Victims can be cross-examined only under vulnerable witness provisions. In any case where the victim is to be cross-examined on their impact statement, a pre-sentence hearing should settle the questions that will be permitted. An unrepresented offender must never be allowed to conduct this cross-examination, and the judge must disallow any and all improper questions.**	Changes to the legislation in all four jurisdictions is required, to clarify that victims can be cross-examined on the content of their impact statement only under vulnerable witness provisions. In all four jurisdictions, the legislation already prevents an unrepresented offender from cross-examining the victim and requires the judge to disallow any and all improper questions. However, new court rules are required in all jurisdictions except for the ACT to implement the proposed victim-focused pre-sentence hearing, which will facilitate the settlement of cross-examination questions. This will require the introduction of the concept of ground rules hearings in Tasmania and changes to the ground rules schemes in Victoria and South Australia, which currently only allow such hearings for child victims or adults with a disability (South Australia) or cognitive impairment (South Australia and Victoria).

(Continued)

Table 5.2 (Continued)

Issue	*Manikis' Canadian model*	*The proposed Australian model*	*Required reforms*
5. Time frames The time frames for preparation of the impact statement	Early disclosure of the impact statement to the defence is required.	**The impact statement should be submitted only if/when the offender has been found guilty.**	No change is required in South Australia, Victoria, or the ACT, as the proposal is consistent with current practice. Our interviews revealed that Tasmanian courts schedule sentencing hearings within hours or days of a conviction. Yet, the Tasmanian Government's Victim Support Service indicates that victims are required to provide their statement to Victims Support Services at least five days before the expected sentencing date. This is inconsistent with current sentencing practice, which should be modified to prevent the hearing of sentencing submissions immediately after a finding of guilt. Tasmanian victims should be given time to prepare and/or finalise their statement and then submit it once the offender has been convicted.

6. Presentation The permissible methods for impact statement presentation	Victims may present their statements verbally to the court.	Victims may present their written statement verbally to the court **or it may be presented verbally by another person of the victim's choosing**. **Victims should always be offered the option to present their statement using the full range of vulnerable witness provisions.**	No change is required in the ACT, as the proposal is consistent with the current approach. In Tasmania, victims are already allowed to present their statement verbally or have it read by the court; in South Australia, they can present their statement verbally or have it read by another person of their choosing. However, the relevant legislation only allows victims to present their statement using some vulnerable witness provisions in specific circumstances, i.e. if they are declared to be 'likely to suffer severe emotional trauma because of the nature of the offence' in Tasmania and if there is 'good reason to do so' in South Australia. This requires amendment, to give all victims the right to present their statement via all the vulnerable witness provisions. Following recent reforms, the Victorian sentencing legislation provides that only admissible parts of an impact statement may be read aloud in open court. This should be amended to allow victims to read the totality of their impact statements, in conjunction with the recommendation above that judicial officers should make clear which parts of the impact statement they do not take into account in sentencing.

NB: the changes between Manikis' and our proposed Australian model are indicated in bold.

of cases. Roberts (2012) summarised findings from a range of studies indicating that impact statements are submitted in somewhere between 14% and 42% of cases. Impact statements are more likely to be submitted in cases where the victim has 'sustained serious harm' (Cassell & Erez 2011: 155), such as sexual assault (Department of Justice Canada 2005). It has also been suggested that women are more likely to submit statements than men (Erez, Ibarra, & Downs 2011).

These issues were touched on by a number of justice professionals interviewed for this study. In contrast to previous research findings, however, they suggested that sexual assault victims may be *less* likely to submit statements than victims of other types of offences, due to the complexity of harm experienced by such victims. For example, according to Tasmanian Prosecutor Michael, 'I've had rape victims who have said, "I don't want that person to know what he has done to me, and what effect he has had on me"'. Similarly, Victorian WAO Hannah said that 'some people choose not to write one, so they don't give the accused the satisfaction of knowing how [the offending] has affected them'.

In some circumstances, the overwhelming experience of being involved in the justice system may also deter sexual offence victims from participating at sentencing. Harriet (WAO, Tas) identified criminal justice fatigue as a reason for victims choosing not to submit statements following a trial:

> I have found, if you get a guilty verdict from the jury, you can find it difficult to convince a person to then sit down and write about it, because they're over it, and they're exhausted. They've done their bit, and they've got the result that they want, and it sometimes doesn't seem for them that important to say more.

Not only do these findings contrast with previous research, but this perspective is strikingly different from that of, for example, South Australian victim August, who said that she viewed her impact statement as 'a chance to have a bit of power, and stand up and have my say'. The views of the quoted justice professionals are also not reflected by the sentencing remarks we analysed; impact statements were submitted in at least 79 of the 100 cases analysed, with a further 11 cases in which it was not stated whether there was an impact statement. This suggests that most victims of sexual offending in Australia do submit impact statements. Nevertheless, Michael and Hannah's comments indicate that choosing not to submit a statement may also be an empowering choice for victims, especially where this allows them to maintain control over their personal information. This view is supported by Samuel (WAO, SA), who said that 'a victim not doing a victim impact statement can be as powerful [for them] as them choosing to do one'. In addition, as Harriet (WAO, Tas) noted above, 'they've done their bit and they've got the result that they want'. The notion that they have 'got the result that they want' may also suggest that victims have found vindication in the verdict itself. This might reduce their need for the therapeutic benefits that could be derived from submitting a statement.

These findings are not the result of a comprehensive examination of this issue. The justice professionals interviewed suggest that victims' reasons for not completing an impact statement may be varied and deeply personal and do not appear to be the consequence of any structural or systemic problem. However, if impact statement processes and procedures are modified in accordance with the model recommended by this chapter, victims' increased understanding of the nature and purpose of their statements may make the choice to prepare one more appealing or accessible. This could be beneficial to the victim as a cathartic or therapeutic experience, as well as to the wider community, through judges' increased ability to impose proportionate sentences and comply with statutory requirements to recognise the victim when sentencing.

Conclusion

The interviews undertaken for this project were designed to achieve a better understanding of sexual offence victims' perspectives of impact statement and sentencing processes and procedures across the ACT, South Australia, Tasmania, and Victoria. These interviews raised two significant problems, the first of which is the lack of clarity around the purpose of victim impact statements. This problem is not limited to Australian jurisdictions. Manikis found that similar issues arise under Canadian impact statement regimes. In response, she developed a model to address these inconsistencies. This chapter used our interview findings to develop an adapted and expanded form of this model for the Australian context. Notably, the solutions proposed in this chapter are largely consistent with current Victorian practice. Accordingly, other Australian jurisdictions can look with confidence to the precedent set by Victoria when reforming their impact statement laws and procedures.

In regard to statement content, we propose an expressive approach, while maintaining certain rules to ensure that statements can also be used instrumentally, without disadvantaging the offender. Under this approach, victims are offered significant flexibility in their expression and the form of their statement. They would also be able to include any information about the harm they have experienced, without limiting this only to the harm caused by the offences for which offenders have been convicted. However, only the actual harm experienced as a consequence of the offending will be considered relevant to the judge's determination of sentence.

Under this approach, prosecutors and victim support and witness assistance officers are not responsible for editing impact statements to remove information that is considered irrelevant to the determination of harm or the sentence. Instead, the judicial officer is responsible for deciding which, if any, parts of the impact statement are relevant to the offender's sentence and must make clear how they have done this. This approach is consistent with the Victorian judicial practice that was in place at the time of our research, but its implementation would now require amendments in all four study jurisdictions.

In regard to the reliability of statements, we recommend a balance between expressive and instrumental approaches. If the judicial officer is able to draw adverse inferences against the offender because of the content of an impact statement, particularly if those adverse inferences lead to an increased sentence, it is vital that the content of a statement be verifiable by the defence. However, under a therapeutic jurisprudence approach, it is crucial that victims not be re-traumatised by the process of cross-examination. Therefore, if cross-examination takes place, victims need to be treated with courtesy and respect and must be offered the opportunity to use vulnerable witness provisions.

The findings of this chapter further support the recommendation made in Chapter 4 regarding the introduction of a victim-focused pre-sentence hearing. This type of hearing would allow the judicial officer to make clear what information from the impact statement would be relied on in passing sentence and would enable the prosecution to make submissions about any matters in the statement the victim would not like to be expressly mentioned in the sentencing remarks. It could further enable the defence to raise any issues with the content of the impact statement and consequently identify any intention to cross-examine the victim on their statement. If such an intention were expressed, the proposed hearing would facilitate the settlement of the questions to be asked in cross-examination. This would act as an additional safeguard to ensure that victims are not re-traumatised by the process of cross-examination.

In regard to statement presentation, we recommend flexibility in the form that impact statements may take, including the use of prose, poems, drawings, and/or songs. This approach is consistent with the current sentencing legislation in Victoria and the ACT. In contrast, the legislation in South Australia and Tasmania allows only for written statements. Accordingly, their legislation should be updated to provide victims with greater choice. Consistent with current approaches in all of the research jurisdictions, victims should always be allowed to present their statement verbally. This must include access to all relevant vulnerable witness provisions during presentation.

As a whole, it is important that the statement guidelines in each jurisdiction be updated to reflect the purpose and permissible content of impact statements accurately.[2] This must include an explicit and clear description of the role of impact statements, including their limitations, and the reasons for these limitations. This should allow victims to make an informed choice about whether to submit a statement. This in turn should reduce the likelihood that victims are surprised by any aspect of the impact statement process and avoid the potential for re-traumatisation.

Under the solutions proposed in this chapter, victims can gain therapeutic outcomes from the process of sharing with the court, in their own words, and with the level of detail they choose, the harm that they have experienced as a consequence of the offending. Therapeutic value can also be gained from the judge's use of the impact statement to determine a proportionate sentence for the offender. It is recognised, however, that the recommendations in this chapter are not a perfect therapeutic jurisprudence solution. The potential for cross-examination of the victim on the content of their statement can only be viewed as anti-therapeutic from the victim's perspective. However, as discussed, if the content of an impact statement does not meet the standard of proof in the event of a challenge from the defence, then it cannot be taken into account by the judge when sentencing. This could also be anti-therapeutic from the victim's perspective. Therefore, this proposed solution has reconciled, as far as possible, the instrumental and expressive approaches to victim impact statements, in order to offer a solution that maximises the potential for a therapeutic experience for the victim (Winick 2009).

Notes

1 This policy was current at the time of the South Australian interviews, which were conducted in 2015. The earlier policy is no longer available online, but is on file with the authors.

2 Provision of accurate information about impact statements' purpose was also identified as deficient in the findings of the Australian Royal Commission into Institutional Responses to Child Sexual Abuse. The Royal Commission recommended that Australian governments should 'improve the information provided

to victims and survivors to better prepare them for the process of making a victim impact statement and give them a better understanding of its role in the sentencing process' (2017: 102).

References

ACT Government (2009). *A Rollercoaster Ride: Victims of Sexual Assault: Their Experiences with and Views about the Criminal Justice Process in the ACT*. Canberra.

Booth, T (2005). 'Restoring Victims' Voices: Victim Impact Statements in the Sentencing Process', *Reform*, 86, 59–62.

Booth, T (2015). *Accommodating Justice: Victim Impact Statements in the Sentencing Process*, Federation Press. Sydney.

Bowden, P, Henning, T & Plater, D (2014). 'Balancing Fairness to Victims, Society and Defendants in the Cross-Examination of Vulnerable Witnesses: An Impossible Triangulation?', *Melbourne University Law Review*, 37, 539–584.

Boyd, R & Hopkins, A (2010). 'Cross-Examination of Child Sexual Assault Complainants: Concerns About the Application of s 41 of the *Evidence Act*', *Criminal Law Journal*, 34, 149–166.

Cashmore, J & Trimboli, L (2005). *An Evaluation of the NSW Child Sexual Assault Specialist Jurisdiction Pilot*, NSW Bureau of Crime Statistics and Research. Sydney.

Cassell, P & Erez, E (2011). 'Victim Impact Statements and Ancillary Harm: The American Perspective', *Canadian Criminal Law Review*, 15, 149–196.

De Mesmaecker, V (2012). 'Antidotes to Injustice? Victim Statements' Impact on Victims' Sense of Security', *International Review of Victimology*, 18, 133–153.

Department of Justice Canada (2005). *Multi-Site Survey of Victims of Crime and Criminal Justice Professionals Across Canada: Summary of Probation Officer, Corrections, and Parole Board Respondents*. Ottawa.

Englebrecht, C (2011). 'The Struggle for "Ownership of Conflict": An Exploration of Victim Participation and Voice in the Criminal Justice System', *Criminal Justice Review*, 36, 129–151.

Erez, E (1999). 'Who's Afraid of the Big Bad Victim? Victim Impact Statements as Victim Empowerment and Enhancement of Justice', *Criminal Law Review*, 545–556.

Erez, E (2004). 'Victim Voice, Impact Statements and Sentencing: Integrating Restorative Justice and Therapeutic Jurisprudence Principles in Adversarial Proceedings', *Criminal Law Bulletin*, 40, 483–500.

Erez, E, Ibarra, P & Downs, D (2011). 'Victim Welfare and Participation Reforms in the United States: A Therapeutic Jurisprudence Perspective', in E Erez, M Kilchling & J-A Wemmers (eds), *Therapeutic Jurisprudence and Victim Participation in Justice: International Perspectives*, Carolina Academic Press. Durham.

Flynn, A (2012). 'Bargaining with Justice: Victims, Plea Bargaining and the *Victims' Charter Act 2006* (Vic)', *Monash University Law Review*, 37, 73–96.

Henning, T (2013). 'Obtaining the Best Evidence from Children and Witnesses with Cognitive Impairments—"Plus ça Change" or Prospects New?', *Criminal Law Journal*, 37, 155–174.

Iliadis, M (2020). *Adversarial Justice and Victims' Rights: Reconceptualising the Role of Sexual Assault Victims*, Routledge. Abingdon.

Ipp, D (1998). 'Lawyers' Duties to the Court', *Law Quarterly Review*, 114, 63–107.

Kennedy, J, Easteal, P & Bartels, L (2012). 'How Protected is She? "Fairness" and the Rape Victim Witness in Australia', *Women's Studies International Forum*, 35, 334–342.

Lens, K, Pemberton, A & Borgaerts, S (2013). 'Heterogeneity in Victim Participation: A New Perspective on Delivering a Victim Impact Statement', *European Journal of Criminology*, 10, 479–495.

Manikis, M (2015). 'Victim Impact Statements at Sentencing: Towards a Clearer Understanding of their Aims', *University of Toronto Law Journal*, 65, 85–123.

Mastrocinque, J (2014). 'Victim Personal Statements: An Analysis of Notification and Utilization', *Criminology & Criminal Justice*, 14, 216–234.

McGovern, D (2013). 'The Therapeutic Potential of Victim Impact Statements for Sexual Violence', *Sexual Abuse in Australia and New Zealand*, 5(2), 21–30.

Meredith, C & Paquette, C (2001). *Summary Report on Victim Impact Statement Focus Groups*, Department of Justice Canada. Ottawa.

NSW Government (2018). *Schedule of Government Response to Recommendations on Victims' Involvement in Sentencing*. http://www.sentencingcouncil.justice.nsw.gov.au/Documents/ Current-projects/Victims/Victims_gov.pdf.

NSW Sentencing Council (2018). *Victims' Involvement in Sentencing—Report*. Sydney.

O'Connell, M (2006). 'Evolving Mechanisms for Engaging Victims in the Sentencing Process: Should Victims Have a Stronger Voice in Court?', Paper presented at the Sentencing Principles Perspectives and Possibilities Conference, Canberra.

O'Connell, M (2009). 'Victims in the Sentencing Process: South Australia's Judges and Magistrates Give Their Verdict', *International Perspectives in Victimology*, 4, 50–57.

Pakula, M. (2018). *Second Reading Speech for the Victims Legislation and Other Amendment Bill 2018*. Legislative Assembly of Victoria, 25 July. Melbourne.

Roberts, J (2012). 'Crime Victims, Sentencing, and Release from Prison', in J Petersilia & K Reitz (eds), *The Oxford Handbook of Sentencing and Corrections*, Oxford University Press. Oxford.

Royal Commission into Institutional Responses to Child Sexual Abuse (2017). *Criminal Justice Report*. Sydney.

Scottish Court Service (2015). *Evidence and Procedure Review Report*. Edinburgh.

Shipman, T & Harper, T (2017). 'Rape Victims to be Spared Court Ordeal', *The Times*, 19 March. https://www.thetimes.co.uk/edition/news/rape-victims-to-be-spared-court-ordeal-q2nd8d29t.

Skvortsova, T & Khazma, R (2017). 'Admissibility of Victim Impact Statements in the ACT', *Ethos*, 245, 26–31.

Tyler, T (2007). 'Procedural Justice and the Courts', *Court Review*, 44, 26–31.

Victorian Law Reform Commission (2016). *The Role of Victims of Crime in the Criminal Trial Process: Report*. Melbourne.

Victorian Office of Public Prosecutions (OPP) (2019). *Policy of the Director of the Public Prosecutions for Victoria*. http://www.opp.vic.gov.au/getattachment/6beb7d86-d539-4443-871f-cc4165557ea4/DPP-Policy.aspx.

Victorian Victim Support Agency (2009). *A Victim's Voice: Victim Impact Statements in Victoria*. Melbourne.

Wexler, D (2000). 'Therapeutic Jurisprudence: An Overview', *Thomas M Cooley Law Review*, 17, 125–134.

Winick, B (2009). 'Therapeutic Jurisprudence Perspectives on Dealing with Victims of Crime', *Nova Law Review*, 33, 535–543.

Wood, J (2004). 'Child Witnesses: The New South Wales Experience', Paper presented at Child Witnesses—Best Practice for Courts Conference, Parramatta.

AUGUST

August met up with the offender and other mutual friends at a pub. The group were all drinking and August drank enough to feel unwell. She had organised to spend a night at a friend's house and she accepted the offender's offer to escort her there. August fell asleep at her friend's house on the sofa-bed in the lounge. During the night, August awoke on three occasions and each time felt fingers inside her vagina. She was still intoxicated and found it difficult to speak and move. On one occasion, she took hold of the offender's wrist while he was penetrating her vagina with his fingers and he apologised, but did not stop. It was when she heard the apology that August realised who was sexually assaulting her.

Some days after the offence, the offender texted August to apologise for what he had done. He ultimately pleaded guilty to one count of rape. After the offender's arrest, August said she would have preferred to have had more contact from the DPP:

> I could see this finished product and I couldn't see how it happened. Because it's me. It's my life. And all of this stuff is happening in the background, and I have no idea what they are doing or why. I think being able to understand that a bit more would have made it a bit better for me.

August also said she would have preferred to be more generally informed of what was going on in terms of the trial process:

> I had one meeting with [the prosecutor]. I had to go over my original statement. Besides that, I saw her when I went to court. I think having more contact with her, and hearing from her what was going to happen, as well as with Witness Assistance, just being a bit more in the loop.

August was informed of the option to complete a victim impact statement by the police officer who investigated her case. The officer gave August a booklet when the matter was first listed for trial, but she was not given any further guidance about the process. About a month before the offender was due to be sentenced, her witness assistance officer provided August with an information brochure with more information. August's rape crisis counsellor helped her finalise the wording of her statement, which was not altered by the prosecutor, and included the following material:

> My life is now implausibly different; my trusted friend circle is very small compared to a once large one. Being raped by someone I considered a friend has not only meant that I have had to move to a different friendship group, but has seeded a never wavering anxiety associated with all friendships … I've lost my capacity to trust. I struggle to partake in many types of social events, as I am always feeling vulnerable and unsafe. Unless I am in a situation where several of my close friends are present and able to always be with me I do not attend these social events, leaving me excluded from all the joyous activities people my age enjoy and isolated me from making new friends … The actions of the offender have left an incredibly exhausting and overwhelming emotional toll … Going through the legal process has been very hard. It has caused additional anxiety and stress in my life. I have had to spread my energy across my commitments finely to retain enough energy to cope. All the feelings and issues I experience are amplified when legal activities are looming, decreasing my capacity to function with the rest of my life … To the offender: It is unacceptable for you to believe and act as if you have power and control over women. It is every woman's right to make their own decisions, but you thought you were entitled to what you wanted and put your needs above mine. You took away my power and control to inflict sexual violence on me. Because of your actions you have to sit there but I am still able to stand here. Your actions have taken away my freedom to live my life in a carefree way but now you face the risk of losing your own freedom through those same actions.

August chose to read her statement out loud. The judge referred to her statement in the sentencing remarks. August would recommend that others in her situation submit an impact statement.

Chapter 6

Victim experiences of impact statements and sentencing

Challenges in communicating with victims

Introduction

As outlined previously, the interviews undertaken with victims and justice professionals revealed two overarching problems around impact statements and sentencing. Chapter 5 concerned the first of these problems, namely the widespread uncertainty about the purpose of impact statements and the corresponding uncertainty about how they can or should be used by the court. This chapter concerns the second identified problem, namely a range of communication difficulties that arise between victims and justice professionals (see also Davies & Bartels 2020). These appear to act as a barrier to justice professionals' fulfilment of their legal obligation to keep victims informed of the progress of their matter, including their obligation to inform victims about sentencing processes.

This chapter begins by identifying the problems raised by the victims interviewed, regarding their lack of knowledge of the progress of their case and of court processes generally, including sentencing. It contrasts these victim experiences with the perspectives of the interviewed justice professionals on the information they believe they are communicating to victims. The chapter then identifies a number of barriers that may prevent the effective sharing of information between victims and justice professionals and proposes a series of evidence-based solutions to resolve the identified communication difficulties.

Victims' need for and right to information

Crime victims' need to be provided with information about the criminal justice system, including information about the progress of their matter, has been long established. As Shapland, Willmore, and Duff (1985: 78) noted, the 'absence of information, both at the investigation and at the outcome stage, seems to be felt very keenly by victims'. Since then, researchers have consistently found that one of the greatest needs for victims throughout their justice system experience is to be provided with timely, accessible, and accurate information (see e.g. Clark 2010; Wemmers 2011; Laxminarayan et al. 2013; Wedlock & Tapley 2016). Consistent with Tyler's (2007) theory of procedural justice, 'victim satisfaction is linked to the amount of information they receive as to the progress of the case' (Shapland, Willmore, & Duff 1985: 48). Furthermore, as the Victorian Law Reform Commission has argued, 'accurate, timely and personalised legal information can help ensure [that] victims have realistic expectations about what the criminal justice system can deliver, and what their role is [in this system]' (2014: 171). In contrast, a lack of information, and the resulting stress and confusion about the justice process, can re-traumatise victims (Konradi 2007; Wemmers 2011).

The importance of providing information to victims is reflected in current victims' rights legislation and charters around Australia. Most provide that a victim has the right to receive information about trial processes generally (see *Victims of Crime Act 1994* (ACT) s4(g); *Victims of Crime Act 2001* (SA) s8(1); *Victims' Charter Act 2006* (Vic) s11(1); *Victims of Crime Assistance Act 2009* (Qld) Sch 1AA, Pt 1, Div 2, cl 3; *Northern Territory Charter of Victims' Rights* (Northern Territory Government 2019: 3); *Charter of Rights for Victims of Crime* (Tas) s7). In addition, all jurisdictions provide the right to receive information about the progress of the case itself, such as information about the charges laid, scheduled hearings and outcomes, including decisions made concerning acceptance of guilty pleas (see *Victims of Crime Act 1994* (WA) Sch 1 s6; *Victims of Crime Act 1994* (ACT) ss4(b), 4(d); *Victims of Crime Act 2001* (SA) ss8(1)(a), (e); *Victims' Charter Act 2006* (Vic) ss9(a), (c); *Victims of Crime Assistance Act 2009* (Qld) Sch 1AA, Pt 1, Div 2, cl 2; *Victims' Rights and Support Act 2013* (NSW) ss6.5, 6.6; *Northern Territory Charter of Victims' Rights* (Northern Territory Government 2019: 4); Tasmanian *Charter of Rights of Victims of Crime* (Tas) 2–4). Table 6.1 illustrates what these rights entail.

The provision of information: problems arising in practice

Information about the justice process

Despite widespread academic appreciation of the need to keep victims informed throughout the justice process and the existing obligations under Australian victims' rights regimes detailed above, each of the six victims we interviewed reported not knowing or understanding

Table 6.1 Informational rights under Australian victims' rights regimes

Victims' informational rights	*Checklist of information that victims are entitled to receive*
The justice system The right to receive information about the justice system and the trial process	Information about: • the role of the prosecution, defence, and judge; • the layout of the court, including where each party is seated; • the types of hearings that may be scheduled, including what may happen at each hearing; • giving evidence, including, if applicable, victims' right to use vulnerable witness provisions; and • victims' right to submit an impact statement, including how and when this can be used.
The progress of the case The right to receive information about the progress of the case	Information about: • the charges laid; • the hearings scheduled; • the outcomes of each hearing; and • decisions made concerning acceptance of guilty pleas.

all or some of the criminal justice process. This included not being kept informed about the progress of their trial and being unaware of the sentencing process. The following quotes demonstrate that the interviewed victims' need for information was not met by the justice professionals who worked with them:

> Being more in the loop would be something that I would [have preferred] … I felt like I was told just: 'be here at this time, this is what is happening', while all this stuff was happening in the background, and that was the stuff I wanted to know.
>
> (August, SA)

> I had no idea what the process was and I would have to ask what was next. They would tell me if I asked, but I had no idea.
>
> (Rachel, Tas)

> Even that he had pleaded guilty, and wasn't trying to fight the charge, I wasn't told for a while. I thought I was still potentially going to trial for quite a while … there were a few holes in the system that meant I was kept out of the loop.
>
> (Laura, SA)

Laura's case, in which she 'wasn't told for a while' that the offender had pleaded guilty, is a particularly alarming example of the failure to keep victims informed in a timely fashion. Timeliness, as noted above, is an important aspect of victims' need for information. Yet a lack of timely information placed two of the victims interviewed in a position where they felt obliged to attend each court hearing in order to remain informed of the progress of their matter. This caused them significant disruption throughout the course of the justice process:

> Had I not made the decision to go to every court hearing, [the justice process] would not have worked for me. Because I wouldn't have had the information I was wanting and when I did get it, it would have been weeks and weeks down the track. It worked for me, because I was there for every step of the process and I therefore knew what was happening as it happened. It got to the point when Witness Assistance would be ringing me and asking me for an update on what was happening.
>
> (Philippa, SA)

> I attended until the end [of the sentencing process] merely to be kept thoroughly in the loop, because the time lapse and wait between hearings until the subsequent court date following adjournments, of sometimes weeks or months, were unbearable and the feedback that followed was a bare minimum.
>
> (Jessica, SA)

Several justice professionals reported being aware of problems around the lack of information provided to victims. For example, Trish said:

> We hear from people all the time about how they feel that they are invisible throughout the legal process, that they are not communicated with regularly, that they aren't talked to about the purposes of the different court hearings and they often don't know whether they are supposed to attend or not. Really basic stuff and they are being left out of the loop.
>
> (VSO, Vic)

Trish therefore confirmed that problems around a lack of information are not exclusive to the victims interviewed for this research. Instead, this appears to be a widespread issue (for an international example, see Englebrecht 2011; see also Iliadis 2020).

During their interviews, many justice professionals indicated that they were aware of the importance of keeping victims informed. When prompted, several shared the approaches they take to ensure that victims are made aware of the justice process. Some of these included:

> [providing] general information about the court process, to more specific information about each step in the process and information about victim impact statements if they get to that stage.
>
> (Suzanna, VSO, ACT)

> [providing] lots of procedural information and lots of practical information about their involvement, their role. And the rules and the etiquette of the court … It's really important that they understand their role in court.
>
> (Samuel, WAO, SA)

> We explain the procedure. For example, where the judge will be, where the jury will be, where counsel will be. We show them the courtroom. We explain examination-in-chief and … cross-examination … and there are witness assistance officers who will take them down and show them the court and will be in regular contact with them.
>
> (Michael, Prosecutor, Tas)

> I explain what happens at a trial from start to finish … and we do court tours … I would explain about taking the oath or the affirmation, giving evidence-in-chief and cross-examination and re-examination.
>
> (Hannah, WAO, Vic)

It is significant that each of these justice professionals described the importance of explaining the trial process to victims, yet none mentioned the importance of keeping victims informed as the trial progresses. Of all the justice professionals interviewed, only Robert (WAO, Tas) described his efforts to ensure that victims are kept informed on an ongoing basis about the progress of their trials:

> Normally what we would do is explain to them over the phone when the first appearance is happening in court and that we would get back to them and let them know what the plea is, either at the first or second appearance. For an indictable matter, when it comes

> to the Supreme Court, [we would keep them updated about] what was happening.

This suggests that some of the justice professionals interviewed may not fully understand that victims' need for information includes the need for timely information about the progress of the trial. An example of the gravity of failing to keep a particular victim updated about the progress of a trial was described by Cathy (VSO, SA), who said 'we had the unfortunate experience where a client was in the waiting room and opened up the newspaper and read about what had happened in court for her matter. No one had told her about it'. Justice professionals should therefore be reminded of the importance of providing victims with information both about the justice process and the progress of the victim's matter. This may be more easily facilitated through the implementation of a victim-focused automated notification system, which is discussed below.

Information about sentencing

For some victims, the lack of information they received extended to a lack of information about the nature of the hearing at which their impact statement was presented. Four of the six victims reported not having been advised prior to this hearing about the substance of a sentencing plea in mitigation. That is, they were not informed that the hearing at which their impact statement would be presented would otherwise be largely offender-focused. This might include favourable submissions about the offender, including, for example, information about the offender's good character or community involvement.

Victims August, Philippa, and Laura (SA) and Rachel (Tas) did not recall being informed about this process at all. Consequently, Laura felt very uncomfortable during the hearing. She explained:

> It would have been good if someone had said, 'don't take it to heart. This is the norm. This is what happens'. Afterward, when I had said 'I feel bad after hearing [the plea in mitigation]', the detective said to me, 'that's just what they do; that's what his lawyers are paid to do'. There wasn't any warning about it. The court process was all very new to me and not well explained at all.

This is another example of an unsatisfactory outcome for victims, stemming from a lack of information. August, Philippa, Laura, and Rachel should have been informed prior to the hearing of the nature of a plea in mitigation. This would have prepared them for the hearing and could have alleviated the distress described by Laura.

Significantly, justice professionals from all jurisdictions spoke of the importance of ensuring that victims are adequately prepared for the content of the offender's submissions in mitigation at sentencing. Two VSOs particularly noted the distress victims may feel upon hearing these submissions and explained the importance of preparing them for the hearing:

> I ensure that if clients are coming along to sit in on sentencing submissions, they know that they will hear things they feel uncomfortable about. They know the offender in one capacity. They know what violence that person is capable of committing. But they will get to hear about the charitable works, the good things about the person. Helping them to psychologically prepare for that experience is important.
>
> (Cathy, VSO, SA)

> [A plea in mitigation] is really confronting … [Victims] often will have in their mind that they are going to hear his sentence, but not factoring in how distressing it can be to hear people get up and speak of his good character. That's something I would prepare them for. I would [explain] it's just part of the court process … I have had clients feel distressed listening to it, so if someone wasn't prepared for it, it would be really distressing.
>
> (Colette, VSO, Vic)

Others also noted how unfair such submissions can feel to victims and consequently emphasised the importance of ensuring they are prepared for the type of submissions that may be made by the defence:

> I always tell them [about the plea in mitigation]. I tell them that it's going to sound really one-sided … [the] defence will go through everything as they try to mitigate … I explain that it is going to seem lopsided … and doesn't seem fair.
>
> (Rose, Prosecutor, Vic)

> If they are going to attend [sentencing], I like to make sure that they know that a lot of it will be about the offender. Some victims go, not realising that they might do character references or they might talk about what a great person the offender is. I think that's really hard for victims to hear those things.
>
> (Suzanna, VSO, ACT)

Many of the interviewed justice professionals revealed awareness of the importance of informing victims about the plea in mitigation and demonstrated how carefully they ensure that victims are educated about this subject. Yet most of the interviewed victims reported not receiving this information. Accordingly, there appears to be a disconnect between the information that justice professionals believe that victims are receiving and the information that victims believe they are told.

Identifying potential communication barriers

This chapter proceeds upon the assumption that both victims and justice professionals are accurately reporting their experiences of information provision. That is, it assumes that justice professionals do attempt to communicate relevant information to victims, but that victims do not actually receive some or all of this information. On that assumption, it explores two significant issues that may act as barriers between justice professionals' communication of information and victims' receipt of that information. The first of these barriers is the current lack of clarity as to who is responsible for the communication of certain types of information to victims, which may explain why victims receive only some of the information to which they are entitled. The second barrier is the problematic approaches that professionals may take when communicating with victims. This may explain why the information that justice professionals believe they are sharing with victims may not be wholly, or even partly, understood by the intended recipients.

Communicating information to victims of crime

Who is responsible for providing information?

In most Australian jurisdictions, including the two in which we conducted the victim interviews, victims' right to information only exists if the victim actively requests that information from the relevant agency. For example, s8(1) of the *Victims of Crime Act 2001* (SA) states that the 'victim should be informed, on request' about information such as the progress of the investigation and the charges laid. The NSW, Queensland, Tasmanian, and Western Australian instruments are all expressed in similar terms; that is, the onus in these jurisdictions is on the victim to contact the police, witness assistance, or DPP to obtain the required information, rather than the obligation resting with those agencies to keep the victim informed.

In contrast, the Victorian legislation states that '[a]n investigatory agency is to inform a victim, at reasonable intervals, about the progress of an investigation into a criminal offence' (*Victims' Charter Act 2006* (Vic) s8(1)) and '[t]he prosecuting agency is to give a victim, as soon as reasonably practicable, the [relevant] information' (s9). The ACT currently also places the obligation to keep the victim informed on the police and prosecution agency; however, recent legislative reforms scheduled to effect in January 2021 will change this. Under s15F(1) of the *Victims Rights Legislation Amendment Act* 2020 (ACT), the police and/or DPP must:

> within a reasonable period before a victim of an offence would be able to make a victim impact statement, tell the victim the following:

(a) who may make a victim impact statement;
(b) that a victim impact statement may be made orally or in writing;
(c) what information a victim impact statement must and may include:
(d) how a victim impact statement may be used in court during a proceeding, including that –
   (i) a copy of the victim impact statement will be given to the offender;
   (ii) the victim may be cross-examined about the contents of the victim impact statement; and
   (iii) the court must consider the victim impact statement in deciding how the offender should be sentenced.

This Act also expands victims' rights in the ACT in a range of other ways and has been described by the current Victims of Crime Commissioner as a 'a crucial opportunity to … better uphold the rights and interests of those affected by crime' (Yates 2020: np).

Our interviews in South Australia and Tasmania suggest that victims' rights instruments in those jurisdictions are operating entirely in accordance with their provisions; that is, the interviewed victims were not apprised of the progress of their case unless they contacted the appropriate agency to seek information. These provisions are therefore problematic because of the negative consequences that arise for victims when they are not kept appropriately informed. These consequences, which were explored above, were summarised by Victorian VSO Colette: 'if the person is left hanging, and there is no communication and no word of what is happening, people can get to highly traumatised states'.

While it is possible that some victims may be aware that it is their responsibility to request information and may also possess the capacity to seek it from the relevant agencies, it is equally possible that victims may not know that the onus is on them to seek such information or may not possess the resilience or capacity to follow this up. This view is supported by Victorian VSO Trish, who argued:

> I think it's unfair to expect someone who is traumatised and going through the pressure of a court case to be able to advocate for themselves or even to be informed enough … to do that. I think that expectation is unrealistic and unfair.

This was certainly the experience of some of the victims interviewed, such as Eve, who said:

> If I have learned anything from this process, it's that nobody actually cares about the victim. I got a phone call out of the blue 15 months after he raped me, saying 'can you come to the DPP's office'. No one got in contact with me after it happened … nobody did any follow-up [with me] … Throughout the 15 months I had to make phone calls to follow up, and I was always put through to different people, because the others were on holidays or whatever. So, it was just bringing it all back every few months that I rang up to ask what was going on.
>
> (Victim, Tas)

Lee (2018) documented a similar experience in her memoir about 'standing up, speaking out and fighting back' against the man who sexually assaulted her. This echoes Eve's experience and confirms that a lack of communication with the victim can result in their re-traumatisation. This is particularly unsatisfactory, given that victims' rights regimes and victim impact statements were introduced as part of reforms intended to reduce the re-traumatisation of victims of sexual offending by the criminal justice process.

Accordingly, it is problematic that victims' rights regimes in some jurisdictions place the obligation on the victim to seek information about the progress of the investigation and trial, rather than placing the onus to provide that information on the police or prosecution agency. As Trish argued, it is not reasonable or fair to expect victims, who are likely to be in a traumatised state, to take responsibility for following up with various agencies to determine the progress of their matters. It is also not satisfactory that an instrument that purports to grant informational rights to potentially vulnerable and traumatised victims is only activated in cases where victims have the personal capacity and resilience to follow up on that right themselves.

We recommend that, in order to increase the level of information provided to victims throughout the justice process, consistency should be achieved across victims' rights instruments. This would require most jurisdictions to remove the responsibility for obtaining information about the progress of the criminal investigation and trial process from the victim and instead place the onus to provide that information on the relevant agency. The recent reforms in the ACT are a step in the right direction. Reforms of this nature should also be supported by training to ensure that agencies are aware of their responsibility to keep victims informed throughout the entire justice process, which could begin to alleviate the problem of victims feeling 'out of the loop'.

Communication barriers that may prevent effective information sharing

As discussed in Chapter 1, we were unable to conduct interviews in the ACT or Victoria. It is therefore not possible for us to compare the difference in experiences or outcomes for victims in jurisdictions where the onus is on the police or prosecution agency to provide information to victims. However, as the quote from Trish above indicates, even victims in Victoria may not receive adequate information and feel left out of the loop. This suggests that there may be problems with the implementation of informational rights, even in jurisdictions where the legislation places the onus on agencies to keep victims informed. This is also supported by the Victorian Law Reform Commission, which was told 'by a parent whose child had been killed, that she was not informed of sentencing hearing dates and was therefore not able to attend' (2016: 107). This suggests that justice professionals' approaches to communication with victims of crime may be problematic. Our interviews demonstrate both that the justice professionals were aware of the need to provide sufficient information to victims about court processes and sentencing hearings and that the victims did not recall being told this type of information. It may be that the interviewed victims were provided with this information, but did not recall it, because they did not fully understand it.

It appears that issues of effective communication have rarely been explored in the context of justice professionals working with victims and little has been written on practical communication strategies in this area. In fact, many communication texts 'devote the majority of their content to specific communication issues and give correspondingly less attention to core communication skills' (Silverman, Kurtz, & Draper 2013: 323). For example, Lewis and Jaramillo (2008) identified many barriers that can affect communication between victims and service providers, but provided few explicit strategies to overcome them. Similarly, a publication by the US Office for Victims of Crime (2005) outlined a list of barriers that can prevent effective communication with victims, without offering practical solutions to overcome these problems. In contrast, medical professionals have long recognised the vast communication difficulties that can arise between doctors and patients. The medical literature is therefore a valuable resource for applied communication skills training.[1]

Silverman, Kurtz, and Draper's (2013) text consolidates a large number of studies on the frequent problems that arise in communication in medical practice. They reported that doctors tend to give sparse information to their patients, often underestimating the amount of information patients actually want. Further, patients frequently do not understand the language that doctors use, including technical language and shorthand. Consequently, patients tend not to understand or recall all of the information imparted by their doctors. This can be compounded by the 'highly emotional nature of illness [that may impede] rational communication and understanding' (2013: 162).

We believe that the same problems may affect communication between justice professionals and victims. It is arguable that prosecutors and witness assistance and victim support officers share information with victims about justice processes that cannot be fully understood. This may be because the information is sparse, victims may not possess a fundamental understanding of the justice process, or they may not understand legal jargon or shorthand, including acronyms such as 'DPP' or 'OPP'. This argument is supported by Hargie, who noted that, in the legal context, 'problems of comprehension [arise] with vocabulary and the technical meaning of some terms that can be at odds with everyday interpretations' (2011: 211). It is also borne out by victim Rachel from Tasmania, who reported 'not knowing who the DPP was'. She stated that 'the prosecutor and witness assistance … deal with these situations, these words, these people, these documents, on a daily basis, but I had no idea. They were saying all these words and I just didn't know'. Similarly, Laura explained:

> I understand that they are busy. But I think it's the little things. They assume that others understand the system enough to understand what is going to happen next. It's easy to assume that if you

> have that knowledge, that other people will have the same knowledge of the system and how it works. I have a decent amount of common sense, but there were things that were worded in ways that weren't clear and they assumed I would understand that if one thing happened, that other things would follow.
>
> (Victim, SA)

These communication difficulties may be exacerbated by the psychological sequelae experienced by victims of crime, including 'difficulties in processing information ... poor concentration, difficulty with memory retrieval ... and a decreased ability to consider long range implications of events' (Reyes, Elhai, & Ford 2008: 176). Rachel also reflected on these difficulties: 'I didn't understand a lot and at the time was overwhelmed ... I was in a frame of mind where they could have talked to me all day and I wouldn't have taken that in'. Consequently, as Ashworth has noted, 'being told is not the same as being made to understand' (1998: 64).

Evidence-based solutions to identified communication barriers

Using Silverman, Kurtz, and Draper's (2013) research, in this section we explore a range of evidence-based solutions to address problems of communication between professionals and victims. These solutions are designed to ensure that appropriate levels of information are provided to victims and can be properly processed and retained by recipients.[2]

As set out in Table 6.1, victims in Australia have the right to receive information about trial processes in a general sense, as well as information about the progress of their case, including information about the charges laid, scheduled hearings, and outcomes, including decisions made concerning acceptance of a guilty plea. In essence, this means that victims are entitled to information about how the criminal justice system operates, starting with the role of the prosecution agency, defence lawyer, and judge. They must be informed prior to each court date of what the hearing might entail, followed by the outcome of hearings as they occur. They must also be informed about their right to submit a victim impact statement, including information about how and when it might be used.

A consideration throughout this should be whether the information is communicated to victims in a form that can be easily understood and processed, both at the time of the communication, as well as later. Silverman, Kurtz, and Draper (2013) have provided a number of strategies to assist medical professionals to impart comprehensible information to patients. These strategies, discussed below, are equally applicable to justice professionals working with victims and include the accessible communication of information verbally and effectively conveying information using visual methods.

Effective verbal communication skills

Silverman, Kurtz, and Draper (2013) have recommended a number of strategies to ensure that verbal information is conveyed effectively. These require professionals to:

1. assess the recipient's starting point prior to giving information, by determining the amount of information or knowledge the recipient already possesses in relation to the subject matter, prior to providing any further information;
2. give information in small, 'assimilable chunks' (2013: 24). The professional must ensure that information is given in small amounts, to enable the recipient to hear and process each piece of information before further information is provided;
3. check the recipient has understood the small chunk of information and use their response as a guide to how to proceed before providing any further information;
4. repeat information if the recipient has not understood;
5. reduce or eliminate the use of jargon; and
6. ask the recipient what other information might be helpful.

Combined, these strategies should ensure that victims are able to comprehend the information presented to them verbally. For example, victim Laura complained that the justice professionals she encountered seemed to 'assume that others understand the system enough to understand what is going to happen next'. This situation could have been avoided if the first strategy listed above had been used. By determining Laura's prior understanding of the justice system, the professionals who worked with her could have avoided the assumption that she understood more than she did and, consequently, could have provided Laura with appropriate levels of introductory information. Further, by avoiding the use of jargon, the justice professionals who worked with Rachel could have avoided the confusion that she experienced when 'they were saying all these words and I just didn't know [what they meant]'.

Consequently, we recommend that, based on the above-described strategies, verbal communication skills training should be conducted with justice professionals to improve their communication when working with victims of crime.

Effective visual communication

Silverman, Kurtz, and Draper (2013; see also Hargie 2011) also recommended using visual methods of conveying information to aid the recipient's recall and understanding. Many victim support agencies and prosecution offices already publish information booklets designed for victims. However, these vary in their accessibility and may not serve as effective aids to victims' understanding. For example, the booklet *Information for Victims of Crime: Treatment, Impact and Access to the Justice System* is published by the South Australian Commissioner for Victims' Rights (2014). This booklet is very comprehensive, but potentially overwhelming; it was 84 pages long at the time of our interviews, although the version on the website in 2020 appeared to have been reduced to 74 pages. When reflecting on the length of such booklets, Rose (Prosecutor, Vic) was sceptical of their utility, commenting that 'for example, 80 pages, that's very big. Ours [the Vic booklet] is quite compact and small … I think you have to assume that although people are sent that information, that they don't really read it'.

A shorter booklet that is less comprehensive, but provides clear and specific information about each stage in the court process, would serve as a greater aid to victims' understanding of the justice system generally. This view is supported by Laura's experience:

> They gave me an information sheet and booklets about the legal process. [These explained] what court is for what sort of offence, and about negotiations and sentencing. But I would have liked a little side bar of minor details about what happens there, because those are the things I didn't know … Like where to sit or where the offender is sitting or who is going to go first. Those little details that add to the stress. I would have liked to be able to mentally prepare myself for it and remain as calm as I could. So, I think that's what is lacking and is probably not hard to fix, because they are very small details.
>
> (Victim, SA)

Her comment is significant, because the South Australian booklet does contain much of the information that Laura desired. The booklet even contains a diagram of both the lower and higher courts, to illustrate the locations of the parties in the room. However, as Prosecutor Rose from

Victoria pointed out, it is unlikely that victims would read a booklet of that length. Accordingly, a shorter and more concise booklet would be preferable. The Victorian OPP (2013) has its own booklet, *Pathways to Justice: A Guide to the Victorian Court System for Victims and Witnesses of Serious Crime*. As set out above, Rose, a Victorian prosecutor, described this as 'quite compact'. However, at 50 pages, it may also be overwhelming in length. It is therefore preferable that victims be provided with condensed versions of these booklets and the option of receiving a copy of the longer publication if desired. The need for 'succinct, victim friendly and accessible' materials for victims was recently accepted by the NSW Government (2018: 13; see also NSW Sentencing Council 2018).

Of key importance in the development of a condensed booklet is the presentation of material in flowcharts, as included the current South Australian and Victorian booklets (see Figures 6.1 and 6.2). A flowchart is ideal, because it assists with visually communicating information, in accordance with Silverman, Kurtz, and Draper's recommendations. The South Australian and Victorian flowcharts have been extracted from the victim booklets and included for illustrative purposes. They are concise, but contain sufficient detail to present the complete course of a criminal prosecution. The justice professionals we interviewed spoke highly of the Victorian flowchart. For example, VSO Colette commented that she frequently uses the *Pathways to Justice* booklet because it 'has a really good flowchart in it'.

The Victorian and South Australian flowcharts are undoubtedly a useful guide for lay people about the various stages of the criminal justice process. However, they are at risk of being overlooked by victims, due to the overall length of the publications in which they are published. Therefore, the inclusion of the chart and other vital information such as legal definitions in a condensed booklet is likely to be of more use to victims.

There is some information for victims in the ACT contained in the Australian Federal Police (2013) *Pocketbook Guide for Victims of Crime*, although the information on court processes appears alongside information on issues such as family violence and home and vehicle security. The ACT Government's Victim Support website acknowledges that '[t]he Court process can be very confusing and intimidating for people who have been a victim of crime' (2020a: np) and provides information about the three levels of court in the ACT (ACT Government 2020b), the role of the prosecution (ACT Government 2020c), and sentencing (ACT Government 2020d), but does not include a visual explanation of the kind we suggest.

We note that Tasmania does not have an equivalent booklet or chart. When asked if a flowchart would have been useful to her, Eve said:

> Yes. To know anything would have been helpful … I think as soon as you say that you want [the defendant] charged, they should give the flowchart to you. And then you would know how long it might take and when they might contact you next, and what would happen at court.
>
> (Victim, Tas)

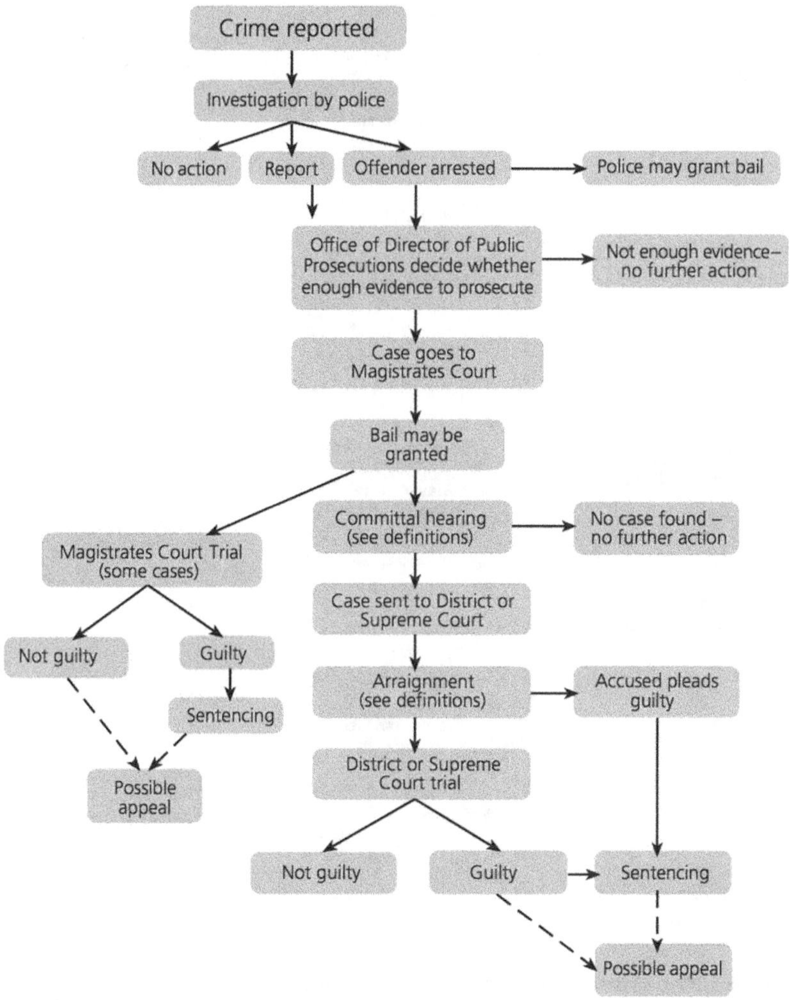

Figure 6.1 South Australian flowchart – the criminal justice system for adult offenders

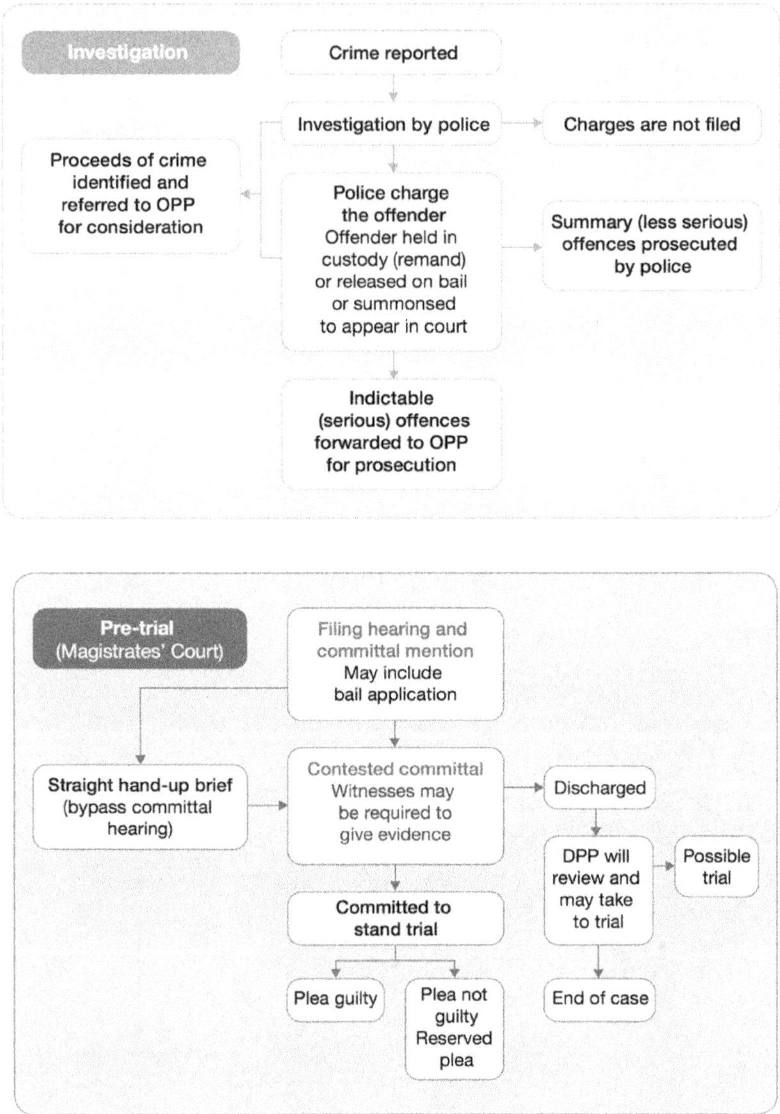

Figure 6.2 Victorian flowcharts on criminal justice processes

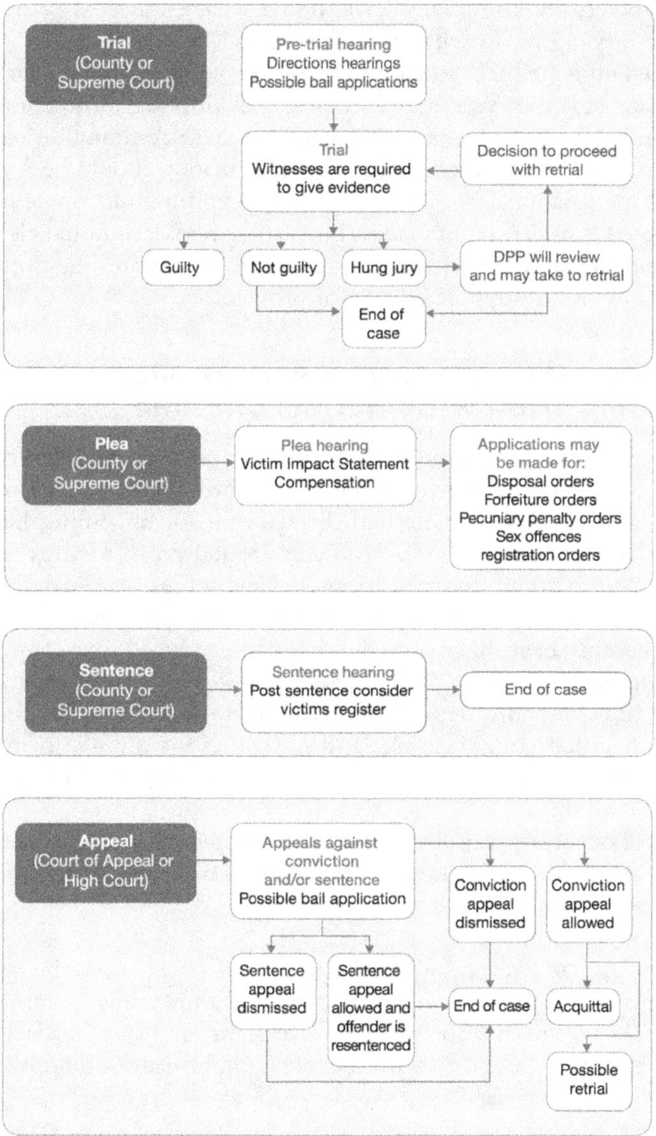

Figure 6.2 Continued

Similarly, Rachel (Victim, Tas) said that 'a summary would have been helpful to actually know why I was doing what I was doing, and what they were going to do with the information I was giving. That would have been quite helpful'. Accordingly, we recommend that similar charts be prepared for the ACT and Tasmania and all other jurisdictions that have similar frameworks, in order to ensure their communication with victims is accessible and effective. This information should be included in short informational booklets that briefly explain court processes and define key terms. To be of practical use, these booklets should also contain adequate space for victims to take notes and write questions they may wish to ask of support services or prosecutors.

Supplementary strategy for improving communication with victims of crime

One further strategy for providing information may complement the approaches proposed above, namely, the introduction of automated systems that provide victims with brief details of upcoming hearings and outcomes. In response to problems around crime victims' receipt of information about court hearings and outcomes, automated methods for communicating with victims have been developed in the US. These systems have been rolled out over nearly 30 years and were operating in 47 states by 2015 (Irazola et al. 2015). These systems provide victims with the opportunity to sign up to receive notifications about scheduled court hearings and outcomes via a range of mechanisms, including telephone, email, and text message (US Department of Justice 2020).

One of our study jurisdictions has also considered this approach, with a recent ACT Government (2018: 21) options paper on victims of crime noting that:

> New Zealand recently introduced a similar text messaging system. England and Wales have introduced a 'track my crime' system where people log in and opt-in to receive alerts, and in Canada victims have access to a secure website to obtain information about offenders who harmed them.

It was suggested that although privacy issues need to be considered, such a system 'would benefit victims and reduce the burden on agencies to provide this information' (ACT Government 2018: 22).

While there is little literature on the operation and effectiveness of such systems, a review by Irazola et al. (2015) found that victims who subscribed to these systems indicated that the notifications helped them to feel more empowered and safe and made them want to be more involved in their case (for discussion, see also Healy 2019). Accordingly, we recommend that similar systems be considered in the Australian context. While this would not alleviate the problems surrounding victims' lack of understanding of the criminal justice system and sentencing more generally, they could help agencies to fulfil their legislative obligations to provide victims with regular and timely information.

Conclusion

In interviews with both victims and justice professionals we identified communication difficulties that seem to act as a barrier to justice professionals' fulfilment of their obligation to keep victims appropriately informed of the justice process, including the sentencing process. Trish (VSO, Vic) summarised the problem clearly:

> [Victims] feel uninformed, they don't understand the process, they feel out of control within the process in terms of how long it takes, what happens and what their role is within it. I think it's a real problem. I think it re-traumatises the vast majority of victims who have experienced sexual assault, by the nature of how the process operates.

Several justice professionals detailed the type of information they usually provide to victims throughout the justice process, yet each of the victims interviewed reported not receiving at least some of the information they were entitled to. This suggests that there is a disjuncture between the information that justice professionals believe that victims are receiving and the information victims recall being told.

The solutions proposed in this chapter are based on the assumption that both victims and justice professionals accurately reported their experiences of information provision. On this basis, we identified two significant problems that may act as barriers between justice professionals' communication of information and victims' receipt of that information. The first is the lack of clarity as to who is responsible for the communication of certain types of information to victims, which may explain why they receive only some of the information to which they are entitled. In response to this problem, we recommended that victims' rights regimes in NSW, Queensland, South Australia, Tasmania, and Western Australia be amended to remove the responsibility for obtaining information about the criminal investigation and trial process from the victim and instead place the onus to provide that information on the relevant agency, as is the case in the ACT, Northern Territory, and Victoria. We also recommended the adoption of automated notification systems, which could further assist agencies to fulfil their obligations to provide victims with ongoing information.

The second identified barrier relates to the problems that may arise when professionals attempt to communicate with victims. This barrier may explain why the information that justice professionals believe they are providing victims may not be wholly, or even partly, understood by the recipients of that information. Based on Silverman, Kurtz, and Draper's (2013) recommendations, we made suggestions for strategies that might improve verbal communication. Together, these strategies should ensure that victims are able to better comprehend and remember the information presented to them verbally. Based on these strategies, verbal communication skills training should be conducted with justice professionals in order to improve their communication with victims of crime.

We also recommended that victims be provided with condensed versions of the existing victim information booklets in South Australia and Victoria. Similar – but shorter – booklets should be developed in all Australian jurisdictions that do not currently offer victims this type of information. This would alleviate the problem identified by Rachel:

> If someone could have told me 'this is probably what is going to happen, this is probably the path that it's going to take', that would have been a really good heads-up … getting my head around that sort of stuff is a task … A cheat sheet would have been great.
>
> (Victim, Tas)

Notes

1 By contrast, the communication theory literature offers much in terms of philosophies around human communication, yet little in terms of applied skills that can be used in practice by justice professionals: see e.g. Heath & Bryant 2000.

2 Effective communication with victims of crime is a complex issue that deserves a level of careful scrutiny and consideration to which we are unable to do justice. Therefore, this section focuses on the issue only in relation to verbal and written information provided to victims by support agencies and prosecutors in the context of victim impact statements and sentencing.

References

ACT Government (2018). *Charter of Rights for Victims of Crime: Options Paper*. Canberra.

ACT Government (2020a). *Court Process*. https://www.victimsupport.act.gov.au/criminal-justice-system/court-process.

ACT Government (2020b). *The Courts*. https://www.victimsupport.act.gov.au/criminal-justice-system/court-process/the-courts.

ACT Government (2020c). *The Role of the Prosecution*. https://www.victimsupport.act.gov.au/criminal-justice-system/court-process/the-role-of-the-prosecution.

ACT Government (2020d). *Sentencing*. https://www.victimsupport.act.gov.au/criminal-justice-system/court-process/sentencing.

Ashworth, A (1998). *The Criminal Process: An Evaluative Study*, Clarendon Press, 2nd ed. Oxford.

Australian Federal Police (2013). *Pocketbook Guide for Victims of Crime*. https://police.act.gov.au/sites/default/files/PDF/Victims-of-crime-booklet-September-2013.pdf.

Clark, H (2010). *'What Is the Justice System Willing to Offer?' Understanding Sexual Assault Victim/Survivors' Criminal Justice Needs*, Australian Institute of Family Studies. Melbourne.

Davies, R & Bartels, L (2000). 'Challenges of Effective Communication in the Criminal Justice Process: Findings from Interviews with Victims of Sexual Offences in Australia', *Laws*, 020, *9*(4), 31. https://doi.org/10.3390/laws9040031.

Englebrecht, C (2011). 'The Struggle for "Ownership of Conflict": An Exploration of Victim Participation and Voice in the Criminal Justice System', *Criminal Justice Review*, 36, 129–151.

Hargie, O (2011). *Skilled Interpersonal Communication: Research, Theory and Practice*, Routledge, 5th ed. Abingdon.

Healy, D (2019). *Exploring Victims' Interactions with the Criminal Justice System: A Literature Review*, Irish Department of Justice and Equality. Dublin.

Heath, R & Bryant, J (2000). *Human Communication Theory and Research: Concepts, Contexts and Challenges*, Lawrence Erlbaum. New Jersey.

Iliadis, M (2020). *Adversarial Justice and Victims' Rights: Reconceptualising the Role of Sexual Assault Victims*, Routledge. Abingdon.

Irazola, S, Williamson, E, Niedzwiecki, E, Debus-Sherrill, S & Sun, J (2015). 'Keeping Victims Informed: Service Providers' and Victims' Experiences Using Automated Notification Systems', *Violence and Victims*, 30, 533–544.

Konradi, A (2007). *Taking the Stand: Rape Survivors and the Prosecution of Rapists*, Praeger. Westport.

Laxminarayan, M, Bosmans, M, Porter, R & Sosa, L (2013). 'Victim Satisfaction with Criminal Justice: A Systematic Review', *Victims and Offenders*, 8, 119–147.

Lee, B (2018). *Eggshell Skull: A Memoir About Standing Up, Speaking Out and Fighting Back*, Allen & Unwin. Sydney.

Lewis, N & Jaramillo, A (2008). *Communication with Victims and Survivors*, National Victim Assistance Academy. Fairfax.

Northern Territory Government (2019). *Northern Territory Charter of Victims' Rights*. Darwin.

NSW Government (2018). *Schedule of Government Response to Recommendations on Victims' Involvement in Sentencing*. http://www.sentencingcouncil.justice.nsw.gov.au/Documents/ Current-projects/Victims/Victims_gov.pdf.

NSW Sentencing Council (2018). *Victims' Involvement in Sentencing—Report*. Sydney.

Reyes, G, Elhai, J & Ford, J (2008). *The Encyclopedia of Psychological Trauma*, Wiley. Hoboken.

Shapland, J, Willmore, J & Duff, P (1985). *Victims in the Criminal Justice System*, Gower. Aldershot.

Silverman, J, Kurtz, S & Draper, J (2013). *Skills for Communicating with Patients*, Radcliff Publishing, 3rd ed. Oxford.

South Australian Commissioner for Victims' Rights (2014). *Information for Victims of Crime: Treatment, Impact and Access to the Justice System*. Adelaide.

Tyler, T (2007). 'Procedural Justice and the Courts', *Court Review*, 44, 26–31.

US Department of Justice (2020). *Victim Notification System*. https://www.justice.gov/criminal-vns/victim-notification-system.

US Office for Victims of Crime (2005). *Listen to My Story: Communicating with Victims of Crime*. Washington, DC.

Victorian Law Reform Commission (2014). *The Role of Victims of Crime in the Criminal Trial Process: Consultation Paper*. Melbourne.

Victorian Law Reform Commission (2016). *The Role of Victims of Crime in the Criminal Trial Process: Report*. Melbourne.

Victorian Office of Public Prosecutions (OPP) (2013). *Pathways to Justice: A Guide to the Victorian Court System for Victims and Witnesses of Serious Crime*. http://www.opp.vic.gov.au/getdoc/9556d0e4-0d59-4fd3-ac0e-f4f60edf2b97/Pathways-to-justice.aspx.

Wedlock, E & Tapley, J (2016). *What Works in Supporting Victims of Crime: A Rapid Evidence Assessment*, Report for the Victims Commissioner for England and Wales. London.

Wemmers, J-A (2011). 'Victims in the Criminal Justice System and Therapeutic Jurisprudence: A Canadian Perspective', in E Erez, M Kilchling & J-A Wemmers (eds), *Therapeutic Jurisprudence and Victim Participation in Justice: International Perspectives*, Carolina Academic Press. Durham.

Yates, H. (2020). 'Opinion: I Am Hoping This is a Turning Point for Victims of Crime', *Canberra Times*, 5 July. https://www.canberratimes.com.au/story/6818695/i-am-hoping-this-is-a-turning-point-for-victims-of-crime/.

LAURA

The offender was a taxi driver who was driving Laura home at approximately 3am. Laura had been drinking with her friends and was quite intoxicated. The taxi driver encouraged Laura to sit in the front seat and, while driving, encouraged Laura to hold his hand, which she did. When the taxi neared Laura's house, she asked the driver to stop. He ignored her request and kept driving. The offender then stopped the taxi and indecently assaulted Laura, including touching her breasts, kissing her, and biting her lip. The offender then drove the taxi further. He pushed his hand under Laura's clothing and touched her vagina. He also took Laura's hand and placed it on his exposed, erect penis. Laura then got out of the taxi. The offender followed Laura after she got out of the taxi, asking that she pay the fare, which she refused to do.

The entire incident was recorded on the CCTV footage in the taxi. The judge said that, upon viewing the footage, it was obvious that Laura was affected by alcohol and was unresponsive at times. This was apparently clear from the fact that the offender had to manipulate the position of Laura's head in order to kiss her.

The offender ultimately pleaded guilty to one count of indecent assault. However, Laura was not kept up to date about the situation. She felt she 'just needed more clarification ... I could tell they really cared. But I would have had six weeks of less stress if I had known about the guilty plea earlier'.

Laura was first informed of her right to submit an impact statement through the WAS officer, who advised Laura that she could submit one if she wanted to. Laura recalled reviewing some guidelines provided to her by the WAS officer.

She found the act of writing the statement to be therapeutic:

> I didn't expect it to [feel like therapy], but it did. Once I started, I really snowballed and kept writing and writing. I was conscious of the fact that I couldn't do too much and wasn't writing an essay. One of the police officers I worked with said that some people write ten pages back-to-back and it might lose its impact if it's that long, so I was just trying to write it out and then compress it into what needed to be said.

Laura's impact statement said:

> Before what happened I led a normal life where I worked, studied and socialised with family and friends. I still do these things today

> but with a feeling of unhappiness that I have lost a sense of trust that I once had in others. Immediately following the incident I felt degraded, taken advantage of and worried for anyone else this may have happened to. On top of this I had to cope with feelings of anxiety, sleeplessness and urges to retreat from my normal life, which I eventually sought counselling for.
>
> I have missed some work and time I would normally have spent studying has been spent at various appointments. It has caused concern for my family and friends, not only for my wellbeing, but for their own safety when catching taxis, something I was not able to do for some time following what happened.
>
> I am hurt that someone in a position of power and responsibility took the right I have to make decisions over my own body away from me at a time when I was vulnerable. To then learn that [the offender] stated that I offered to be treated this way was even more distressing.
>
> I wish you had thought about what you did before you did it – and I hope that if you had done, you would have chosen to act differently. That said, you have changed me nonetheless and for what I feel is for the worse. But I hope you have come to understand and realise that what you did is not how a person should treat another and that you never will again. I hope that you can take responsibility for your action, and understand that they were your choices, no one else's, and that they were wrong.

Laura's statement was not edited by the WAS officer. She recalled asking if it was OK and the WAS officer confirmed it was fine.

Laura attended court for the offender's sentencing, but chose not to read her statement out loud:

> I had to decide if I wanted to have it handed up, or have it read out in court, or have me read it in court. I didn't really want to read it out in court, I didn't want him to look at me. So I asked for it to be read out for me. The prosecutor read it out … It was hard, but I wanted to be there for it. I had people there holding my hand. I almost didn't have it read out, I almost said 'just give it to the judge', but I wasn't sure whether or not that would lead to him actually reading it. So my therapy of writing it might have gone to waste.

She also explained:

> At the start of the court case, the prosecutor stood up and said 'I'm going to read the victim impact statement', and the magistrate said

> 'oh, I would normally read that myself,' which made me feel stupid. I thought maybe I shouldn't have done that, but I was given that option from the beginning. … It was hard to get to that point, to build up the courage to do it. So when the judge [sic] said that, it felt like being punched in the stomach. But the judge said 'never mind, read it to me'. So it started out a bit funny, but it was all right after that.

When the prosecutor read the statement aloud, Laura felt quite overwhelmed:

> It felt very surreal, the whole ordeal. I sat there and I didn't want to look up. I put my head down and closed my eyes. It's very weird to hear my words that were sensitive, and made me feel really vulnerable, read out to a courtroom of strangers. So in a way I wanted to hide. But afterward, I was really glad that it happened. But in the moment, it was scary. I felt naked.

The magistrate made the following reference to Laura in the sentencing remarks:

> I make it clear that I take into account the impact of the victim and those close to her of this defendant's appalling treatment of her. It is but one of a number of factors that I need to take into account, but it is a significant one … This was appalling behaviour. It was a serious breach of trust. He preyed on an innocent, young, vulnerable victim.

Laura commented that this all happened very quickly:

> Yes, he was talking about it all, and then he just did the sentencing. It was all part of the speech, he talked about the crime and how the offender acted, and said 'based on this, this is what the sentence is'. It was done really quickly.

Laura viewed the impact statement as being a communication tool between herself and the offender:

> Through the whole process, I hadn't really ever had an opportunity to hear what he thought, or to know that he had heard what I was thinking or feeling. Whether or not he listened, I don't know. But it gave me a chance to try and have him hear what I wanted to say to him. That's the main reason. And I guess, inadvertently, it helped to

get the jumble out of my brain and put it into some sort of sense in words on a piece of paper. Which made me realise I did have a lot circling in my mind, that I had to get out.

I think the bit where I got to, hopefully, get through to him in some way that was probably the scariest, but most therapeutic part of it. Because you never have an opportunity to say anything to them. They're locked up and there's a barrier between you and the other person, from day dot. I almost didn't want to communicate with him, ever. But that little fighter inside said 'just do it.' So that was the most important part, for me.

Chapter 7

Conclusion

Introduction

On the release of the Victorian Law Reform Commission's (2016) report on the role of victims in the criminal justice process, the Chair of the Commission and former Supreme Court judge the Hon Phillip Cummins (2016: np) observed that '[c]ourts need to change. The distress of a trial cannot be completely eliminated, but there are specific steps we should take to reduce trauma'. Since the 1980s, legislative and policy reforms in Australia have increased the role that victims play in the justice process, including through the introduction of victim impact statements at sentencing. As discussed in Chapter 1, these reforms were intended, at least in part, to address barriers that contributed to high attrition rates in the prosecution of sexual offences and reduce the anti-therapeutic aspects of victim involvement in the criminal justice process. However, there is little research on victims' experiences of impact statements and sentencing. This is particularly so for research focusing on victims of sexual offending and involving interviews with victims themselves. Some of the research that has been conducted describes the therapeutic benefits that victims derive from judicial acknowledgement of their impact statement at sentencing, but little research has explored or quantified judicial practice in this area.

We sought to address these gaps by conducting in-depth interviews with six victims of sexual offending and 15 justice professionals who work with victims throughout the impact statement and sentencing process. We also analysed 100 sentencing transcripts from sexual offence matters to explore judicial acknowledgement of impact statements at sentencing. At the time of our research, victim impact experiences of victims of sexual offending had not been explored in this way, in Australia or elsewhere. This combination of research approaches allowed for a unique and rich analysis of victim experiences. This chapter consolidates our findings and recommendations and summarises their implications for legislative and policy reform. It also identifies future research directions arising from the recommendations.

Gaining a better understanding of victim perspectives of impact statements and sentencing

As set out in Chapter 1, the first aim of our research was to gain a better understanding of victims' perspectives of impact statement and sentencing processes in sexual offence cases. This was accomplished through interviews with victims and justice professionals. Three key findings arose from our interviews. The third aim of our research was to make recommendations for policy and/or legislative reform to achieve best practice from a victim-focused perspective. In accordance with this, the summary of each relevant finding is followed by our reform recommendations.

Finding 1: the unclear purpose of victim impact statements

The first significant finding from our interviews was that the participants experienced numerous practical difficulties because the Australian impact statement legislation, case law, policies, and guidelines are inconsistent in their guidance around the actual purpose of impact statements. Consequently, justice professionals are unable to provide coherent and consistent advice to victims about the type of information they can include in their statement and how the statement may be used by the court. This finding is not unique to the Australian context; similar issues have arisen in Canada. In response, Manikis (2015) developed an impact statement model designed to reconcile the instrumental and expressive approaches of impact statements and achieve clarity and consistency in their purpose. We used a combination of the fundamental principles of criminal justice, Australian law and policy, and our interview findings to review the applicability of the Manikis model to the Australian context.

Recommendations for a proposed model to achieve impact statement consistency

We recommended the adoption of a modified and expanded version of Manikis' model for the jurisdictions covered by this research. Our proposed model promotes an expressive approach to impact statements, while maintaining certain rules to ensure that statements can also be used instrumentally, without disadvantaging the offender. Under this model, victims would be offered significant flexibility in their expression and in the form of their statement. They could present their statement in a variety of ways, including prose, drawings, poems, and/or songs. Victims may also choose to present their statement verbally, using vulnerable witness provisions, or have someone else present it verbally on their behalf.

Under the proposed approach, the victim would be allowed to include within their statement any information about the harm they have experienced, without limiting this to the harm caused only by the offences for which the offender has been convicted. However, only the actual harm suffered by the victim in respect of these offences would be considered relevant to the determination of the offender's sentence. Prosecutors and witness assistance officers would not be responsible for editing impact statements to remove information that may be considered irrelevant. Instead, the judge would be responsible for deciding which, if any, parts of the statement are irrelevant to the offender's sentence and must make clear if and how they have done so. If a victim was to be cross-examined on the content of their statement, a pre-sentence 'ground rules' style hearing would facilitate the settlement of questions to be asked. This would act as an additional safeguard to ensure victims are not re-traumatised by the process of cross-examination. The model and the reforms required to give effect to it are set out in more detail in Table 5.2.

Finding 2: problems affecting victims' right to information

The second significant finding arising from the interviews was that each victim interviewed reported not receiving some or all of the information they were entitled to receive about the justice system. This included information about court processes and sentencing processes generally, as well as the ongoing progress of their individual case. We determined that this problem may arise, in part, from a misplaced burden of communication on the victim.

Recommendations for reforms to victims' rights frameworks

In most Australian jurisdictions, including the jurisdictions in which the victim interviews took place, victims' right to information only exists if victims actively request the information from the relevant agency. This places the onus on the victim to contact the relevant agency to obtain information about the progress of their case, rather than placing the obligation on those agencies to keep the victim informed. In contrast, some other jurisdictions place the burden of communication on the relevant agency instead.

It was evident from the victim interviews that victims in South Australia and Tasmania are not kept apprised of the progress of their case unless they contact the appropriate agency to seek information, in accordance with the current framework. However, we argued that it is not reasonable or fair to place this obligation on victims, who are likely to be in a traumatised state. We consequently recommended that all Australian jurisdictions adopt frameworks that place the burden of communication on the relevant agency, rather than on the victim. This change should reduce the risk of victims feeling 'out of the loop' about the progress of their case.

All Australian and other relevant jurisdictions should also consider implementing automated notification systems. These systems allow victims to sign up to receive notifications about scheduled court hearings and outcomes. The notifications can be provided via a range of forms, including telephone, email, and text message. This would not alleviate the issue of victims' lack of understanding of the criminal justice system generally, but would help agencies to discharge their obligations to provide victims with ongoing and timely information as their case progresses and might help victims feel safe, empowered, and more willing to be more involved in their case (Irazola et al. 2015).

Finding 3: communication barriers between justice professionals and victims

The third significant finding from our interviews was the identification of several communication barriers between justice professionals and victims. It emerged that prosecutors and witness assistance and victim support officers may share information about justice processes that is not fully understood by victims. This may be because the information is lacking, because victims may not possess a fundamental understanding of legal processes, and/or because victims do not understand legal jargon or shorthand.

Recommendations for communication skills training for justice professionals

We relied on Silverman, Kurtz, and Draper's (2013) evidence-based communication skills research to recommend a range of strategies that may alleviate communication barriers between victims and justice professionals. In summary, these strategies require justice professionals to: assess the victim's starting point prior to giving information; ask what information might be helpful; give information in small pieces; check that the victim has understood the information; and use the victim's response as a guide to how to proceed before providing any further information. Justice professionals should also repeat information if the victim has not understood it and reduce or eliminate the use of jargon. Based on these strategies, verbal communication skills training should be conducted with justice professionals, in order to improve their communication with victims.

We also recommended that victims be provided with succinct information about court processes in visual form, including relevant definitions and flowcharts depicting the justice process. To be of most practical use, this information should be presented in booklets that contain adequate space for victims to take notes and write questions they may wish to ask of support services or prosecutors.

Identifying current judicial sentencing practice

The second aim of our research was to explore judicial practice in relation to the use of and reference to impact statements at sentencing. We achieved this through an analysis of 100 sentencing remarks from sexual offence cases, as well as our findings from the interviews with both victims and justice professionals. These findings are briefly explained below, before setting out our recommendations in response.

Finding 4: current judicial practice around the acknowledgement of victims at sentencing

We found that victims and their impact statements were acknowledged in 95 of the 100 cases examined, with harm to victims' families also mentioned in 15 cases. Victoria was the only jurisdiction in which the judge acknowledged the victim sentencing in all cases; as this was also the jurisdiction with the largest number of cases, it should be regarded as a best practice model in this context. There was no reference to the victim in 14% of cases in the ACT, compared with 5% in South Australia, and 6% in Tasmania. This aligns with Booth's (2015) assertion that it is rare for judicial officers not to refer to victims' impact statements.

The ideal extent to which a judicial officer should refer to or acknowledge a victim at sentencing had not been previously established, although victim support and witness assistance officers speak highly of judges who speak in detail about victims, as opposed to those who provide minimal or 'tokenistic' acknowledgement (Victorian Department of Justice 2014: 59). The justice professionals we interviewed agreed that acknowledgement consisting of a mere sentence is problematic, because of the risk that victims will not feel they were taken seriously. This would negate the potential benefit or validation victims might otherwise gain from more detailed acknowledgement.

The findings from the sentencing remarks analysis and victim interviews demonstrated that detailed judicial acknowledgement can be therapeutically beneficial for victims, but the interviews also demonstrated that too much detail can have negative consequences for some victims. These results reveal the significant challenges that judicial officers face when crafting therapeutically effective sentencing remarks.

Recommendations for best judicial practice when acknowledging victims at sentencing

Chapter 4 proposed two recommendations to ensure that judicial officers are educated on the possible therapeutic and anti-therapeutic consequences of their acknowledgement of victims at sentencing. The first recommendation was the publication of a victim-focused benchbook to guide judges concisely and clearly through the 'dos and don'ts' of victim acknowledgement at sentencing. This publication should contain real-life examples, like those included in Chapter 4, to illustrate particular judicial approaches that appear to have effectively and therapeutically met the needs of the victims involved. It should also flag matters of particular sensitivity to victims, such as sharing details about their mental health, and suggest more therapeutic ways to handle this sort of information.

Our second recommendation was the introduction of a mechanism to enable judges to be informed, prior to sentencing, if there is material in a victim impact statement that is particularly sensitive and should therefore not be outlined in detail in the sentencing remarks. This would require the judicial officer to convene a short pre-sentence hearing with prosecution and defence counsel, where any particularly sensitive material could be identified by the prosecutor. The hearing would also benefit the defence, by providing an opportunity for the judicial officer to make clear what information from the impact statement would be relied on in passing sentence. This hearing would also allow the defence to raise any relevant issues with the content of the impact statement and facilitate the settlement of any questions to be asked of the victim in cross-examination.

Future research directions

We recognise the limitations of the small sample size for the victim interviews and that the participants were self-selected. In addition, although we examined judicial use of impact statements at sentencing by analysing 100 sentencing remarks, we did not have access to copies of the impact statements in those matters. Accordingly, some aspects of our analysis are speculative in nature. Third, financial and time constraints prevented the further understanding that would have been gained by also interviewing judicial officers, and also meant that we were only able to conduct research in four of the eight Australian states and territories. It is quite possible that beneficial practices go unacknowledged in the remaining Australian (and other) jurisdictions. Furthermore, some of our recommendations may not be applicable to other legal frameworks.

As a result of these limitations, there are several avenues for future research. This should include research in the Australian jurisdictions that were not subject to examination in this book and increased sample sizes. Future research should also include judicial participants' perspectives on how they acknowledge victims in their sentencing remarks, as well as the views of defence practitioners. Furthermore, the reform proposals arising out of our findings or future impact statement research must be subject to feedback and scrutiny from victim support and witness assistance officers, judicial officers, and experienced prosecution and defence practitioners, whose views must be sought to properly inform the reform process.

In addition, there is a need for urgent research on two of our recommendations. Specifically, research is required to inform the implementation of a victim-focused pre-sentence mechanism to settle both prosecution and defence issues around impact statements, as well as automated notification systems to help keep victims informed throughout the justice process. This research should investigate the potential effects and outcomes of these proposals on victims, judicial officers, legal practitioners, and, more broadly, the resources of the courts and agencies that would implement the proposed mechanisms.

Conclusion: implications for victim impact statement policy and practice

As outlined above, we took a unique approach to our research on victims' experiences of impact statements and sentencing, combining qualitative interviews with victims and justice professionals with a thematic analysis of sentencing remarks. We have presented the first analysis of sentencing remarks to quantify judicial reference to victims and their impact statements at sentencing in Australia. Informed by established literature on victims' justice needs (see e.g. Daly 2014), we identified practices that are therapeutic and anti-therapeutic from a victim-focused perspective. Our recommendations, particularly the publication of a victim-focused benchbook, will provide judicial officers in Australia with clear, evidence-based guidance for effective acknowledgement of victims at sentencing.

This book also contains an analysis of the first in-depth interviews undertaken to explore the experiences of Australian victims of sexual offending in relation to impact statements. The divide between expressive and instrumental approaches to impact statements has been sporadically explored in previous research (see e.g. Roberts 2003; Booth 2015; Manikis 2015). However, that research did not identify the significant practical problems that this divide can cause for justice professionals, who consequently cannot provide accurate and comprehensive information to victims about current impact statement schemes. Victims' need for information about the justice process has been long established (Shapland, Willmore, & Duff 1985) and is well understood by both academics and the justice professionals interviewed for this book. Consequently, the finding that information provision problems continue to affect victims was unexpected. We therefore demonstrated the significant benefits from directly interviewing victims when investigating victims' experiences of the justice system, rather than the common practice of relying solely on the perspectives of the professionals who work closely with them. It is strongly recommended that any future researchers continue to investigate victims' experiences of impact statements directly.

In conclusion, we have both empirically confirmed and built upon the findings of previous impact statement research. We also elucidated the significant implications of the past and present research findings for the day-to-day practice of judges, justice professionals, and the victims with whom they work. In addition, we recommended a number of practical and clear solutions to each of the problems identified by the research; if implemented, they will achieve the therapeutic jurisprudence goal of minimising the unintended anti-therapeutic effects of impact statement processes and maximising the potential for healing for victims (Winick 2009).

In her memoir, Miller wrote that, after her statement was released, she felt she 'had power', but subsequently awoke to the 'excruciatingly long process of substantive change, how huge and imbedded systems are, how impossible they are to dismantle, how tiny I was' (2019: 303). We acknowledge that our research likewise constitutes but a small contribution to the broader search for substantive change and more therapeutic outcomes for victims of sexual offending. Nonetheless, our findings and recommendations support the development of a best practice model for the use of impact statements in Australia.

Victim impact statements are used in a range of countries, including Canada, Ireland, the Netherlands, New Zealand, South Africa, the UK, and the US. Accordingly, our research has relevance for all jurisdictions seeking to promote a victim-focused model for the use of such statements. In particular, our recommendations have the potential to create more therapeutic outcomes for victims of sexual violence and thereby help them know that they 'can't be silenced … justice was served … [and] we are getting somewhere' (Miller 2019: 357).

References

Booth, T (2015). *Accommodating Justice: Victim Impact Statements in the Sentencing Process*, Federation Press. Sydney.

Cummins, P (2016). *Respect the Rights of Victims of Crime in Court: VLRC Report*, Media release, 22 November. http://www.lawreform.vic.gov.au/media/respect-rights-victims-crime-court-vlrc-report.

Daly, K (2014). 'Reconceptualizing Sexual Victimization and Justice', in I Vanfraechem, A Pemberton & F Ndahinda (eds), *Justice for Victims: Perspectives on Rights, Transition and Reconciliation*, Routledge. Abingdon.

Irazola, S, Williamson, E, Niedzwiecki, E, Debus-Sherrill, S & Sun, J (2015). 'Keeping Victims Informed: Service Providers' and Victims' Experiences Using Automated Notification Systems', *Violence and Victims*, 30, 533–544.

Manikis, M (2015). 'Victim Impact Statements at Sentencing: Towards a Clearer Understanding of their Aims', *University of Toronto Law Journal*, 65, 85–123.

Miller, C (2019). *Know My Name: A Memoir*, Viking. New York.

Roberts, J (2003). 'Victim Impact Statements and the Sentencing Process: Recent Developments and Research Findings', *Criminal Law Quarterly*, 47, 365–396.

Shapland, J, Willmore, J & Duff, P (1985). *Victims in the Criminal Justice System*, Gower. Aldershot.

Silverman, J, Kurtz, S & Draper, J (2013). *Skills for Communicating with Patients*, Radcliff Publishing, 3rd ed. Oxford.

Victorian Department of Justice (2014). *Victim Impact Statement Reforms in Victoria—Interim Implementation Report*. Melbourne.

Victorian Law Reform Commission (2016). *The Role of Victims of Crime in the Criminal Trial Process: Report*. Melbourne.

Winick, B (2009). 'Therapeutic Jurisprudence Perspectives on Dealing with Victims of Crime', *Nova Law Review*, 33, 535–543.

Index

Page numbers in *italics* indicate figures and page numbers in **bold** indicate tables.

www.ingramcontent.com/pod-product-compliance
Lightning Source LLC
LaVergne TN
LVHW011131300926
849160LV00008B/602
9780367524227